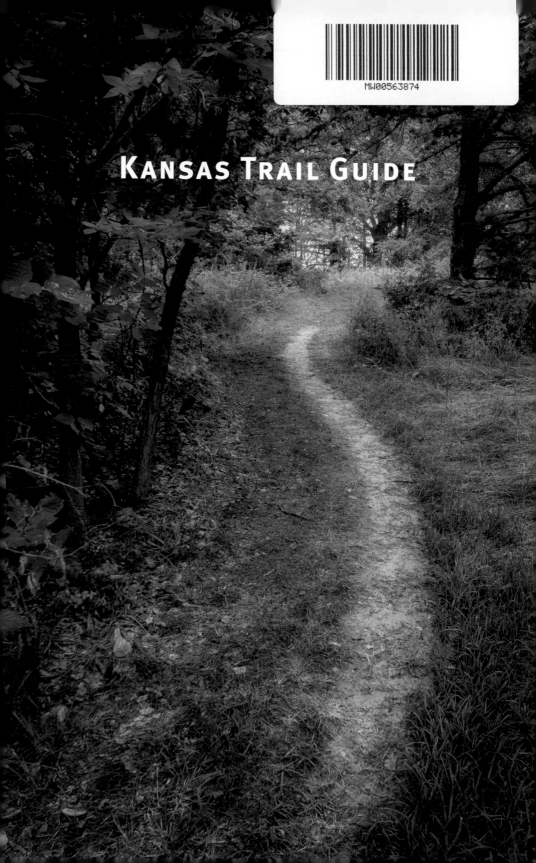

KANSAS TRAIL GUIDE

KANSAS TRAIL GUIDE

THE BEST HIKING, BIKING, AND RIDING IN THE SUNFLOWER STATE

JONATHAN CONARD AND KRISTIN CONARD

FOREWORD BY MARCI PENNER

University Press of Kansas

Publication was made possible, in part, by a grant from the Federal Highway Administration's Recreational Trail Program, administered by the Kansas Department of Wildlife, Parks, and Tourism.

Published by the University Press of Kansas (Lawrence, Kansas 66045), which was organized by the Kansas Board of Regents and is operated and funded by Emporia State University, Fort Hays State University, Kansas State University, Pittsburg State University, the University of Kansas, and Wichita State University

Library of Congress Cataloging-in-Publication Data

Conard, Jonathan.
    Kansas Trail Guide : the best hiking, biking, and riding in the Sunflower State / Jonathan Conard and Kristin Conard ; foreword by Marci Penner.
    pages   cm
    Includes bibliographical references and index.
    ISBN 978-0-7006-2066-1 (pbk : acid free paper) 1. Hiking—Kansas—Guidebooks. 2. Trails—Kansas—Guidebooks. 3. Kansas—Guidebooks. I. Conard, Kristin. II. Title.
    GV199.42.K2C66 2015
    796.5109781—dc23
                        2014045936

British Library Cataloguing-in-Publication Data is available.

Printed in China

10 9 8 7 6 5 4 3 2

CONTENTS

FOREWORD

Whether you are an avid hiker or prefer to be propelled forward by a bicycle or a horse, or even if you are just looking for a splendid way to spend a beautiful Kansas day, this book should be in your possession.

The brother-sister team of Jonathan Conard and Kristin Conard has spent years examining every detail of Kansas trails to make trail-going easy for the rest of us. This book uncomplicates the details of knowing where to go, when to go, what to expect, and so much more. The Conards' passion for trails comes through in the specifics, the maps, and the pictures.

Kansas has an incredible legacy of trails, as explained in the first chapter. And after reading it, you'll feel like it's your duty as a Kansan to get to a trailhead and forge ahead. Between our wide-open sky and prairie soil are more trails than you can imagine, and they will take you on a remarkable journey of Kansas geography and history.

As the authors explain, Kansas has eleven different physiographic regions, which means that the trails in each region look a bit different. You can really get to know Kansas by hiking at least one trail in each region. But watch out — if you do that, you'll only want to do more!

If you enjoy the trails, let your friends know. Find a way to brag about your trekking adventures in Kansas (through Twitter or Facebook, for example). You'll find rock formations, lakes, creeks, woods, and sights that leave you breathless. With their book, the Conards have given us a great launching pad to do some boasting.

I already have my own favorite trails, but my new quest as a Kansas Explorer Club member will be to experience every trail in the Conards' book. It may take some time, but I'm going to do it — and I'll thank Jonathan and Kristin with every step.

Marci Penner
Executive Director, Kansas Sampler Foundation

Preface and Acknowledgments

The trails of Kansas don't always get the respect they deserve, and the state's reputation as a flat land with little to see is not limited to outsiders. However, for those willing to venture beyond the pavement, there are trails throughout Kansas that highlight some of the best and most scenic natural areas in the state. From the windswept plains to the majestic Flint Hills, the subtle beauty of the Sunflower State is best appreciated from these trails. Spending the better part of a year hiking and biking our way throughout the state has been an amazing experience, and we hope the knowledge and insights we've gained will be a valuable resource for those who want to explore Kansas.

We couldn't have done this without a lot of help. We'd like to thank Maddie Estrada at Garmin for letting us test and use the company's devices to help us create the maps, and Cathy Kruzic and Janie McCullough at Kruzic Communications for making introductions to tourism boards. For their support and answers to many questions, we are grateful to Liron BenDor at Overland Park Tourism; Susan Rathke at Emporia CVB; Kristi Lee at Franklin County CVB; Marcia Rozell at Manhattan CVB; Jim Thomas, Kansas Horse Council director; Clark Coan, former director of development at Kanza Rail-Trails Conservancy; Doug Walker, vice president of Kanza Rail-Trails Conservancy Inc.; and Wendy Bowles at Kanopolis State Park. We'd also like to thank the photographers who let us use their photos of some of the trails: Judd Patterson, David Welfelt, Scott Bean, Marciana Vequist, Billie Hufford, Chris Harnish, Amanda Botterweck, and Randy Van Scyoc. We appreciate all the volunteers and park employees across the state who work so hard to keep the trails in good shape — it's a more difficult job than many can imagine. And thanks to our editor for his support for the project from the beginning.

More than anything, we'd like to thank our family: our brother Andrew and his wife Nicole for their help with and enthusiasm for this book and for opening up their house; Mark and Joyce, our parents, for being endlessly supportive, helping to pick us up on the longer trails, taking pictures, giving guidance, and tackling many of the trails with us; and Melissa, Jonathan's wife, for being patient and encouraging after long days on the trail and for supporting our dream of writing this book. Finally, we are grateful to God for such a wonderful world to explore.

To Katie, John, Jenna, and Anne: we finished this, so you know that anything's possible.

CHAPTER 1

INTRODUCTION

These things — the air, the water, the scenery and we who fill these scenes — hold many and many a man to Kansas when money would tempt him away. . . . Here are the still waters, here are the green pastures. Here, the fairest of the world's habitations.

WILLIAM ALLEN WHITE, CIRCA 1912

Olathe Prairie Center. Photo by Kristin Conard

Kansas is widely perceived as a flat state that is best known for its tornadoes and *The Wizard of Oz*. But hiding in plain sight are hundreds of miles of trails waiting to be explored by hikers, cyclists, and horseback riders.

HISTORY

Those who set out to explore the trails of Kansas are following in some famous and historical footsteps. Native Americans traveled across Kansas to hunt game, visit religious sites, and trade with other tribes. Spanish explorer Francisco Vasquez de Coronado traveled through what is now Kansas in 1541, following Cabeza de Vaca's stories of wealth in the region. It is thought that Coronado and his men stood atop a hill northwest of what is now Lindsborg and looked out over the valley. That hill is now aptly named Coronado Heights.

Some 260 years later, the Lewis and Clark expedition made camp on the banks of the Kansas River and spent time exploring the region during the summer of 1804. As might be expected, their journals included entries on the high heat that is common during a Kansas summer, but they also reflected on the area's scenery.

Coronado Heights in the Smoky Hills. Photo by Scott Bean

Clark wrote in his journal on July 4, 1804: "We Camped in the plain one of the most butifull Plains, I ever Saw, open & butifully diversified with hills & vallies all presenting themselves to the river covered with grass and a few scattering trees a handsom Creek meandering thro at this place the Kansaw Inds."

As Lewis and Clark returned to the East after their expedition, Zebulon Pike set out across Kansas in 1806 with the mission of exploring the southern portion of the lands acquired in the Louisiana Purchase. Pike started his journey through what is now southeast Kansas and trekked northwest, spending time in the Flint Hills and the Smoky Hills and along the Arkansas River. His journals record the area's wildlife and scenery, but his overall impression was that the land was not desirable for settlement. In fact, in one entry he wrote, "Our citizens being so prone to rambling and extending themselves on the frontiers will, through necessity, be constrained to limit their extent on the west to the borders of the Missouri and Mississippi, while they leave the prairie incapable of cultivation to the wandering and uncivilized aborigines of the country."

Pike was certainly wrong in his assessment that the vast prairies of Kansas would limit exploration and travel through the region. From the 1820s to 1860s, before the spread of the railroad, traders and settlers began to move west by trail, and the most important routes went through Kansas. The 2,000-mile Oregon Trail had its start in Kansas, with wagon trains gathering in Kansas City, St. Joseph, Leavenworth, and Atchison. Ruts from the trail can still be seen in various locations, including the Oregon Trail Nature Park in Wamego. Another famous trail, the 750-mile Santa Fe Trail, ran from the Missouri River, through Kansas, to Santa Fe, New Mexico. It was used primarily as a supply route for traders and the military.

In addition to the westbound trails crossing the state, Kansas is well known for the trails used to drive longhorn cattle north from Texas. The Chisholm Trail, the most famous of these cattle trails, initially ran north from Texas through Indian territory to a trading post operated by Jesse Chisholm near the present-day city of Wichita. The trail was extended to Abilene in 1867 to expedite the shipment of vast herds of longhorns to stockyards and markets in the East.

With the development of the railroad and the automobile, many of these trails, which were once the main routes of transportation, became places of leisure and exploration.

GEOLOGY AND GEOGRAPHY

While exploring the Kansas trails, you'll notice a marked difference in the landscape, depending on where you are in the state. Kansas is made up of eleven physiographic regions, and these differences developed over millions of years. The oldest part of the state, in terms of geology, is the limestone and chert of the Ozark Plateau, deposited in the southeastern corner of the state more than 330 million years ago. This region does the most to challenge the stereotype of Kansas as flat

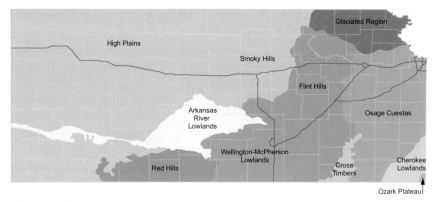

Physiographic regions

and treeless. It receives more rainfall than any other part of the state, and it is forested and hilly, with caves and steep stream valleys.

The Cherokee Lowlands has fewer trees than the Ozark Plateau, although it is forested along stream banks and hills. It features gently rolling hills and shallow stream valleys on shale and sandstone.

The small sliver of the Cross Timbers, or Chautauqua Hills, that extends into southern Kansas from Oklahoma is composed of sandstone deposited between 286 million and 320 million years ago. Vegetation in the area includes a mix of grassland and hardwood trees such as scrub oak.

The majority of southeast Kansas is within the Osage Cuestas region. *Cuesta* is Spanish for slope, and the rolling hills of the region typically have steep east-facing ridges rising 50 to 200 feet, with gently descending slopes on the opposite side. These hills have underlying layers of sandstone, limestone, and shale that were deposited during the Pennsylvanian period, 290 million to 323 million years ago.

The landscape of the Glaciated Region in the northeast corner was carved by the advance and retreat of two glaciers from 600,000 to 1.6 million years ago. Glacial deposits of rocks that originated farther north, such as Sioux quartzite, can be found throughout the region. The dominant flora of the hilly area is a mix of tallgrass prairie and deciduous forest.

The Flint Hills are formed of limestone and shale. The chert in the limestone resulted in rocky soil and steep streambeds, which made farming difficult. As a result, this region has been preserved as one of the country's largest contiguous tracts of native tallgrass prairie. The dominant plant species are warm-season grasses, including switchgrass, Indian grass, little bluestem, and big bluestem, which can reach an impressive 10 feet tall during years with abundant rainfall. These hearty grasses thrive in the prairie, as they are well adapted to flourish in the harsh combination of drought, fire, and grazing that characterizes these areas.

The Arkansas River Lowlands and the Wellington-McPherson Lowlands are similar topographically and geologically. Both are alluvial plains formed from river and stream deposits over the past 10 million years. In addition, these regions contain inactive sand dunes covered with grass and scattered wetland marshes that are important for migratory shorebirds and waterfowl.

Another region that bucks the flat Kansas stereotype is the Red Hills. In southern Kansas, red shale, sandstone, and siltstone were deposited with gypsum and dolomite 260 million years ago. This resulted in sinkholes and flat red hills topped with dolomite or gypsum. The waters here were sacred to the Plains Indians, and because of the calcium and magnesium sulfate in the waters from the rock, they have therapeutic properties.

The Smoky Hills in north-central Kansas, named for the haze that collects in the valleys, are made up of three distinct formations. The Dakota Formation is composed of sandstone and contains buttes and hills amongst the plains. To the west is the Greenhorn Limestone, with its chalky limestone and shale. The Niobrara Chalk at the western edge of the region features spires and towers of chalk remnants.

The High Plains are predominantly windswept, flat, and treeless. Stretching across nearly the entire western third of the state, the region has swaths of flatlands interspersed with gently rolling hills. It also contains the Ogallala Formation, which is mostly underground and includes the aquifer from which western Kansas gets its water; however, occasional outcrops of the formation can be found aboveground. From east to west within the region, there is a gradual elevation gain.

FLORA AND FAUNA

Kansas has a variety of ecosystems, from tallgrass and shortgrass prairies to woodlands to riparian forests. Moving from west to east across the state, average annual precipitation increases. This rainfall gradient drives the transition from arid shortgrass prairie in the west to tallgrass prairie and mesic woodlands in the east. During the spring and summer, prairie wildflowers and redbuds are in bloom, and the dense, green woodlands provide shaded canopies for many of the trails, particularly in the eastern portion of the state.

In winter, with the leaves off the trees, there's a better chance of spotting wildlife. However, many of the trails provide amazing opportunities for wildlife observation year-round. Since the trails outside of urban areas are more lightly used, animals such as white-tailed deer and wild turkeys can often be spotted. Some trails may offer an opportunity to see iconic Kansas animals such as the American bison, ornate box turtle, and prairie dog, along with less common animals such as the black-footed ferret, American badger, or bobcat.

Birding is popular in Kansas, and the state is part of the Central Flyway — a bird migration route through the Great Plains from Mexico to Canada. Turkey vultures soar overhead in summer; in spring and fall, sandhill cranes and the occasional

White-tailed deer. Photo by Judd Patterson

endangered whooping crane, along with other migratory shorebirds and water-fowl, pass through; and in winter, you can spot bald eagles at several Kansas reservoirs. Great blue herons make their homes along the lakes and streams, prairie chickens perform their elaborate dances out on the prairie, and red-tailed hawks perch on fence posts as they rest between hunting flights.

CLIMATE AND WEATHER

As the geographic center of the Lower 48, and with no major bodies of water impacting weather conditions, Kansas has a classic continental climate characterized by a wide variation in temperatures across seasons, with hot summers and cold winters. But as long as you plan ahead (think extra water in the summer and plenty of warm layers in the winter), you can enjoy the trails year-round.

Some of the best times of the year for exploring the trails are spring and fall, when temperatures are typically balmy. With spring rains, the prairies turn green and native wildflowers begin to bloom. In the fall, the changing color of the leaves, particularly in the eastern portion of the state, is inspiring. It's worth taking the

Great blue heron at Milford Lake. Photo by Chris Harnish

same trail at different times of the year to see the dynamic impact the changing seasons have on the vegetation and wildlife.

From December to February, trails can best be enjoyed on the mild, sunny days that occur sporadically throughout the winter. One of the prime benefits of winter hiking is the peace and solitude on the trails at this time of year, and the practical advantages include fewer bugs, less overgrowth, and often less wind. As vegetation becomes dormant during the winter, it may also be easier to spot wildlife along the trail, and a light dusting of snow reveals the tracks of even the most secretive species. Some species are actually most likely to be seen during the winter, including the bald eagle, which spends the winter months along reservoirs and rivers in the central and eastern parts of the state.

Be aware that the weather can change quickly, particularly in fall and spring;

what started out as a warm day could turn cold, and vice versa. So plan ahead and bring layers of clothing. No matter the season, wind is likely. On average, the wind speed in Kansas is over 10 miles per hour. For trails with little tree cover, this is a consideration, as is sun exposure.

With the possibility of rapidly changing conditions, you should be prepared for adverse weather on the trail. Thunderstorms can come up quickly in Kansas, and lightning strikes from these storms are the primary threat. If you see lightning in the area, quickly descend to lower ground and avoid exposed ridges, bluffs, or lone trees until the storm passes.

Tornado season is typically April through June, as humid, warm air from the Gulf of Mexico collides with dry, cool air from the Rockies. Much of the state's yearly rainfall occurs between April and September. The average annual precipitation in Kansas ranges from 45 inches in the southeast to less than 20 inches in the west. The Rocky Mountains are actually responsible for the arid climate in western Kansas. The mountain range creates a rain shadow effect: moist air from the Pacific is pushed upward as it moves east across the Rocky Mountains and loses moisture prior to reaching western Kansas.

In cool temperatures, hypothermia can occur when the body is unable to generate enough heat to maintain core body temperature. Hypothermia can occur gradually and is characterized by shivering, confusion, and lack of coordination. Prevent hypothermia by carrying additional layers of clothing that can be worn if the weather becomes cooler. Avoid cotton-based clothing, which provides little insulation if it becomes damp from perspiration or rainfall.

KNOW BEFORE YOU GO: ADVICE AND PRECAUTIONS

> The stranger [to Kansas], if he listened to the voice of experience, would not start upon his pilgrimage at any season of the year without an overcoat, a fan, a lightning rod, and an umbrella.
>
> John James Ingalls, "In Praise of Blue Grass," 1875

A sense of adventure, comfortable shoes, water, snacks, and a dose of common sense should get you through any Kansas trail with lots of enjoyment and few mishaps. But it's always good to know what hazards you might encounter and to be prepared for them.

GEAR AND CLOTHING

If you're experienced in the outdoors, bring whatever works for you. Following are some basic recommendations, not a complete list.

Always bring plenty of water. You can help prevent dehydration by drinking water throughout your time on the trail, particularly in the summer. Pack plenty of water, since the majority of trails do not have potable water available along the route, although in some cases there may be water available near the trailhead or the parking lot. Water in streams and reservoirs should be properly filtered and purified prior to drinking.

Other recommended items include sunscreen, insect repellent (particularly in summer), a small first-aid kit, and a cell phone, although coverage may not be available in all locations. For longer day trips, it's wise to carry a flashlight or head-lamp. And having a few tasty energy snacks is never a bad idea.

Wear or bring layers of clothing, including a waterproof jacket if there's a chance of rain. As noted earlier, cotton clothing won't provide insulation if it gets wet, and it dries more slowly than synthetic materials. Closed-toed shoes are best for all trail users. For those on foot, most of the trails can be hiked with a good pair of walking or running shoes, rather than heavier-duty hiking boots.

Cyclists should wear helmets and bring spare tubes, a multitool, and a repair kit. Equestrians should wear long pants and, ideally, helmets; they should carry items for tack repair, a hoof pick, and an extra lead rope.

REPTILES AND INSECTS

While not common, snakes are present throughout Kansas, though few are venomous. The four species of venomous snakes with established populations in the state are the timber rattlesnake, copperhead, prairie rattlesnake, and massasauga. The timber rattlesnake and copperhead are found in eastern Kansas and are associated with woodland areas. The massasauga is found in a variety of habitats,

Copperhead snake. Photo by Kristin Conard

including prairies, rocky hillsides, and open wetlands. The prairie rattlesnake is found in the western half of the state, and there is an isolated population in Kanopolis State Park. Although these snakes are venomous, they are typically not aggressive unless provoked. Paying close attention to rock ledges and exposed rocks helps avoid unwanted encounters. If you see or hear a snake, give it a wide berth as you walk around it.

Mosquitoes can be a minor annoyance, but they can also spread serious diseases such as West Nile virus. Mosquitoes are most active at dawn and dusk and during the summer. Protect yourself by using an insect repellent and wearing long sleeves and long pants.

Mosquitoes aren't the only insect pests to be aware of. If you're walking through high grass, chiggers can be a problem. Their bites are irritating and itchy, but chiggers don't carry diseases and are easily removed with a warm, soapy shower.

Of more concern are ticks, which can carry Rocky Mountain spotted fever and Lyme disease. Areas with deer are likely to have higher populations of ticks. Try to avoid rubbing up against vegetation, use insect repellent (permethrin-infused clothing is ideal, as DEET doesn't stop ticks), and wear long sleeves and long pants. Check for ticks after every outing, since you may not feel a tick bite, and remember to search the scalp, groin, armpits, and in the ears. Equestrians should check their horses for ticks as well. If you find a tick, remove it immediately by taking tweezers and firmly grasping the tick at the base of the head and pulling steadily. Make sure the mouthparts are removed along with the rest of the tick. If you have concerns or develop a rash or a fever after a tick bite, consult a doctor.

POISONOUS PLANTS

The most common poisonous plant along the trails in Kansas is poison ivy. Poison ivy occurs throughout the state and is typically found in woodlands and along woodland edges. Exposure to the plant can cause itching, skin irritation, and a rash. Poison ivy commonly grows either as a spreading ground cover or as a vine climbing up into trees. The key identifying characteristic of poison ivy is a pattern of three large leaflets: "Leaves of three, let it be." Wearing long sleeves and long pants can help prevent accidental contact with poison ivy. If you've been exposed to poison ivy, clean the affected area with rubbing alcohol or wash as soon as possible. Wash any exposed clothing, too, as it can carry the poison ivy oils, which can cause an outbreak.

HUNTING SEASON

Many state parks and wildlife areas allow hunting during specific seasons. Some trails may cross public hunting areas, and it is advisable to contact officials in the area you will be visiting to determine the specific dates and locations of hunting. Some trails may be closed for use during hunting season. If you're on a trail that's open during hunting season, be mindful and respectful of hunters, and make sure they can see you. Wear blaze orange headgear and a minimum of 100 square inches of blaze orange on both your front and your back.

ROUTES

The trails are well described and mapped out in this book, but it's always a good policy to carry a GPS with spare batteries, a map, or a compass. Let others know where you're going and the approximate time you expect to return. Don't assume you'll get consistent cell phone coverage on the trail. Unexpected storms or other events can result in obstructions on the trail, and some trails are better maintained than others. When in doubt, or when faced with a blocked or undefined trail, the most sensible option is to turn back.

RESPONSIBLE TRAIL USE

While on the trail, be courteous of others and practice a "leave no trace" policy by traveling only on marked trails, packing out all your trash, and leaving natural objects where you find them. Unless otherwise noted in the trail descriptions, dogs are allowed on the trails if they are leashed.

Avoid heading out on the trails after a recent rain. Trail use after a heavy rain can leave deep ruts that are difficult to smooth out after they dry. Some trails are closed during and after wet weather; respect all signs regarding trail openings and closings.

Many of the trails are multiuse — with cyclists, hikers, and riders all using the same trail — and some basic courtesies should be followed. Cyclists should yield to both hikers and horses. Hikers should yield to horses. Let others know you're coming with a friendly hello, and identify your general location if you're passing someone from behind ("On your left!"). Trail traffic should stay to the right and pass to the left. If you're approaching someone on horseback, check in with the rider before passing so you don't spook the horse. Cyclists should keep their speed under control and ride within their limits. Cyclists traveling downhill should yield to those coming uphill.

COSTS

All Kansas state parks charge a fee for vehicle access. Daily or annual permits are available for purchase, with reduced rates for seniors and for disabled individuals. For updates on the fee schedule, check the website for the Kansas Department of Wildlife, Parks, and Tourism: http://www.kdwpt.state.ks.us/news/State-Parks/Park-Fees. Many of the non–state park trails are free, but if there is a fee, it is noted in the trail description.

CAMPING INFORMATION

Cabins or campsites are available in many Kansas state parks, and a camping permit is required in addition to the motor vehicle permit. Daily, long-term, or annual camping permits can be purchased. Many campsites have hookups for water and electricity; others are more primitive, with only a grill for cooking and a driveway for parking.

Currently, many of the state parks accept reservations for some of their sites, while the others are available on a first come, first served basis. A two-night stay may be required for weekend reservations, and holiday weekend reservations require a five-day stay for campsites and a three-day stay for cabins. For more details, check the website: http://www.kdwpt.state.ks.us/State-Parks/Reservations. Reservations can be made through www.reserveamerica.com.

Along with campsites, many of the state parks have cabins for rent. Primitive cabins provide a place to sleep and not much else. Modern cabins offer true camping luxury, with furnished living rooms, bedrooms, bathrooms, and kitchens, along with heat and air-conditioning. Just bring your own bedding, towels, and toiletries.

CONTACTS AND RESOURCES

Each featured trail includes specific contact information and hours of operation for the trails themselves (though the hours of the on-site park offices may differ). For the most up-to-date information on trail openings and closures, access details, and camping fees for state parks, contact the Kansas Department of Wildlife, Parks, and Tourism, 512 SE 25th Avenue, Pratt, KS 67124; 620-672-5911; http://www.kdwpt.state.ks.us.

The Kansas Trails Council (PO Box 695, Topeka, KS 66601-0695; http://www.kansastrailscouncil.org/) is a nonprofit dedicated to maintaining and promoting the Kansas trails system. The Kansas Cycling Association (http://kscycling.org) promotes cycling at every level and provides information on all races and results in Kansas. Promoting mountain biking and maintaining and building single-track trails in south-central Kansas is the mission of the Kansas Singletrack Society (http://www.kssingletrack.com). For details about cycling clubs around the state, consult Kansas Cyclist (http://www.kansascyclist.com).

For information on equestrian events throughout the state and for maps, contact the Kansas Horse Council (8831 Quail Lane, Suite 201, Manhattan, KS 66502; 785-776-0662; http://www.kansashorsecouncil.com).

Volunteer nonprofits committed to building, maintaining, and promoting many of the rail-to-trail initiatives in Kansas include the Sunflower Rail-Trails Conservancy Inc. (sunflowertrails.org) and the Kanza Rail-Trails Conservancy (info@kanzatrails.org; http://kanzatrails.org/).

HOW TO USE THIS GUIDE

The state has been divided into seven regions: Kansas City metropolitan area, northeast, southeast, north-central, south-central, northwest, and southwest. The longer rail trails that span multiple regions have their own chapter.

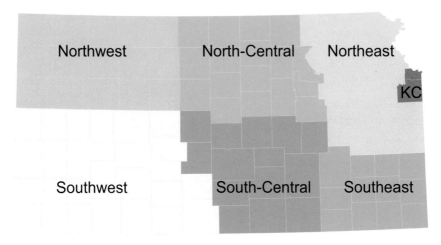

Kansas

Trails are listed within a region alphabetically by the park name. A broad overview of the park or area is followed by an in-depth description of the featured trails for that park or area, along with contact information, hours of operation, and cost. Featured trails are those that best showcase the particular area and were, at the time of writing, in good shape and recommended for use. These trails are 1 mile or longer round-trip and mostly on nonpaved surfaces. Some areas have multiple featured trails, some have a few shorter trails that combine to make up a longer featured trail, and some areas have only one featured trail. Not all trails in all areas are mapped, and some longer trails may have a featured segment with a listing for any additional nearby trails or continuations of the featured trail.

Each featured trail entry starts with the trail name(s), its method of access (hike, bike, bridle), its distance, and whether it's one-way or a loop. The descriptions of all featured trails include GPS coordinates for notable spots along the trail, and all featured trails have an accompanying detailed map.

Each description ends with directions on how to get to the trailhead, additional trails in the area, and information on camping (if available). For recommendations on places to eat and sleep other than campsites, check the book's companion website: kansastrailguide.com.

Disclaimer: The information provided is believed to be correct and true at the time of publication. GPS locations are estimated to be accurate to within 5 to 15 feet; however, there is no assumption of liability or responsibility in case of any discrepancies. Unexpected changes on the trails, such as flooding or fallen trees from storms, can make previously passable trails impassable. Exercise your best judgment in using this guide and on the trails.

TOP TRAILS

Although each trail has its own unique charm, some stand out. Here are our picks for the best of the best.

 ## BIKE

Most college towns have a good bike trail or two nearby, and this was a hard list to narrow down. But these well-marked, fun-to-ride bike trails with quick climbs and flowing recovery sections should not be missed.

Camp Alexander, Bike Loop — Northeast

Clinton Lake, North Shore Trails — Northeast

Fall River Lake, Badger Creek North Trail — Southeast

Lawrence River Trails — Northeast

MacLennan Park, Red Trail — Northeast

Manhattan, River Trail — North-central

Wilson Lake, Switchgrass Mountain Bike Trail — North-central

Wyandotte County Lake Park, East Dam Trails — Kansas City

 ## BRIDLE

Hundreds of miles of bridle trails can be found throughout Kansas, but some stand out because they are easily accessible and well taken care of and offer great views.

Hillsdale State Park, Saddle Ridge SE Red Trail — Northeast

Kanopolis State Park, Horsethief Canyon Trail — North-central

Lake Scott State Park, Multiuse Trail — Southwest

Melvern Lake, Crooked Knee Horse Trail — Northeast

FAMILY FRIENDLY

The whole family can enjoy these easily accessible, shorter trails over gentle terrain.

Chaplin Nature Center, River Trail — South-central

Chisholm Creek Park, Cottonwood Trail — South-central

Dillon Nature Center, Woodard Trail — South-central

Melvern Lake, Marais des Cygnes River Nature Trail — Northeast

Prairie Dog State Park, Steve Mathes Nature Trail — Northwest

Prairie Park Nature Center, Nature Trail — Northeast

Quivira National Wildlife Refuge, Migrant's Mile — South-central

HISTORICAL

With Native Americans, explorers, Civil War soldiers, pioneers, and settlers all influencing the history of the state, some trails take you through and past that history.

Allegawaho Memorial Heritage Park, Kanza Trail — North-central

Black Jack Battlefield and Nature Park, Battlefield and Nature Trails — Northeast

Cimarron National Grassland, Companion Trail — Southwest

Green Memorial Wildlife Area, Oregon Trace Trail — Northeast

Lake Scott State Park, Multiuse Trail — Southwest

Oregon Trail Nature Park, Sea of Grass Trail — Northeast

WILDLIFE AND WILDFLOWERS

A visit to one of these trails, particularly during spring and summer, almost guarantees some showy wildflowers or a chance to see some native wildlife.

Baker Wetlands, Nature Trails — Northeast

Olathe Prairie Center, Nature Trails — Kansas City

Prairie Park Nature Center, Nature Trail — Northeast

Quivira National Wildlife Refuge, Little Salt Marsh Trail — South-central

Tallgrass Prairie National Preserve, Scenic Overlook Trail — South-central

TOP 10

Well-maintained, easy to follow, and with some of the best scenery in the state, these trails are our overall top 10.

Cedar Bluff State Park, Agave Ridge Nature Trail — Northwest

Elk City State Park, Elk River Trail — Southeast

Kanopolis State Park, Horsethief Canyon Trail — North-central

Konza Prairie, Kings Creek Loop — North-central

Lake Scott State Park, Multiuse Trail — Southwest

Perry Lake, National Recreation Trail — Northeast

Prairie Spirit Trail and Southwind Rail Trail — Ottawa to Humboldt

Shawnee Mission Park, Orange, Violet, and Red Loops — Kansas City

Tallgrass Prairie National Preserve, Scenic Overlook Trail — South-central

Wilson Lake, Switchgrass Mountain Bike Trail — North-central

CHAPTER 2
KANSAS CITY METROPOLITAN AREA

If the Garden of Eden exceeded this land in beauty or fertility, I pity Adam for having to leave it.

HORACE GREELEY, NEAR SPRING HILL, 1859

Ashley Masoni at Shawnee Mission Park. Photo by Kristin Conard

Kansas City metropolitan area

1. Ernie Miller Park and Nature Center
2. Kill Creek Park
3. Olathe Prairie Center
4. Overland Park Arboretum and
   Botanical Gardens
5. Shawnee Mission Park
6. Wyandotte County Lake Park

Kansas City was founded at the confluence of the Kansas and Missouri Rivers, an area used by the Kansas, Osage, and Pawnee tribes. In 1804 Lewis and Clark observed that it would be a good site for a settlement. Some 120 years later, the city became a birthplace of jazz and barbecue, and it is now known as a city of fountains. Within this urban setting, there are a handful of parks that let you get away from the bustle of the city and get closer to the wild.

Kansas City and its surroundings are within the Glaciated Region. Some 400,000 to 600,000 years ago, what is now northeast Kansas was entirely covered in ice. As the glaciers melted and retreated, they left behind the quartzite boulders they had broken off and carried with them from places as far away as present-day Iowa, Minnesota, and South Dakota. The terrain in this region is hilly, and trails can be fairly rocky.

The area has some prairie paths, but most of the trails are partly or entirely through trees. And thanks to its dedicated mountain bike clubs and trail organizations, Kansas City has some of the state's best-kept biking trails. Overall, the trails here are typically hiding in plain sight, and they provide an easily accessible and pleasant respite from the city.

ERNIE MILLER PARK AND NATURE CENTER

The City of Olathe (*Olathe* means "beautiful" in Shawnee) purchased 113 acres of land south of the K-7 Highway in 1966, turned it into a park, and named it for Ernie Miller, who died that year. Miller, newspaper columnist and editor for the *Olathe Mirror*, was an active community member; he was named the first "Mr. Olathe" in 1964. The park has a few miles of trails running through it, and it features a prairie restoration area, an amphitheater, and a nature center with indoor exhibits housing live turtles, snakes, and amphibians and outdoor exhibits that include a butterfly and hummingbird garden.

Contact: Ernie Miller Park and Nature Center, 909 N. Highway 7, Olathe, KS 66061; 913-764-7759; Johnson County 24-hour park information line: 913-312-8833; erniemiller.com.

Hours: Daylight hours.

Cost: Free.

FEATURED TRAIL: SOUTH TRAIL, UPPER AND LOWER RIDGE TRAILS, AND BITTERSWEET TRAIL

Trail access: Hike. No dogs allowed.

Distance: 1.7-mile loop.

None of the longer trails at Ernie Miller Park and Nature Center is a closed loop, but by combining trails, you can make your own loop and vary its distance, depending on how you're feeling or any changes in the weather. This entry describes a combination of four of the park's trails starting at Shelter 1, although you

19

can also start at the Nature Center. Behind the parking lot for Shelter 1 (38.89653, −94.83922), the South Trail heads south and west into the timber. The dirt trail is wide and easy to follow through the trees. Despite its accessibility, you're likely to have the trail mostly to yourself during the week, unless there's a school group out taking a hike. The trail winds its way south and west along gentle inclines and declines. Keep an eye out for exposed roots and occasional rocks. The woods are primarily deciduous trees such as hackberry, black walnut, and American elm, as well as a fair amount of eastern red cedar. Spring and summer bring green fullness to the park's trees, along with blooming wildflowers; fall features bright tree colors and migratory birds; and in winter, the lack of vegetation means a better chance at spotting wildlife such as Canada geese, downy woodpeckers, and white-tailed deer.

About 0.3 mile into the South Trail, you'll pass a wooden bench near an opening in the forest canopy that overlooks a small prairie section. After the bench, head back into the woods and stay there for the next 0.75 mile. The trail heads east and south, with a small stream crossing (38.89246, −94.83658) 100 feet or so before the trail turns west. As the trail heads back north, you'll pass a trail junction (38.89116, −94.83988). If you turn left, you'll intersect with the Fire Road Trail and pass a pit toilet. The South Trail continues to the right. It winds north through the trees, following an easy path until it crosses a short log bridge just before the intersection of the Ridge Trails and the Amphitheater Trail. Turning right (east) takes you past the amphitheater and back toward the Nature Center. Continuing straight (north) follows the South Trail, and turning left (southwest) leads you over a bridge along the Lower Ridge Trail.

Crossing the bridge over Little Cedar Creek takes you toward the Ridge Trails. If you'd prefer a creek-side stroll that's less strenuous and shaves 0.3 mile off the 1.7-mile loop, take the first and nearly immediate right (north) after the bridge for the Lower Ridge Trail. For something a bit more strenuous, take the steep but short uphill portion to the Upper Ridge Trail. The Upper Ridge Trail also intersects with the Southwest Trail, which, after 0.28 mile, connects with the Rolling Ridge Trail (see Additional Trails). The Upper Ridge Trail intersects with the Lower Ridge Trail at the northern end, and the Lower Ridge Trail continues north until you cross Little Cedar Creek. This easy creek crossing involves stepping across carefully placed boulders within the creek bed (38.89699, −94.84360). At this point, you're relatively far away from K-7, so there's little traffic noise, and you can enjoy the views of the creek and the surrounding woodlands in relative peace. The Lower Ridge Trail curves back east and intersects with the Bittersweet Trail. Take the Bittersweet Trail southeast to the South Trail intersection (38.89646, −94.84181). If you continue straight onto the South Trail, you'll pass the back of the amphitheater and a small pond. Or you can bear left (east) to stay on the Bittersweet Trail and head back toward the Nature Center. Stop by the Nature Center to grab snacks and water and to check out the exhibits, or continue back onto the South Trail southeast of the Nature Center (38.89645, −94.84069) and follow it for 0.1 mile past the park's prairie restoration area and back to the Shelter 1 parking lot.

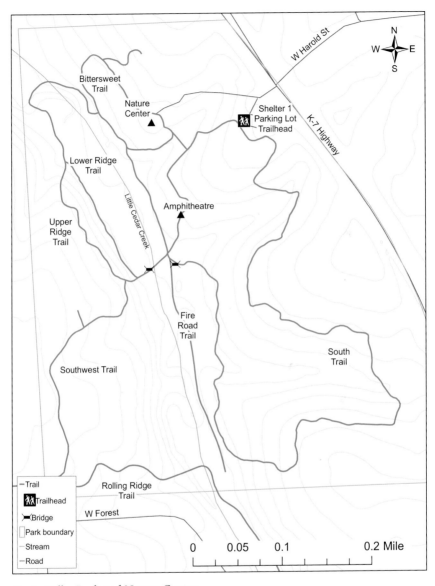

Ernie Miller Park and Nature Center

Directions to the trailhead: The park entrance is at the intersection of W. Harold Street and K-7. Trailheads can be accessed from north and east of the Nature Center — turn right (north) at the entrance, or they can be accessed at the parking lot for Shelter 1 — turn left (southwest) at the entrance.

Additional trails: The Rolling Ridge Trail, for hikers and bikers, can be accessed from the Southwest Trail, which links with the Upper Ridge Trail. The Rolling Ridge Trail is a 2.5-mile asphalt trail primarily along Little Cedar Creek between the Prairie Center Park to the north and Alta Lane and Ferrel Drive to the south, a few blocks from Rolling Ridge Elementary School.

Camping: As this is an urban hike, nearby camping is hard to come by. RV camping is available about 15 miles northeast at Walnut Grove RV Park (10218 Johnson Drive, Merriam, KS 66203; 913-262-3023; walnutgroverv.com). For the closest tent camping, Hillsdale State Park is about 23 miles south, off of K-7 (26001 W. 255th Street, Paola, KS 66071).

KILL CREEK PARK

This park, one of the newer ones in Johnson County, has a lake, a marina, a beach, a playground, and a dozen miles of trails. The 880-acre Kill Creek Park was opened in 2001, and the trails take you across streams, past lakes, and through the woods and the prairie. The 28-acre lake is stocked with largemouth and smallmouth bass, crappie, and channel catfish. The hiking, mountain bike, and equestrian trails that run through Kill Creek Park can be combined in different ways for a new experience each time.

Contact: 11670 Homestead Lane, Olathe, Kansas 66061; 913-831-3355; Johnson County 24-hour park information line: 913-312-8833.
Hours: Daylight hours.
Cost: Free.

FEATURED TRAIL: HIKING TRAIL

Trail access: Hike.
Distance: 1.2-mile to 3-mile loops.

The hiking trail and the mountain biking trail both start behind Shelter 1 (38.91477, −94.97404). The hiking trail bears right toward the northeast along a paved sidewalk. With trees to the left, the start of the trail is exposed, and after a few hundred feet is the wooden prairie observation deck to the west. Check out the view overlooking part of the 23 acres of restored upland prairie with hundreds of plant species; it's particularly beautiful during the summer when the flowers are in bloom. From the observation deck, the trail becomes a dirt track along the edge of the woods that border the prairie restoration area. Close to the end of 115th Street, the hiking trail and the equestrian trail intersect (38.92027, −94.97354). To stay on the hiking trail, bear right (northwest) at the intersection.

From here, the trail takes you into the woods. During the summer, the narrow, single-track trail is easy to follow, although it may be overgrown. About 1,000 feet after the intersection at 115th Street, you'll cross Kill Creek (38.92269, −94.97423). Large boulders have been strategically placed to help ensure a dry crossing, even if there is water. Shortly after the creek crossing, the trail splits and you can continue straight or turn left; this is the beginning (or end) of an approximately 0.75-mile loop. Taking the loop all the way around and continuing back to the parking lot

Sunset and storm near the Kill Creek Park entrance. Photo by Billie Hufford

totals a 1.4-mile round-trip; alternatively, there is an extension of the hiking trail about halfway through the loop.

If you take the trail to the left (west), you'll have to cross Kill Creek a few times, and the trail can be a bit hard to follow. Keep an eye out for the hot-pink ties on tree limbs to help you stay on the right path. The trail to the left is easier in terms of elevation gain, as the trail that continues straight (north) heads uphill. Both trails intersect with the equestrian trail, and about halfway through the loop you'll reach the intersection with the continuation of the hiking trail (38.92584, –94.97637).

Shortly after the hiking loop intersects with the northwestern portion of the hiking trail, the trail crosses Kill Creek again (38.92582, –94.97657) and continues northwest. Leading through a brief break in the trees (as well as across the creek again), the trail turns left (west) near the base of a low stone ridge. After another 0.25 mile through the trees (and another creek crossing near the end of the northernmost stretch of the trail), it heads south between the forested areas and South Spoon Creek Road. The trail is relatively flat and easy going here, as it leads toward the intersection of the mountain bike trail and the paved trail (38.92180,

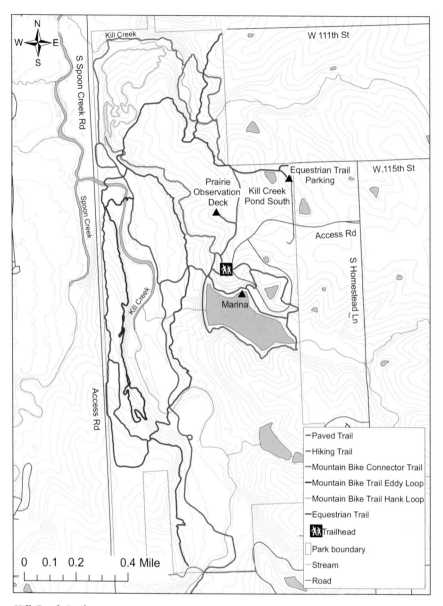

Kill Creek Park

–94.98248). From there, it's 1 mile back to the parking lot via the paved trail, or 0.8 mile on the mountain bike trail back to the start.

Additional trails: To the south of the parking lot is a marina and a small lake. If you follow the paved trails around the lake, you'll find a short hiking trail through the trees along the south side of the lake (38.91121, –94.97367). From the parking lot, around the lake, and past the marina and beach, it's a 1.2-mile round-trip.

FEATURED TRAIL: CONNECTOR AND HANK TRAILS

Trail access: Hike or bike.
Distance: 2.5-mile loop.

Starting from the parking area near Shelter 1 (38.91477, –94.97404), the paved trail heads north into the woods. After the first turn is the start of the connector mountain bike trail, heading northwest into the woods. The single-track trail is typically cleared of vegetation, although there may be occasional rocky sections and exposed roots. After traveling 0.8 mile along the trail through the woods, with an occasional up and down and past an old stone fence, you'll cross the equestrian trail (38.92134, –94.98098), and 400 feet after that intersection is the start of the Hank Trail.

The Hank Trail is the easier of the two mountain bike loops at Kill Creek (see "Additional trails" for the harder one). Head straight (north) along the rock wall, and you'll come to a three-way intersection (38.92407, –94.98182). This is the start of the loop of the Hank Trail, which you can take either way and end up back at this intersection. It's designed as a beginner–intermediate trail, with some rocky parts that lean more toward the intermediate side; however, it's a good place to test

Nate Backer at Kill Creek Park. Photo by Kristin Conard

your skills as you ride through the trees. The trail can be soft after a recent rain, so wait a couple of days to allow it to firm up. The loop is 1.6 miles. To get back to the start after finishing the loop, you can either retrace your ride along the connector trail or, for a change of scenery with more prairie views, take the paved trail back. For a greater challenge, and for advanced riders only, add on the Eddy Trail.

The Eddy Trail heads south from the intersection of the connector trail and the paved trail (38.92164, –94.98234). After going 0.2 mile south on the paved trail, you'll arrive at the start of the Eddy Trail. It crosses the creek, and there are two log jumps (with optional routes around the obstacles) at the start. The trail is a "lollipop" — an out-and-back mile of trail heading south with a loop at the end. You can take the loop either way; if you take it to the right (counterclockwise), it heads uphill near Kill Creek.

FEATURED TRAIL: EQUESTRIAN TRAIL

Trail access: Bridle.
Distance: 5.8 miles total.

The parking area for horse trailers is just east of Kill Creek Pond South, and the equestrian trail starts there (38.91949, –94.96955). Note that the bridle trail will be closed if it's wet. The dirt trail starts out exposed through open prairie and heads just north of the pond. The trail is mostly flat with occasional dips, and it intersects with the hiking trail and the end of W. 115th Street (38.92027, –94.97354). From there, head into the woods until you hit a three-way intersection (38.92185, –94.97549). If you turn right (north), the trail will cross the hiking trail loops and the creek, with a gradual uphill ride to the end of W. 111th Street.

If you continue straight at the intersection, you'll be in the timber, with some dips and turns for 0.3 mile before you emerge from the woods and head southwest along the prairie. The prairie views to the northeast while you ride are particularly pleasant during the summer when the wildflowers are in bloom. Take in the scenery before heading back into the woods. Keep an eye out here for bikers and hikers, as the equestrian trail crosses the mountain bike trail (38.92134, –94.98098). After crossing the mountain bike trail, the trail splits, and you can head either right or left for a 2.7-mile loop in the southern portion of the park. The trail crosses the creek on both sides of the loop — once on the western side, just past an intersection of the equestrian trail and the paved trail (38.91997, –94.98098), and once on the eastern side, also just past an intersection of the paved trail and the equestrian trail (38.90752, –94.97839).

The loop section offers a couple of alternatives. If you take the trail clockwise after the creek crossing, the trail emerges from the trees and you'll reach a four-way intersection (38.90569, –94.97998). The trail heading back northeast takes you to the park's southern boundary. You can continue along the prairie either west-northwest or south — both options take you to the southern edge of the large southern loop. From the end of the loop, ride the mile back to the start.

Directions to the trailhead: From K-10, take the Kill Creek exit and head south toward 115th Street for 2.8 miles. Turn right (west) onto W. 115th Street. For the hiking and biking trailhead behind Shelter 1, take the first left (south) onto S. Homestead Lane; then take the first right (west) onto the access road and follow it 0.6 mile to the parking lot. For horse trailer parking, take the second left off W. 115th Street onto the access road; the circle parking lot is a few hundred feet off of W. 115th Street.

Additional trails: In the southern part of Heritage Park (16050 Pflumm Road, Olathe), the Mid-America Combined Training Association (MACTA) has 4.72 miles of trails that are open to the public when events are not being held. South of Kill Creek Park between Gardner and Edgerton, the Lanesfield Historic Site (18745 S. Dillie Road, Edgerton, KS 66021) has a short nature trail for hiking and a one-room limestone schoolhouse that is open for tours on Friday and Saturday afternoons or by appointment.

OLATHE PRAIRIE CENTER

No place in the Kansas City area offers visitors a more in-depth or immediate immersion into the tallgrass prairie than the Prairie Center. But it's not just prairie. On the 300 acres of protected preserve, you can also find wetlands and riparian woods. What was once farmland was purchased in 1968 to be used as an educational space. In 1990 the Kansas Department of Wildlife, Parks, and Tourism took over the property, and the educational focus continues. School groups are frequent visitors to the center, and teacher workshops are held throughout the year.

Annual controlled burns keep the trees and shrubs out of the grassland, and the wildflowers, accompanied by bees and butterflies, put on a show that changes with the seasons. In spring, you might see wild strawberry and the endangered Mead's milkweed; in summer, black-eyed Susan, purple prairie clover, and prickly poppy; and in fall, goldenrod, blue sage, and smooth aster. And no matter the season, you can bring in a meal to enjoy at the picnic area overlooking a 5-acre lake that is open for fishing, as is the stream (for catch and release).

Contact: 26235 W. 135th Street, Olathe, KS 66061; 913-856-7669.
Hours: Daylight hours.
Cost: Free.

FEATURED TRAIL: NATURE TRAILS (TOP WILDLIFE AND WILDFLOWER TRAIL)

Trail access: Hike. No dogs allowed.
Distance: 3-mile loop, 6 miles total.

It's easy to mix and match the different trails, depending on how long you want to spend exploring the prairie. Parking is available near the main entrance off S. Cedar Niles Road in the northeast corner of the park, and the barn, pit toilets, and trailhead are close by (38.88299, –94.89053). After walking 150 feet on the wide

Olathe Prairie Center. Photo by Kristin Conard

gravel path, you have the choice of continuing straight or turning left (east). Either way, the trails loop back and connect several times, with little overall change in elevation, so the direction you choose at this point doesn't make much of a difference. If you continue straight, the trail takes you past a wooden platform, open only for special programs. Following the gravel pathway, you'll come to an intersection with a mowed grass trail (38.88068, –94.89452). To cut straight to the picnic area and pond, stay on the gravel pathway. Following the mowed grass trail to the right (northwest) leads you along the edge of the woods until you reach another intersection (38.88054, –94.89926). You can cut back to the left (east) to meet the picnic area trails or turn right (west) to cross Cedar Creek. The creek crossing is across pavement, and a couple hundred feet beyond it is another trail intersection (38.88030, –94.90033), where you can turn left or right. If you turn left, the trail continues through a mix of light woodlands; to the right is the more strenuous (relatively speaking) portion of the trail that takes you up some low limestone bluffs. It's a gradual but noticeable elevation change, after the smooth paths encountered thus far. The reward for this uphill trek is the view across the prairie and woodlands from one of the park's highest points. The first trail intersection along the bluffs is with a 0.1-mile spur to W. 135th Street. From this intersection, the main trail turns left (southwest) and continues uphill to the intersection (38.88092, –94.90414) with the main trail and the 0.3-mile connector to the W. 135th Street parking area.

Continue downhill and back into the woods to a T-junction in the trail. The right (south) trail follows the main trail to its southern edge, while the left (northeast) trail connects back with the Bluff Loop near the Cedar Creek crossing. If you take the trail to the right (south) back into the woods, you'll find a spur trail to the west that leads to an archery range as well as the Moonlight Road entrance. The main trail heads south and then curves north and east and crosses Cedar Creek several times. You emerge from the trees at the picnic area near the pond. Along with the picnic tables, there are pit toilets and a small deck overlooking the pond. It's a great place to stop and take in the views before finishing up your hike. To get back to the main parking area from the picnic area, take either of the trails south of the pond for new views of the reseeded prairie; they both come together at the eastern edge of the park. The southernmost trail is 0.2 mile longer and takes you out through the prairie, while the other trail puts you between the prairie and the wooded area.

Directions to the trailhead: From K-7, turn west onto W. 135th Street. Continue for 3 miles and turn left (south) onto S. Cedar Niles Road; the entrance is about 300 feet ahead on the right. To get to the second W. 135th Street parking lot,

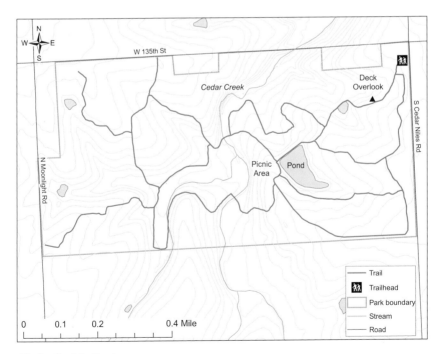

Olathe Prairie Center

continue on W. 135th Street for 3.8 miles; the parking lot is on the left (south). For the west entrance on Moonlight Road, continue on W. 135th Street another mile after S. Cedar Niles Road and turn left (south) onto Moonlight Road; the trailhead is another 0.5 mile on the left (east).

Additional trails: Ernie Miller Park and Nature Center is nearby. See the featured trail above.

Camping: Primitive camping is available with special permission.

OVERLAND PARK ARBORETUM AND BOTANICAL GARDENS

In 1996 the Erickson Water Garden was the first display that opened at the Overland Park Arboretum and Botanical Gardens. Over the years, the gardens have grown to include the Xeriscape Garden, with water-efficient plants, and the Monet Garden, complete with a green bridge over Margaret's Pond, which was inspired by Monet's gardens in France. The 300-acre arboretum was designed to be a recreational and educational destination devoted to preserving natural ecosystems, and the botanical gardens are all about stunning colors and plant design. The nearly 5 miles of trails through the mixed woodland ecosystems, across and along Wolf Creek and limestone cliffs, are wide and covered in wood chips. The trails are mostly shaded, with water stations and benches along the way, making them ideal for family outings. The mix of loops and connecting trails means that if you're feeling energetic, you can easily combine different loops without too much backtracking or overlap, and if you get tired, it's easy to head back. The spring blooms are impressive, particularly along the Rocky Ridge Trail, and in the fall, the foliage makes a stunning background for your walk.

Contact: 8909 W. 179th Street, Overland Park, KS 66013; 913-685-3604; www .opkansas.org.

Hours: Open 8 a.m. to 7:30 p.m. from mid-April to the end of September; open 8 a.m. to 5 p.m. from October to mid-April.

Cost: $3 for those aged 13 and older, $1 for children 6 to 12, and free for children 5 and younger; free every Tuesday.

FEATURED TRAIL: BLUFF LOOP, ROCKY RIDGE TRAIL, AND COTTONWOOD TRAIL

Trail access: Hike.

Distance: 2.2-mile loop.

From the Environmental Education Visitors' Center, head south along the International Sculpture Garden Trail. This asphalt trail is a 0.4-mile loop, and at about the 0.25-mile point, it intersects with the mulched Cottonwood Trail, just past several impressive sculptures by Chinese and American artists. The exhibit is semipermanent; the eleven sculptures will eventually be part of a much larger sculpture garden on the neighboring Kemper Farm. For now, they help guide the way to the 0.4-mile Cottonwood Trail. From the paved trail, turn southwest at the

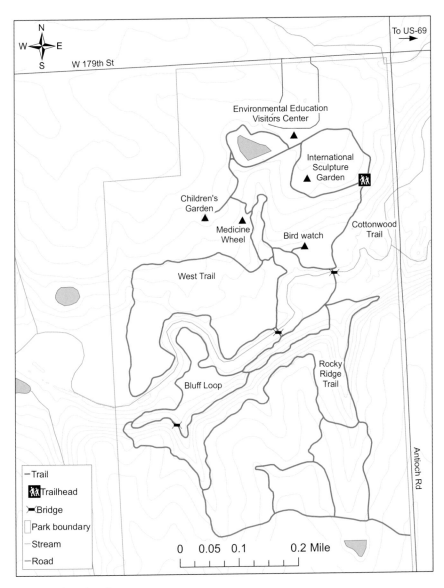

Overland Park Arboretum

Cottonwood Trail trailhead (38.80032, −94.68730). The Cottonwood Trail links the International Sculpture Garden Trail and the Bluff Loop at a bridge over Wolf Creek (38.79841, −94.68847), which bisects the arboretum. If you follow the Cottonwood Trail to the west instead of heading south across the bridge, you'll pass a bird blind and the paved garden trails, which eventually connect to the West Trail (see the following featured trail).

After crossing Wolf Creek on the large wooden bridge, you'll arrive at the eastern intersection of the Bluff Loop and Rocky Ridge Trail. Wooden signs point out different options. For an easier route with little elevation change, take the 1-mile Bluff Loop. For something a bit more strenuous, the 1-mile Rocky Ridge Trail heads uphill along the limestone bluffs south of the creek. This trail takes you through the most diverse range of ecosystems in the arboretum, including the dry oak-hickory forest at its start; this type of forest, which is common through-out central North America, consists of post oak, shagbark hickory, and black oak. Heading through the woods and uphill, you'll cross a small bridge and come to an intersection, where you can continue south to the prairie section or turn west to stay on the Rocky Ridge Trail. Past the bridge, there's a water station and benches — a good place for a break. Continuing north and then west again, you may notice a subtle change in your surroundings. Within the wooded draws just south of the creek, you may find different kinds of vegetation such as red cedar, elm, and rough-leaf dogwood.

At the southernmost point of the Rocky Ridge Trail, it splits (38.79338, –94.69295). Heading left (south) takes you toward open prairie, which is part of a 10-year restoration project; heading right (northwest) keeps you on the Rocky Ridge Trail. On the western edge of the Rocky Ridge Trail, the ecosystem is me-sic oak-hickory forest. This part of the arboretum has some of the largest trees, thanks to the moist soil along the Wolf Creek floodplain. Along with red oak and shagbark hickory trees, it has white ash and pawpaw trees. The Rocky Ridge Trail heads downhill and ends at a water station and the western end of the Bluff Loop (38.79505, –94.69551).

From this intersection, either side of the 1.1-mile Bluff Loop can be taken back to the east. The south side of the Bluff Loop is 0.5 mile; the north side is 0.6 mile and takes you along the creek. Taking the north side offers more options, as it also includes a bridge across Wolf Creek to the West Trail. Along the north side, the trail follows the bends of Wolf Creek through stands of cottonwoods and syca-mores until you reach the end of the loop at the intersection of the Rocky Ridge Trail. From there, backtrack along the Cottonwood Trail to the right (northeast) or head left (west) to link up with the West Trail or to explore the botanical gardens.

FEATURED TRAIL: WEST TRAIL

Trail access: Hike.
Distance: 1.5-mile loop.

Head southwest along the paved trails past the Environmental Education Visi-tors' Center and along the south side of Margaret's Pond. The paved trails spiral and twist around the different gardens, and the start of the West Trail is south of the Marder Woodland Garden. The West Trail is essentially a loop, with the start and finish about 50 feet apart off the paved garden trail (38.79897, –94.69038). The easy wood-chip trail can be taken in either direction, with little change in ele-vation. If you take the trail clockwise, after just over 0.1 mile you'll come to a large

Overland Park Arboretum West Trail. (Photo by Kristin Conard)

wooden bridge across Wolf Creek. You can connect with the Bluff Loop on the other side or stay on the West Trail. The trail is almost entirely within the dry oak-hickory ecosystem, characterized by black oak, post oak, and shagbark hickory.

Along the creek, you may see white-tailed deer. Although the paved trails near the entrance can be crowded, it gets quieter as you head farther into the woods, and you might even hear the telltale tap of woodpeckers. After following the creek for about 0.5 mile, the trail turns right (north) through the woods for 0.25 mile and then turns right (east) again. Emerging from the woods to cross open ground and a park access road, the trail takes you south of the Medicine Wheel and the Children's Garden as the loop closes back at the paved trail. Head back north through the rest of the gardens or continue exploring the woodlands.

Directions to the trailhead: The Overland Park Arboretum is southwest of the intersection of W. 179th Street and Antioch Road. Take the W. 179th Street exit off of US-69 and continue west on W. 179th Street for 0.8 mile past Antioch Road. Turn left (south) into the arboretum.

Additional trails: Paved trails twist and turn through the gardens, and they are handicapped accessible as well as being ideal for strollers.

Heritage Park is northwest of the arboretum at 16050 Pflumm, Olathe, KS. The Mid-America Combined Training Association (MACTA) has 4.72 miles of horse trails in the southern part of the park that are open to the public when events are not being held.

Camping: The closest camping is south and west at Hillsdale State Park, off of K-7 (26001 W. 255th Street, Paola, KS 66071).

SHAWNEE MISSION PARK

The 1,600-acre park in Shawnee was dedicated on May 30, 1964, and is the most visited park in Kansas. With a 120-acre lake open for boating and fishing, a disc golf course, plenty of picnic areas and playgrounds, an archery range, and trails for hikers, bikers, and equestrians, its popularity is not surprising. If you pull up to Shawnee Mission Park in the evening, there's likely to be dozens of cars in the parking lot, as local road cyclists, mountain bikers, trail runners, and walkers come out to enjoy the trails after work. With paved multiuse areas; winding, sometimes rocky single tracks for beginners to experts; and enough short climbs and descents to get your heart pumping, the park has something for just about everyone. The bike trails are well maintained, and hundreds of hours have been spent keeping the trails in good shape.

Contact: 7900 Renner Road, Shawnee, KS 66219; 913-888-4713; 913-312-8833 (24-hour park information line for possible trail closings); info@jcprd.com.

Hours: 6 a.m. to 8 p.m.

Cost: Free.

FEATURED TRAIL: ORANGE LOOP, VIOLET LOOP, AND RED LOOP (TOP 10 TRAIL)

Trail access: Hike or bike.

Distance: Orange, 2.5-mile loop; Violet, 2-mile loop; Red, 3.4-mile loop.

The well-marked and -maintained Shawnee Mission Park single-track trails through the woods are some of the rockiest in the area. They give even expert mountain bikers a good workout and a fun ride. The trails are flowing and shady, with three different loop options: the Orange Loop is the easiest, the Violet Loop is the most difficult, and the Red Loop is the longest total distance. But since there are a few different starting points and intersection points, you can mix and match to create a different experience each time you ride. The trees are mostly deciduous, and in the spring you can spot redbuds in bloom. In the fall you can enjoy a ride through trees in full color while keeping an eye out for white-tailed deer — the park has a large population of them. To start with the easiest part of the trail, set out on the Orange Loop. If you want to bypass the Orange Loop altogether and go straight to the hard stuff, you can access the Violet Loop from 79th Street, west of the parking lot near Shelter 4 and the tennis courts (38.98572, –94.80918).

To start with the Orange Loop, from the parking lot for Shelter 4 (38.98761,

Billie Rhodes running at Shawnee Mission Park. (Photo by Kristin Conard)

−94.80027), cross the park road and the paved shared-use trail for the eastern Orange Loop trailhead (38.98821, −94.80107). The trail can be taken clockwise or counterclockwise through the woods. To ease into your ride without much elevation change, head to the left at the trailhead to take the loop clockwise. Keep an eye out for rocks and roots as well as other trail users on this twisty, flowing trail. With a gradual uphill to the north, the trail curves back south and west and reaches the western trailhead for the Orange Loop (38.98719, −94.80343). From that intersection, the trail bears sharply right (north) and continues north and then west, uphill to the intersection with the Violet Loop (38.98803, −94.80574). This is about the halfway point for the Orange Loop.

Novice riders should follow the Orange Loop back to the start, while advanced riders can continue onto the Violet Loop, which can be taken either clockwise or counterclockwise. For quick access to the Red Loop and to bypass the most difficult portions of the Violet Loop, take the trail to the right (north). By taking the Violet Loop counterclockwise, the hill at the northernmost portion of the loop becomes a downhill rather than an uphill section.

For a challenge — to hit the hardest parts of the Violet Loop first and take the northern hill section uphill — bear left and go down the hill, following the trail for 0.3 mile to its intersection with the Violet Loop trailhead (38.98572, –94.80918). From the Violet Loop trailhead, the trail becomes tricky and extremely technical, with lots of rocks and quick ups and downs. About 0.6 mile from the Violet Loop trailhead is a trail off to the left (west) that connects with the access road, which can be ridden south to 79th Street (38.99064, –94.81084). From there, the main trail bears east and brings you to the intersection of the Violet Loop and the Red Loop (38.99119, –94.80870). To continue on the Violet Loop, bear right at the intersection. The trail heads uphill past the intersection with the equestrian trail and intersects with the Red Loop a second time (38.99252, –94.80432). From the Red Loop intersection, you can head south again to the intersection of the Orange and Violet Loops.

For the Red Loop, start from the western intersection with the Violet Loop (38.99119, –94.80870), bear left, and start winding your way north through the trees. At about 0.15 mile from the intersection, you'll pass through a cleared space in the trees for a set of power lines. After the power lines, the trail takes you up- and downhill along a ridge. The reward for your hard work as you ride west and north is open views out over the grasslands near the northern edge of the trail. From the vista point, the trail goes downhill for a bit before another uphill section begins. The trails here were built with the ideals of FDR's Civilian Conservation Corps in mind — that is, the trails are intended to be in place for many years for future generations to use and enjoy. Although this trail (like the rest here) can be rocky, sections of barbed wire have been removed, so bikers don't have such high stakes when it comes to controlling speed around turns. The trail emerges from the trees on the east side, crosses an access road, and then goes beneath the power lines before connecting with the Violet Loop.

Directions to the trailhead: The bike trails are accessible from 79th Street near Shelter 4. The park is south of Shawnee Mission Parkway, north of W. 87th Street, and between US-435 and K-7. From Shawnee Mission Parkway, turn south onto Midlands Drive; after just less than a mile, turn right (south) onto Ogg Road and follow it into the park. Turn right (west) on 79th Street; the parking area for the trails is on the left (south) near the tennis courts and Shelter 4.

Additional trails: In late 2013, workers began extending the trail, adding another 1.3 miles, which should bring the total distance to around 5 miles.

A paved shared-use trail runs along the northern edge of the park. For a more rugged trail, the South Shore Trail follows the south side of the lake. This trail is a relatively easy 3-mile one-way ride, with views of the lake through the trees, so you can go for a 6-mile out and back. Alternatively, if you start hiking from the east end and lock a bike up at the west end before you start, you can enjoy a mostly downhill paved ride along the road back to your car at the east trailhead. This trail can get a bit overgrown in the summer, and it is less popular than the nearby bike trails. The South Shore Trail also runs through the off-leash dog area.

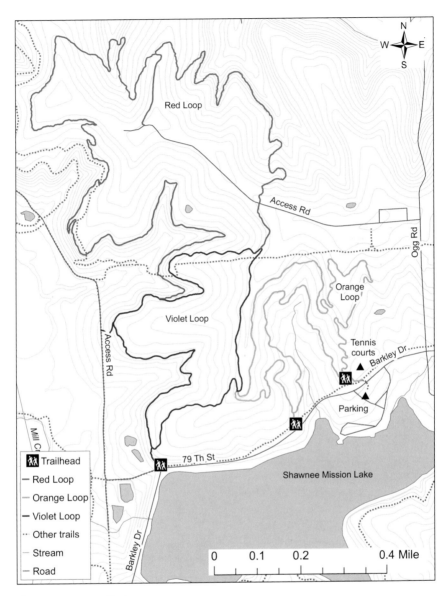

Shawnee Mission Park

For equestrians, an 8.3-mile bridle trail starts at the southwest corner at the archery range. It runs up and across the northern edge of the park, past the park buildings in the northeast corner, and ends alongside the South Shore Trail.

Northwest of Shawnee Mission Park is Mill Creek Streamway Park. The paved Gary L. Haller National Recreation Trail is a 17-mile rail trail that runs from the Kansas River at Nelson Island south to Olathe. Nearby Black Hoof Park (9053

Monticello Road, Lenexa, KS), has a 2-mile trail around Lake Lenexa that is open to hikers and bikers.

Camping: Camping at Shawnee Mission Park is available by reservation only for not-for-profit youth organizations.

WYANDOTTE COUNTY LAKE PARK

The 456-acre Wyandotte County Lake was built by the Works Progress Administration (WPA) in the 1930s. You can boat and fish on the lake, and it's the practice spot for the Kansas City Rowing Club. Inside the 1,500-acre park, you can have a meal at one of the many picnic shelters, play at the playgrounds, or explore the trail system's options for hikers, bikers, and equestrians. Throughout the hills around the lake, it's primarily oak-hickory hardwood forest, with some sycamores along the lake itself.

Contact: Leavenworth Road and 91st Street, Kansas City, KS 66109; 913-596-7077; parksinfo@wycokck.org.

Hours: 6 a.m. to midnight.

Cost: Free.

FEATURED TRAIL: EAST DAM TRAILS (TOP BIKING TRAIL)

Trail access: Hike or bike.

Distance: White Tail Loop Trail, 3 miles; Mason's First Linear Trail, 2.75 miles; Boy Scout Loop Trail, 2.5 miles; Oz Loop, 1 mile. Total miles of trail in production: 11.5 miles.

Around Shelter 9 and Boy Scout Cove, intersecting trails wind through the trees and alongside the lake, giving hikers and cyclists all kinds of options. These well-maintained trails — which are being expanded by the EarthRiders, the local mountain bike club — have a handful of fun as well as some not-so-fun obstacles along the way, such as low-hanging branches and protruding roots, but these are all clearly marked with yellow or pink tape. The trails are constructed to prevent erosion and dry up quickly after a rain, unlike the bridle trail that winds around the lake. There are plenty of trail intersections, which means you can have a new experience each time, with different distances and different combinations of trails. However, it can also be a bit confusing, especially your first time. Check the map at every intersection to ensure that you know where you are.

The trails start at the south end of the parking lot for Shelter 9 (39.16305, −94.77032). Immediately, you're faced with a decision about which way to go. From the trailhead, you can take the White Tail Loop (3 miles) either clockwise or counterclockwise. The single-track trail flows through the hardwood forest and is clear and easy to follow. Going clockwise, you'll reach a connector trail to the southwest at 0.5 mile in, which connects with the gravel park road (39.16153, −94.77317). To continue on the trail, take the switchback back to the east. Not

Log obstacle on the trail at Wyandotte County Lake Park. (Photo by Kristin Conard)

long after, you'll come to one of the log obstacles scattered along the trails. For all such obstacles, there's the option of going around it if you're not feeling up to going over it. After another 0.25 mile, you'll reach a connector trail to the main road (39.16278, –94.77424). To continue on the trail, bear to the right; the trail starts to wind back on itself, gradually bearing north and east toward the lake and Shelter 7. A connector trail near Shelter 7 (39.16454, –94.77701) can take you west to the 357 Loop Trail (see Additional Trails). To continue on the White Tail Loop, head downhill toward the lake. The trail tracks south again before reaching the lake, and there's another junction with a connector trail (39.16486, –94.77752). This connector trail, near the halfway point of the White Tail Loop Trail, heads north to Mason's First Linear Trail. If you follow the White Tail Loop Trail back toward the start of the loop, you'll come to a break in the trees, which is noteworthy on these wooded trails (39.16395, –94.77403). This break in the trees also marks a four-way intersection with the White Tail Loop Trail and Mason's First Linear Trail (39.16394, –94.77349). Bear right (south) at the junction after the clearing, and it's a winding 0.5 mile back to the trailhead. There's another intersection with Mason's First Linear Trail south of the clearing intersection.

If you bear left (northeast) at the junction near the clearing, you'll be on the eastern portion of Mason's First Linear Trail, which connects with the Boy Scout Loop Trail near the lake. At 0.2 mile past the clearing junction, there's a Y-intersection of Mason's First Linear Trail and a connector trail that links it with the Boy Scout Loop Trail (39.16599, –94.77300). You can either take Mason's First Linear Trail back to its southern intersection with the White Tail Loop Trail or take the trail to the left (northwest) to the Boy Scout Loop Trail. A few hundred feet downhill from the intersection is boat storage for the rowing organizations that practice on the lake. Head uphill to the open picnic area, and check out the view of the lake before heading back into the trees. After the picnic area, you're presented with another choice. The Boy Scout Loop begins (or ends) here, and there are a handful of connections to other trails along the way to either shorten or lengthen the trail. You can take the loop clockwise or counterclockwise. Hugging the side of the lake on the northern side of the loop (clockwise), you get glimpses of Boy Scout Cove through the trees, and after another 0.25 mile, you'll come to the Oz Trail offshoot. This 1-mile section is more technical and is best attempted only by advanced riders.

If you continue past the Oz Trail offshoot on the Boy Scout Loop, you'll reach a Y-junction where you can head to the right and cut 0.5 mile off the loop. Or you can continue along the edge of the lake for the full Boy Scout Loop. The Boy Scout Loop meets up with the end of Mason's First Linear Trail at a four-way intersection (39.16696, –94.76985). The first right to the east is a connector trail to the park road, the second right is Mason's First Linear Trail, and the first left is the continuation of the Boy Scout Loop. Both trails gradually take you back south and west, along winding hills. The Boy Scout Loop Trail is about twice as long, with more switchbacks and turns, as the Mason's First Linear Trail, which runs between the Boy Scout Loop Trail and the park road. The two trails intersect again to the southwest (39.16439, –94.76621) and then one more time near the northern end of the Shelter 9 parking lot (39.16481, –94.77000). From this intersection, you can head up through the trees to the parking lot. If you're on the Mason's First Linear Trail, you can take it for another 0.5 mile to the southern intersection of the White Tail Loop Trail. If you're on the Boy Scout Loop Trail, you can take it back up to

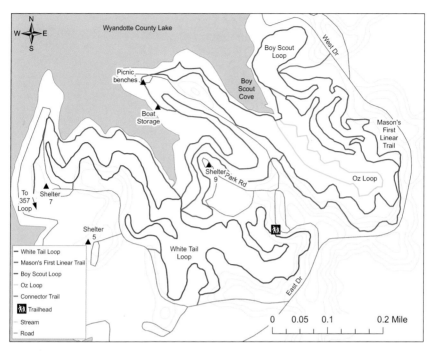

Wyandotte County Lake Park

the picnic area near the lake and then take the Mason's First Linear Trail back toward the trailhead.

Directions to the trailhead: Take I-435 north from I-70 to K-5/Leavenworth Road (exit 15). Continue east on Leavenworth Road for 0.7 mile. Turn left (north) on N. 83rd Street; after 0.4 mile, bear left onto County Lake Park Road and then bear right (east) onto East Drive and follow it for 1 mile to Shelter 9.

Additional trails: In late 2013 and early 2014, the 1.25-mile 357 Loop Trail and the 0.5-mile Lollipop Loop Trail were finished (located to the west of Shelter 5 and Shelter 7). For mountain bike experts looking to work on their technical trail riding, the Oz Trail is a 1-mile offshoot from the Boy Scout Loop that is in a state of flux with different hazards and improvements.

Hard-core trail runners and those on horseback may enjoy the 9-mile bridle trail that circumnavigates the lake. Built in the 1930s with a bulldozer, this trail has several steep sections, and its surface has ruts and holes, so use caution.

To the west of the dam are a couple of shorter loop trails near the archery range and the off-leash dog area.

Camping: No camping is available. RV camping is available at the Blue Ox Campground at the Kansas Speedway, about 7 miles northwest of the lake (400 Village W. Parkway, Kansas City, KS 66111; 913-328-3347).

CHAPTER 3

NORTHEAST KANSAS

We were spinning along through Kansas, and in the course of
an hour and a half we were fairly abroad on the great Plains.
Just here the land was rolling — a grand sweep of regular el-
evations and depressions as far as the eye could reach — like
the stately heave and swell of the ocean's bosom after a storm.

MARK TWAIN, *ROUGHING IT*

Sunflowers at Melvern Lake. Photo by Kristin Conard

1. Baker University Wetlands
   Research and Natural Area
2. Banner Creek Reservoir
3. Black Jack Battlefield and
   Nature Park
4. Blue River Rail Trail
5. Camp Alexander
6. Clinton Lake
7. Green Memorial Wildlife Area
8. Hillsdale Lake
9. Kaw River State Park

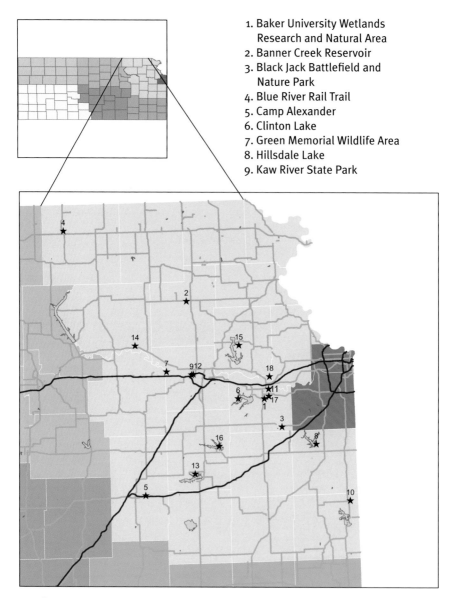

Northeast Kansas

10. La Cygne Lake
11. Lawrence River Trails
12. MacLennan Park
13. Melvern Lake
14. Oregon Trail Nature Park
15. Perry Lake
16. Pomona Lake
17. Prairie Park Nature Center
18. University of Kansas Field Station

Northeast Kansas is graced with an abundance of hills and broad valleys within the Osage Cuestas and Glaciated Region, making for a plethora of diverse trails. Along with the state capital, Topeka, and college towns such as Lawrence and Emporia, the area has many wonderful and popular trails that traverse the prairie and the woodlands and are often located along reservoirs, rivers, creeks, or wetlands. The Oregon and Santa Fe Trails both ran through northeast Kansas, and you can still see ruts from the wagon wheels on some of the trails. History buffs know that Black Jack Battlefield near Baldwin City was the site of the first shots fired in the Civil War. Along with top historical trails, this region also has some of the state's best biking and bridle trails.

BAKER UNIVERSITY WETLANDS RESEARCH AND NATURAL AREA

One of the most diverse ecosystems in northeast Kansas can be found in the Baker Wetlands. Native people of the Kanza tribe used this floodplain of the Wakarusa and Kansas Rivers, and by 1854 the land was being homesteaded and farmed. The wetlands south of Lawrence was designated a National Natural Landmark by the National Park Service in 1969, and the 927-acre site is protected for its valuable wetlands habitat. It has taken time to restore the wetlands. In 1969 less than 8

Baker Wetlands after a storm. (Photo by Marciana Vequist)

percent of the area was natural habitat, but with annual controlled burns, usually in the spring, and the dedicated work of researchers, students, and volunteers, the area is being returned to a natural mix of wet meadows, woodlands, prairies, and marshes. The Discovery Center, opened in 2015, has exhibits with information on the area's wildlife and habitat.

Contact: Roger Boyd, director of natural areas and emeritus professor of biology, 785-594-3172; rboyd@bakerU.edu.

Hours: Daylight hours.

Cost: Free.

FEATURED TRAIL: RESTORATION AREA NATURE TRAILS (TOP WILDLIFE AND WILDFLOWERS TRAIL)

Trail access: Hike.

Distance: 3-mile loop, 6 miles total.

Walk carefully and quietly here for the best chance of seeing wildlife, and it's a good idea to have binoculars handy. At the west entrance to Baker Wetlands, a newly restored portion of wetlands is open for exploration. Tracts A and B were wetlands before the land was farmed in the 1800s, and they were returned to their natural state in 2008. The trails that start near the parking area (38.92064, −95.24854) crisscross, which means they can be taken in lots of different ways. For those with kids or anyone who wants a short trail with maximum wildlife viewing opportunities, head south to walk along the boardwalk in the Tract B Restoration Area and then go diagonally across the wetlands.

The trail can be taken to the right or left from the trailhead; both options intersect on the other side of the Education Pavilion a few hundred feet from the parking lot. The pavilion has information placards about the wildlife as well as information about the wetlands' development. The boardwalk section starts to the right after the Education Pavilion. Boy Scouts from Baldwin City built the recycled plastic lumber boardwalk between 1992 and 1994, along with the nearby observation blind. If you're on the boardwalk in spring or early summer, you may see water beneath the boardwalk itself, but it may be dry the rest of the year. Along the boardwalk are benches where you can rest and take in the tranquil scenery. The wetlands here provide habitat for muskrats, fairy shrimp, pond snails, and many more creatures. Hundreds of different species of birds have been spotted here, and it has been a nesting site for green herons, robins, great horned owls, and at least a dozen other bird species. The boardwalk curves back around and meets up with a dirt trail that can be taken to the left (west) to the observation blind or to the right (east) back to the east entrance of the boardwalk.

From the east entrance of the boardwalk, walk north back toward the Education Pavilion and turn right (east) to take the trail across the Tract B Restoration Area. It's a flat, wide trail that runs for 0.5 mile to E. 1400 Road. From there, you can cross the road and link up with the original wetlands trails, or you can take a

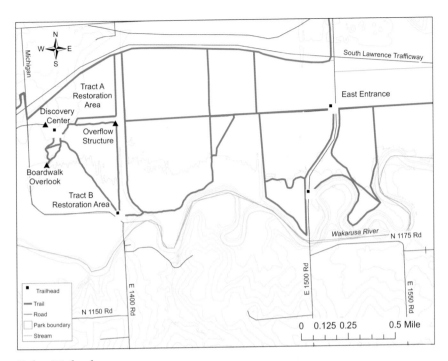

Baker Wetlands

sharp left (north) and walk for 0.5 mile parallel to the road to the concrete over-flow structure that helps control flooding inside Tract B. Turn left (west) at the overflow structure and continue back to the trailhead for a 2-mile trek. To add on a mile, cross 35th Street (N. 1250 Road) 0.23 mile after the overflow structure (38.92078, –95.24603). This flat, easy trail encircles the Tract A Restoration Area. From the road, it's 0.26 mile back to the west entrance.

Directions to the trailhead: Three different entrances are available. For the west en-trance for the featured trail, take Louisiana Street south out of Lawrence and turn right (west) on W. 31st Street. After 0.4 miles, turn left (south) onto Michigan Street and turn right (east) on N. 1250 Road. The parking lot for the trailhead is on the right.

Additional trails: Encircling the original wetlands are 3 miles of trails, and the trail system is expanding to the east for a total of around 10 miles. Prairie Park Nature Center is nearby (see the featured trail later in this chapter).

Camping: No camping is available at Baker Wetlands. The closest camping is at Clinton State Park (798 N. 1415 Road, Lawrence, KS 66049; 785-842-8562).

BANNER CREEK RESERVOIR

Thirteen miles of trails wind around the 535-acre lake near Holton. The hike and bike nature trail encircles the entire lake, with the most scenic portions along the

Banner Creek Reservoir from the dam. (Photo by Kristin Conard)

shelters, a disc golf course, three boat docks, and a swimming beach. Anglers can fish for channel and flathead catfish, crappie, largemouth bass, and walleye.

Contact: Banner Creek Reservoir Headquarters, 10975 Highway K-16, Holton, KS 66436; 785-364-4236; bannercreekreservoir@yahoo.com.

Hours: 5:30 a.m. to 10:30 p.m. in season (typically late spring, summer, and early autumn); off-season and winter hours may vary.

Cost: $2 vehicle entrance fee.

FEATURED TRAIL: NORTH CAMP LOOP TRAIL, DAM TRAIL, AND TWIN OAKS LOOP TRAIL

Trail access: Hike or bike.

Distance: North Camp Loop, 2-mile loop; Dam Trail, 1.2 miles one-way; Twin Oaks Loop Trail, 1.2 miles one-way.

The North Camp Loop trailhead (39.46192, –95.77962) is close to the entrance to the Banner Creek Reservoir headquarters, where you can get a parking permit before starting on the trail. The trail splits near the beginning, and you can head east or south. Bear right (south) at the trail intersection near the trailhead, along the exposed gravel trail to the west of the paved sidewalk. After 0.5 mile, the North Camp Loop Trail crosses the park road to the left (southeast) and along the edge of the tree line. If you bear to the right (south-southwest) near the bridge, the trail links up with the Sunset Ridge Trail, which follows part of the northern side of the lake. Continuing on the North Camp Loop Trail, you wind through the trees along the edge of the lake. The trail may become indistinct here, so be sure to keep the campsites to your left and the lake to your right as you make your way around the loop. Across a bridge and uphill near the park chapel, the trail becomes more distinct. Past the swimming beach and the boat ramp, you can close the loop and head back to the trailhead, or you can link up with the Dam Trail.

Downhill and past the boat ramp, the Dam Trail heads along the edge of the lake and across open fields, which may be a difficult ride on a road bike. The trail up the dam is a bit steep, but there are lovely views out across the lake at the top. The trail here is mowed grass, making it a challenge if you're on a bike, and it stays that way until you reach the opposite side of the dam and the beginning of the Twin Oaks Loop Trail (39.45210, –95.76493).

The Twin Oaks Loop Trail twists and turns along the southwestern edge of the lake, with blue blazes and markers on the trees to help you stay on the trail. Along the way you'll see interpretive signs with information on some of the species that make up the ecosystem here, such as the belted kingfisher, shagbark hickory tree, copperhead snake, and ticks. The trail in this section is mostly shaded, but it's

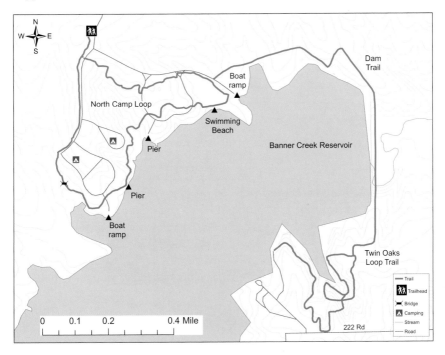

Banner Creek Reservoir

narrow and challenging, with exposed roots and some quick ups and downs. A couple of benches and bridges along the way can act as landmarks and places to rest as you weave through the timber to the parking area at the end of the Twin Oaks Loop Trail (39.45227, –95.76949). From there, you can continue to explore the southern side of the lake or backtrack across the dam to the north side.

Directions to the trailhead: From US-75, drive into Holton. Turn south on W. 4th Street, and after 1.7 miles turn left (south) onto the park road. The entrance and trailhead are to the right.

Additional trails: You can continue on the trails around the western edge of the lake, with trailheads along M Road near 222nd Road.

The 9-mile Banner Creek Horse Trail is on the north side of the lake. It's a mix of trails through the woods near the shoreline and along country roads.

Camping: Near the headquarters building at the north entrance is the Camp Host. RV and tent spaces are available.

BLACK JACK BATTLEFIELD AND NATURE PARK

Black Jack Battlefield, near Baldwin City, was the site of one of the first battles of the Civil War. In fact, the National Geographic show *Diggers* described it as the place where the first shots of the Civil War were fired. It was designated a National Historic Landmark in 2012. This location also has some wagon ruts from the Santa Fe Trail.

Before the Civil War, Kansas was such a violent place that the state was referred to as "Bleeding Kansas." The events leading up to the battle at Black Jack Battlefield were as follows: Pro-slavery forces led by Henry C. Pate of Missouri burned Lawrence on May 21, 1856. Shortly after the Lawrence incident, abolitionist John Brown and others executed five pro-slavery men at Pottawatomie Creek. Pate then took three anti-slavery men prisoner, two of whom were Brown's sons. Brown led the June 2, 1856, fight against Pate's forces at Black Jack Battlefield. The three- to five-hour battle ended with a victory for Brown's side. His sons were released in exchange for the pro-slavery men who had been captured.

Self-guided tours of the site are available. A brochure explains the history of the battle and describes the nine stops on the tour, including Pate's position, the point of surrender, and Brown's position. Free guided tours are conducted every Saturday and Sunday at 1 p.m. from May through the third weekend of October. Linked to the shorter self-guided tour path is a nature trail and mowed grass trails through a prairie restoration area. It's a pleasant walk, and the trails are well taken care of and easy to follow, with signs on the nature trail identifying different plants and trees.

Contact: 163 E. 2000 Road, Wellsville, KS 66092; 785-883-2106.

Hours: Daylight hours.

Cost: Free.

Black Jack Battlefield. (Photo by Kristin Conard)

FEATURED TRAIL: BATTLEFIELD TRAILS AND PRAIRIE RESTORATION TRAILS (TOP HISTORICAL TRAIL)

Trail access: Hike.

Distance: 2 miles total.

The trail starts south of the Black Jack Battlefield Monument (38.76387, –95.13071). A small pavilion should be stocked with brochures explaining the different sites in the park. If you take the trail toward the north and then west, you'll pass by two sites where Santa Fe Trail ruts are still visible. The western trail ruts are close to where Pate's men surrendered and reportedly where Brown took Pate prisoner. The trails near the battlefield are through woodlands and along a gentle slope (which reportedly gave Brown an advantage in the battle).

Combine a walk through the battlefield with one through the restored prairie area for some nice habitat diversity. From the battlefield trail, follow signs to the nature trail and restoration area. Turn left (southwest) before you get to the silo (38.76311, –95.13349). Along the edge of the restored prairie area, you can choose among several different routes on the mowed grass paths, shortening or lengthening your hike and having a new experience each time. The perimeter route along the west and south is out in the open, along the edge of the trees, until the trail loops north again and heads back into the trees. The trail through the timber has a bit more variation in elevation, but it's still relatively easy going. Crossing a small wooden bridge along the nature trails that link to the prairie trails takes you back to the intersection of the nature trails and the battlefield trails. You can retrace your steps through the battlefield or pass by the Robert Pearson house. Pearson, who was living in the area when the battle took place, heard the fighting and took up arms for the Free Staters. After the battle, he purchased the land and built his farmhouse in 1890.

To add on 0.5 mile, instead of heading back through the battlefield, turn right (south) at the sign to the nature trail and make a loop around the southwestern prairie portion. Cross a bridge across Captain's Creek and then pass through a grove of sugar maples. Pearson planted the trees, in their evenly spaced rows, and his descendants tapped the trees to make maple syrup. The sugar maples put on a show in the autumn, making it a particularly nice time to visit.

Directions to the trailhead: From US-56, turn south onto E. 2000 Road. The trailhead is on the right.

Additional trails: Baker Wetlands is 20 miles northwest near Lawrence. See the previous featured trail.

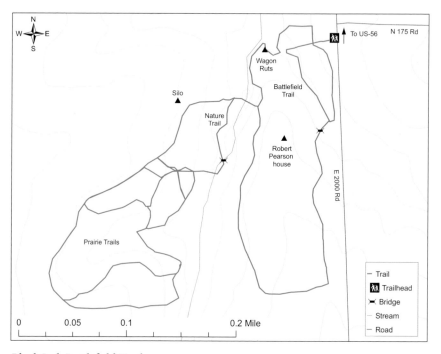

Black Jack Battlefield Trail

Camping: No camping is allowed at Black Jack Battlefield and Nature Park. The closest camping is at Hillsdale Lake (26001 W. 255th Street, Paola, KS 66071; 913-783-4507) or at Clinton Lake (798 N. 1415 Road, Lawrence, KS 66049; 785-842-8562).

BLUE RIVER RAIL TRAIL–MARYSVILLE

The rich legacy of trails in Kansas is particularly evident in Marshall County, which has been designated the "Trails Capital of Kansas" by the Kansas Sampler Foundation. Pioneers following the Oregon Trail, riders for the Pony Express, and drivers along the Overland Stage Route have traversed the countryside surrounding the Blue River. The town of Marysville was the site of a Pony Express home station, and the original stone barn housing the station is still standing and open to the public as a museum. Although the historic trails have faded into the depths of

Blue River Rail Trail. (Photo by Jonathan Conard)

the past, the Blue River Rail Trail provides current hikers and bikers with a great opportunity to experience the same landscapes seen by so many early travelers on their way west.

Contact: Marshall County Connection Inc., c/o Maureen Crist, 1129 Juniper Road, Marysville, KS 66508; brrt@bluevalley.net.

Hours: Daylight hours. Closed during rifle season.

Cost: Free.

FEATURED TRAIL: BLUE RIVER RAIL TRAIL — MARYSVILLE TO OKETO

Trail access: Hike or bike.

Distance: 8.7 miles, one-way.

The Blue River Trail was established in 2011 and follows the Big Blue River north from Marysville to Oketo along a shaded and quiet route. The marked trailhead in Marysville (39.86021, −96.65291) is the best access point to start the route. From the trailhead, the old Union Pacific rail bed runs north roughly parallel to the Big Blue River. Within the first 0.5 mile, the trail approaches the Big Blue River, and there's a convenient covered bench where you can pause and take stock of the scenery. Continuing from this point, the trail turns northeast through a shady gallery forest along the east bank of the river. Slightly over 0.75 mile from the Marysville trailhead is one of the highlights of the trail: the beautiful covered bridge that spans the gently flowing waters of Rocky Run Creek (39.86895, −96.64508). From the covered bridge north to Harvest Road, the trail leaves the confines of the river corridor and passes through more open farmland. After crossing Harvest Road, the trail continues through open country past mile marker 3, where it bends slightly east. You'll enter a woodland area bordered by tall limestone bluffs (39.90226, −96.64559). There's a long footbridge crossing the point where the quickly flowing waters of Blodgett Creek course into the Big Blue River. From here, the trail continues north to Frontier Road. Continuing north from Frontier Road, the trail crosses a long railroad bridge over Brommer Creek before skirting the western edge of the tiny town of Marietta. For these first 7.2 miles, the crushed limestone trail is smooth and wide, with distance markers at each mile. However, from this point north to Oketo, the trail currently lacks a crushed limestone surface. Although the route north of Deer Trail Road is rougher, it is generally cleared of ballast and is certainly passable for hikers and mountain bikers.

Marietta was established when the Union Pacific was looking for a suitable location around Oketo to lay side tracks. When the railroad found an acceptable spot south of Oketo, Marietta was quickly platted, and a grain elevator, stockyard, and depot were built by 1889. Angus McLeod and his brother William built and operated the first grain elevator, and they were responsible for establishing the first farmer-owned cooperative elevator system in the state of Kansas. Although the stockyard, depot, and other businesses in Marietta have long since closed, the elevators owned by the current Farmers Co-op Association still stand tall — a monument to the concept started by the McLeod brothers well over a century ago. At Marietta, the trail crosses Deer Trail Road and passes west of the town's grain elevators, continuing north toward Oketo. This part of the trail is generally more open, with long views of plowed fields and prairie pastures adjacent to it. North of Marietta, the trail again parallels the river and crosses under Highway 233/Cherokee Road. In this vicinity, the historic Oketo Cut-Off Trail crossed the Blue River. In 1862 the Oketo Cut-Off was established by Ben Holladay as an alternative for

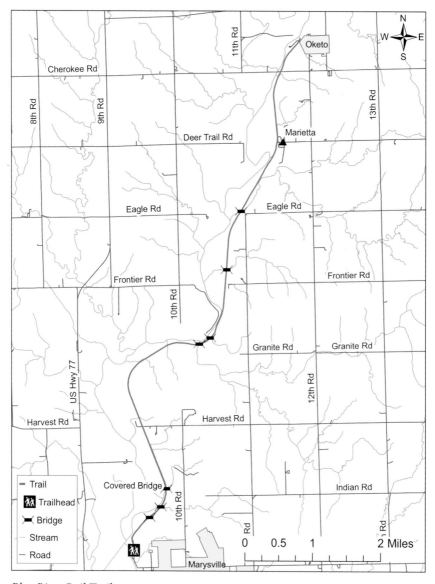

Blue River Rail Trail

stagecoaches traveling west on the Overland Stage Route. This option was intentionally designed to bypass Marysville, but the cutoff route was short-lived, and the majority of traffic returned to the main route through Marysville by 1863.

From this point, the Blue River Trail continues north to the western edge of the town of Oketo. The trail extends north along the railway bed to connect with the Chief Standing Bear and Homestead Trail. This allows trail users to cross the state line and continue all the way to Lincoln, Nebraska.

Directions to the trailhead: From the intersection of US-77 and US-36 in Marysville, go west on US-36 (Center Street) until you reach 8th Street. Turn north on 8th Street and continue north for 1 mile. Turn west onto Jayhawk Road and follow this road for 0.5 mile as it bends to the north and dead-ends at the gravel parking area for the trail.

Additional trails: Visitors should check out the Alcove Spring Historic Site, located south of Marysville; there's a turnoff to the west from US-77. The Alcove Spring Historic Site was near the Independence Crossing of the Oregon Trail, and it was used as a campsite by travelers along the route. There is a small seasonal waterfall flowing over a limestone rock formation.

Camping: Primitive and utility campsites are available at the Marysville City Park (10th and Walnut Streets), along with picnic tables, restrooms, and a playground. Marysville is known as the "Black Squirrel City," and they can often be seen cavorting throughout the park.

CAMP ALEXANDER–EMPORIA

E. J. Alexander, a former slave from North Carolina, bought 9 acres of land in Kansas in 1886. Eventually, he expanded his farm and landholdings to around 40 acres. When he died in 1923, he donated his land and his savings to the children of Lyon County, and the day camp bears his name. The trails are fun, challenging (think hills and single tracks through the woods, with a handful of obstacles), and well maintained. The trails are open to visitors, who must stop by the camp office near the parking lot (38.41750, –96.10782) to get a pass to display if the camp is in use.

Contact: 1783 Road P5, Emporia, KS 66801; 620-342-1386.
Hours: 24/7.
Cost: Free.

 ## FEATURED TRAIL: CAMP ALEXANDER TRAILS (TOP BIKE TRAIL)

Trail access: Hike or bike.
Distance: 3.8-mile loop.

If camp is in session (if you see kids running around), stop by the camp office to register and pick up a badge to wear around your neck identifying you as an

Camp Alexander. (Photo by Kristin Conard)

authorized visitor. The trail starts south of the camp office (38.41729, –96.10725), and there are markers indicating which way to go (it's intended to be taken clock-wise). Near the beginning, several trails intersect, and there's one trail past an old train car and a small pond. The packed-dirt single-track trail has some quick ups and downs. Proceeding through the crisscrossing trails in the woods, you'll cross a dirt camp road, and the trail comes out into the open as it passes south of the camp garden before taking you back into the woods and north along the river. Along these stretches through the woods, the trail has some log obstacles, and you'll occasionally pass under some wooden arches, presumably made from large branches that have fallen along the trail. This variation in the trail design and the heart-pumping hills later on make this one of our top bike trails.

At the two Y-intersections, one shortly after the other, signs direct you to bear left for both. The trail winds north and then turns back south through the Y-intersections, again heading left. You cross a bridge and then go up and around a break in the trees. Along the last of the northern wooded loops, you encounter the steep Heartbreak Hill, which takes you up and out into the open. The trail continues around the camp's swimming pond and across some camp roads before

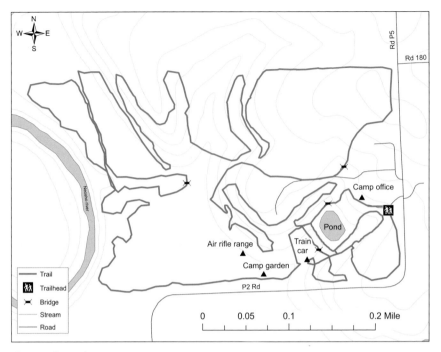

Camp Alexander

ascending another hilly portion in the northeast corner of the camp. West of some camp buildings, the trail bears south over a small bridge, across a gravel section, and then back west past a challenge course and near the pond again. The final push is back into the trees for some switchbacks past a small pond and up to the trailhead. Make sure you return your pass to the camp office before leaving.

Directions to the trailhead: From I-35, take exit 135 toward County Road R1 and travel north on County Road R1 for 0.7 mile. Turn left (west) onto Road 180, and after 0.8 mile, turn left (west) onto Road P5. The camp is about 0.1 mile on the right.

Additional trails: North of I-35 and Emporia State University are a few miles of single-track bike trails near the Neosho River.

Camping: No camping is available at Camp Alexander. The closest camping is at Melvern Lake to the northeast (29810 S. Fairlawn Road, Osage City, KS 66523; 785-528-4102).

CLINTON LAKE

Southwest of Lawrence is Clinton Lake. The reservoir was created in the 1970s, but the lake wasn't opened up to recreational activities until 1981. It was created to help control flooding in the Wakarusa Valley, and thousands of people rely on the

Clinton Lake. (Photo by Scott Bean)

reservoir for their drinking water. If you want to learn more about the history of the area and the lake itself, stop by the Wakarusa River Valley Heritage Museum in Bloomington Park East. The US Army Corps of Engineers manages a couple of the parks around the lake, including Woodridge Park on the west side of the lake.
Contact: US Army Corps of Engineers–Clinton Lake, 872 N. 1402 Road, Lawrence, KS 66049; 785-843-7665.
Hours: 24/7.
Cost: Free.

FEATURED TRAIL: GEORGE O. LATHAM TRAIL

Trail access: Hike.
Distance: 2.5-mile loop.
   While the North Shore and Rockhaven Park Trails are heavily used by mountain bikers and horseback riders, respectively, the George O. Latham Trail is the top choice of hikers and backpackers. The trail is named for George O. Latham, a Lawrence resident who was a strong and early proponent of establishing a

network of trails throughout Kansas. His favorite trail at Clinton Lake, now carrying his name, passes through a scenic wooded area in Woodridge Park and along a peninsula that reaches out toward the lake. This trail provides one of the few true backpacking experiences available in the state. Primitive tent camping is allowed throughout the Woodridge public-use area, and the small clearings alongside the trail provide backpackers with perfect backcountry campsites. The majority of these tent clearings are found along short spur trails within the first mile of the route. Open fires are allowed only in established fire pits within these areas. The trail is marked to be hiked counterclockwise, and the entrance to the trailhead is on the southeast side of the parking area. The trail starts east from the trailhead (38.92613, –95.43489) and heads toward the lake as the rocky dirt path descends through a heavily shaded mixed hardwood forest. The trail continues to descend until it nears the shores of Clinton Lake and angles to the northeast, parallel to the shoreline.

During the summer months, thick foliage obscures the lake along most of this part of the route, but there are several choice locations where the trees open up to allow expansive views of the lake (38.92784, –95.42461). The trail angles sharply back to the northwest and passes mile marker 2 before reaching an old hay loader (38.93881, –95.42246), left over from the days prior to the reservoir when the area was farmed extensively. The trail gradually climbs in elevation as you return to the

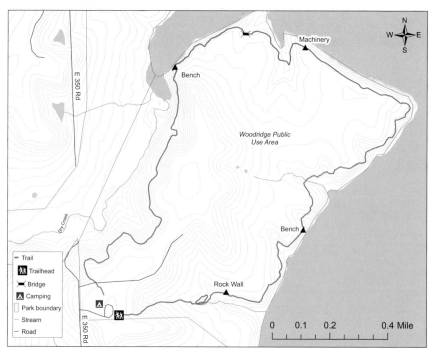

Clinton Lake, George O. Latham Trail

trailhead, and a strategically placed bench provides an excellent spot to rest your legs and reflect on the beauty of the landscape before continuing up to the end of the trail, on the opposite side of the parking area from where you began.

Directions to the trailhead: From US-40, turn west onto County Road 442/N. 1600 Road/Stull Road. Drive for 4.6 miles and then turn left (south) onto County Road 1023/E. 250 Road. After 3.5 miles, turn left (east) onto N. 1250 Road, and take the first left (north) onto E. 350 Road. The trailhead is near the second right.

CLINTON STATE PARK

Consisting of 1,500 acres along the northeastern edge of Clinton Lake, Clinton State Park was dedicated in 1975. More than half a million people visit the park each year to enjoy its attractions, which include an archery range, swimming beach, mountain bike skills course, cross-country ski trail (one of the few in the state), playgrounds, picnic areas, sand volleyball, disc golf course, trout pond, and kid's fishing pond. The lake and surrounding state park provide good habitat for wildlife, and in 1989 the branch of the lake along Deer Creek became the first recorded bald eagle nesting site in Kansas since the species had been driven to the brink of extinction. In addition to bald eagles, watch for other interesting birds in the area, including wood ducks, American kestrels, and red-bellied woodpeckers.

Contact: Clinton State Park Office, 798 N. 1415 Road, Lawrence, KS 66049; 785-842-8562.

Hours: 24/7.

Cost: State park fee.

FEATURED TRAIL: NORTH SHORE BLUE TRAIL (TOP BIKE TRAIL)

Trail access: Hike or bike.

Distance: 8.4-mile loop.

The North Shore Trails at Clinton State Park are scenic, well maintained, and favorites of local mountain bikers. The trail network consists of two main segments — the Blue Trail and the White Trail. The White Trail has a slightly higher level of difficulty and offers more technical challenges for mountain bikers. The Blue Trail stays closer to the shoreline and is moderately difficult, with rocky sections, steep climbs, and tight turns.

The trails run in parallel as they wind around the contours of the reservoir, but there are several points where they cross, so it is possible to combine both trails and create your own custom loop. To keep on track, just follow the blue- and white-colored blazes that designate the respective trail segments. To take the Blue Trail, start from the trailhead (38.93954, −95.34082) and follow the blue blazes as the trail descends sharply across rocky terrain toward the lake. The trail loops and crosses a park road (38.93512, −95.34954) before reaching the 2-mile marker. After that marker the trail emerges from the woodlands at small, pleasant

Lake Henry. This 4-acre impoundment is popular with anglers, since it is stocked with trout during the winter months. To stay on the Blue Trail, continue straight across the Lake Henry dam and then take the left fork. The Blue Trail crosses a small stream and reaches a point in the trail marked "Lands End" (38.92902, –95.35401). Shortly after this point, you can either take the Red Trail to the left, which leads along the shoreline of the reservoir, or continue straight and stay on the Blue Trail. The Red Trail descends to the edge of the reservoir and passes along a rocky section of shoreline before rejoining the Blue Trail. The Blue Trail continues under the thick, shaded canopy of the mature hardwood forest, and shortly after the 5-mile marker it emerges at a point with great views of the lake before passing under a unique arch constructed of tree branches (38.93090, –95.37344). The trail continues north and west from this point. If you want to take a break and play in the water, the trail passes a point with access to a sandy beach (38.93518, –95.37785). There are also several cross trails leading down concrete staircases from campsites toward the lake.

The trail bends to the north, and there are two options: cross a paved park road (38.93973, –95.38738), or keep going to intersect with the White Trail and take it back to the trailhead. Across the road is a designated skills loop area that offers some serious opportunities for mountain bikers to test their skills as they ride through a variety of treacherous obstacles, including a bridge, a teeter-totter, and ramps. Use this area at your own risk, and make sure your skills are up to the

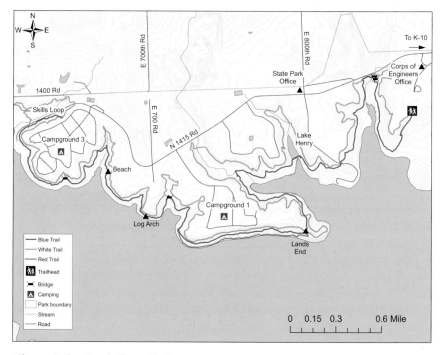

Clinton Lake, North Shore Trail

challenge before venturing too far onto this course. It is also possible to continue past the skills loop area and head west along Cactus Ridge before looping back and meeting the White Trail, which can be taken back to the trailhead.

Directions to the trailhead: From US-40, exit onto K-10E/S. Lawrence Trafficway. After 1.7 miles, take the Clinton Parkway exit. Turn right (northwest) onto E. 900th Road, and then take the first left (southwest) onto N. 1402 Road. The trailhead is on the right.

Additional trails: On the north shore of the lake, additional hiking trails include a connecting trail to Sanders Mound, which can be accessed from a turnoff near the start of the North Shore Trails. Nature trails along the north shore of the reservoir include the Backwoods Nature Trail (0.6 mile) and the Discovery Trail (0.5 mile), with trailheads located behind the US Army Corps of Engineers visitors' center.

Camping: Two designated camping areas are close to the North Shore Trails. Campground 1 is closer to the trailhead, and Campground 3 is a large campground on the west side of the state park that provides good access to both the trails and the lake.

GREEN MEMORIAL WILDLIFE AREA

Uniontown was a town before Kansas was a state or even a territory. It was a stop for travelers on the Oregon and Pikes Peak Trails, since a natural rock ford of the Kansas River was located nearby. It's hard to imagine the challenge of taking a wagon across the rocky, bumpy terrain here, but wagon-wheel ruts are still visible on the Oregon Trace Trail, proving that it happened right where you're now standing.

Uniontown was burned in 1849 because of a cholera scare — the same epidemic that wiped out hundreds of Pottawatomie Indians living in the area. In 1850 the town was rebuilt, and a river ferry began operating. Sadly, the town's heyday was short-lived. In 1855 it was abandoned, and in 1859 the town was burned again. To see the graves of cholera victims and other settlers, you can visit the Green Cemetery — which some say is haunted — situated across the road from the Green Memorial Wildlife Area. Members of the Green family were farmers from the 1870s to the 1960s. In July 1984 the Green family donated 83 acres to the Kansas Department of Wildlife, Parks, and Tourism (KDWPT) for the creation of a wildlife area.

Although it encompasses a relatively small area, there is a diverse range of habitat — from oak-hickory woodlands in the northern part to riparian vegetation along Post Creek to tallgrass prairie to the east. Controlled burns help prevent the invasion of woody species, and fishing, trapping, and hunting are prohibited, which makes it a haven for wildlife.

Contact: KDWPT Area Office, 785-945-6615.

Hours: Daylight hours.

Cost: Free.

Green Memorial Wildlife Area. (Photo by Kristin Conard)

 ### FEATURED TRAIL: OREGON TRACE TRAIL AND POST CREEK RIDGE TRAIL (TOP HISTORICAL TRAIL)

Trail access: Hike.
Distance: The Oregon Trace Trail and Post Creek Ridge Trail are each 0.8-mile loops.

Both trails are relatively short and easy, with access from the same parking area and trailhead; however, the Oregon Trace Trail is the easier of the two. At the trailhead (39.08394, –95.93792) is a picnic table; there should also be pamphlets available there that provide information about the numbered wooden trail markers. The markers start with the Post Creek Ridge Trail, so bear right at the trailhead. Near the trailhead is the homesite of the Green family, and as you head west along the mowed grass trail, you'll see their old farming equipment. Farming in the area (not just by the Greens) damaged the natural ecosystem, allowing nonnative trees such as the honey locust to grow in what was once tallgrass prairie. With controlled burns, portions of the wildlife area are being returned to their natural state.

The trail takes you into the timber, with post oaks and redbuds growing along the way. During the summer, the trail might be overgrown and hard to follow through the woods, and you should beware of poison ivy. The trail turns north and then south as you head downhill toward Post Creek. The trail here is rocky for a bit, so take it slow through the woods — a mix of smooth sumac, northern red oak, and black walnut. Pointed stumps along the western edge of the trail are the mark of beavers, which eat the bark. As the trail turns west, you'll pass a bench. The trail then reverts to mowed grass as you head back uphill to the trailhead.

To take the Oregon Trace Trail before moving on, turn right (south) just before the parking area (39.08371, −95.93855). The trail is shaded through the woods for just over 0.1 mile before it opens up into a reclaimed prairie area. In spring and summer the wildflowers will be in bloom, including black-eyed Susans and Illinois bundleflowers. The Oregon Trace Trail splits into a loop (39.08199, −95.93847). To follow the markers, take the loop to the left. After you pass a bench, the trail becomes a bit rocky and more shaded as it heads downhill to a spot north of a set of ruts from the Oregon Trail (39.08042, −95.94041). The trail turns back north and east after passing a couple more benches where you can stop and do some wildlife spotting. The eastern deciduous forest, with its oak and hickory trees, provides food and habitat for wild turkeys, red squirrels, and other creatures. Following the trail back around, you'll pass through the prairie again before emerging from the woods near the trailhead.

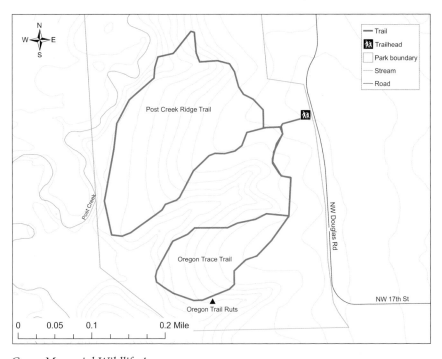

Green Memorial Wildlife Area

Directions to the trailhead: From Topeka, head west on I-70. Take exit 346 for Carlson Road to the right (north). After 2.3 miles, and before you cross the Kansas River, turn right (east) onto W. 2nd Street, which dead-ends in 5 blocks. Take a right (south) onto Gilkerson, which turns into NW Douglas Road, and continue for about 0.5 mile. The trailhead is on the right (west).

Additional trails: Oregon Trail Nature Park is the closest trail system. See the featured trail later in this chapter.

Camping: No camping is allowed at Green Memorial Wildlife Area. The closest camping is at Mill Creek Campground and RV Park in Paxico (22470 Campground Road, Paxico, KS 66526; 785-636-5321; millcreek@kansas.net). It's about 15 miles west off I-70.

HILLSDALE LAKE

The US Army Corps of Engineers built Hillsdale Lake in 1982, making it one of the state's newest reservoirs. The Kansas state park system leased the surrounding land in 1989, and the area was opened up to recreation in 1994. It is a popular area for trail users, with 30 miles of equestrian trails and a few miles just for hikers and bikers, primarily through oak-hickory woodlands and some open, grassy meadows. The 7,000-acre park also offers hunting, a remote-controlled airplane flying field, and plenty of places to get out on the water for boating, jet-skiing, or fishing. Bald eagles have nested at Hillsdale Lake since 1993. They are most likely to be spotted around lakes in Kansas from November to March.

Contact: Hillsdale State Park, 26001 W. 255th Street, Paola, KS 66071; 913-783-4507. US Army Corps of Engineers–Hillsdale Lake, 913-783-4366.

Hours: 24/7.

Cost: State park fee.

FEATURED TRAIL: HIDDEN SPRING NATURE TRAIL

Trail access: Hike or bike.

Distance: 1.2-mile loop.

Behind the Corps of Engineers visitors' center and northeast of the dam is a nature trail. Though short and shaded, the trail presents a bit of a challenge, with occasional steep and rocky sections. From the parking lot by the visitors' center, follow the sidewalk west toward the trailhead (38.66331, –94.89172). You can take the trail in either direction (clockwise or counterclockwise). The trail to the left, which is relatively wide and consists of packed dirt, heads downhill into the timber. After about 0.5 mile you'll come to a wooden bridge and three benches. Shortly after the first bridge is a second one, and the trail divides. If you turn right (northeast), the trail goes uphill back to the trailhead, 0.3 mile away. To continue and complete the full trail, take a left (southwest). Almost immediately is another trail intersection. You can take this loop in either direction, as both head down toward the lake and back up. Along the loop is another wooden bridge and a set

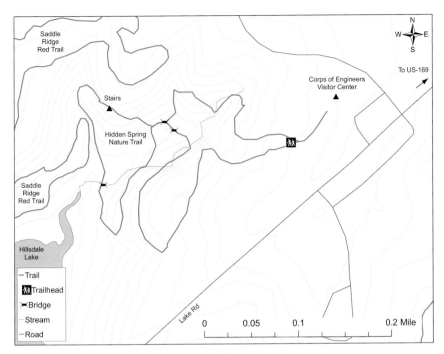

Hillsdale Lake, Hidden Spring Nature Trail

of wooden stairs installed to help protect the ridge from erosion. After taking the lakeside loop, you'll reach the bridge intersection with the first loop, and if you bear left (northeast), you'll be 0.3 mile from the trailhead.

Directions to the trailhead: From the south and west: Take I-35N toward Kansas City. Take the K-68 exit toward Ottawa/Louisburg. Turn right (east) onto K-68. After nearly 16 miles, turn left (north) onto Osawatomie Road, which turns into Lake Road. Cross the dam, and the entrance for the visitors' center is the first left after the end of the dam.

From the north and east: Take I-35S. Take the US-169S exit, exit 215, toward Paola. Turn left onto US-169S. Take the 255th Street ramp and follow W. 255th Street to the west for 2.5 miles. Continue onto Lake Road and take the first right after Harmony Road, followed by an immediate left. The visitors' center is a few hundred feet down the road.

FEATURED TRAIL: HIKE AND BIKE TRAIL

Trail access: Hike or bike.
Distance: 4.7 miles, one-way.

The Hike and Bike Trail connects all the campgrounds in the Russell Crites area along the southwestern side of the lake, and the trail can be accessed from any one of them. The eastern trailhead is near the park entrance for the Jayhawk Marina (38.64648, –94.91899), a few hundred feet northwest of the self-pay station off Lake Road. This trail is almost entirely exposed, with little shade, and it may be hot in the summer. However, you get good views of the lake, and the gravel trail is relatively flat and easy. The first spot you'll pass as the trail heads west is the Sunflower Day Use Area. The dead trees sticking out of the lake serve a couple of purposes. First, they remind you that, like most of the lakes in Kansas, this is not a natural lake. Second, they provide habitat for thriving populations of walleye, bluegill, crappie, catfish, and largemouth bass.

Past the Sunflower Day Use Area, the lake is intermittently hidden behind the trees as you pass the Scott Creek and Rabbit Ridge Campgrounds. As the trail winds north and east, you'll get good views of the lake before heading north and crossing the park road (38.65240, –94.92804). Here, the trail splits to the left and right and makes a couple of smaller, intersecting loops. Heading right takes you close to the swimming beach and Pintail Point Campground. Heading left takes you to Shelter 3 and Crappie Cove Campground.

Directions to the trailhead: From the south and west: Take I-35N toward Kansas City. Take the K-68 exit toward Ottawa/Louisburg. Turn right (east) onto K-68. After about 16 miles, turn left (north) onto Osawatomie Road. This turns into W. 271st Street, after which you bear left (north) onto Lake Road. The Jayhawk Marina entrance is on the left.

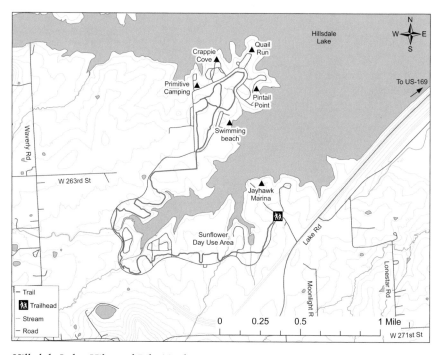

Hillsdale Lake, Hike and Bike Trail

From the north and east: Take I-35S. Take the US-169S exit, exit 215, toward Paola. Turn left onto US-169S. Take the 255th Street ramp and follow W. 255th Street to the west for 2.5 miles. Continue onto Lake Road for another 2.5 miles across the dam. The Jayhawk Marina entrance is the first right after the dam.

FEATURED TRAIL: SADDLE RIDGE SE RED TRAIL (TOP BRIDLE TRAIL)

Trail access: Hike, bike, or bridle.
Distance: 9.5-mile loop, 32 miles total.

Though they are technically multiuse trails, the Saddle Ridge Trails are most popular among those on horseback. At the equestrian camp, you can access the northern Blue Camp Trail or the Red Trail. For the Red Trail, go south at the trailhead (38.67085, –94.89801) and into the timber. The shaded, single-track dirt trail twists and backtracks along the lakeside hills, and occasional red reflectors help keep you on the right track. Yellow reflectors designate side, connector trails. One of these is located a few hundred feet past the gravel road crossing, 0.3 mile from the trailhead. Following the Red Trail takes you closer to the lake, which

Out for a ride at Hillsdale Lake. (Photo by Kristin Conard)

is visible through the trees in winter. Although the trail is popular, it may have some overhanging branches and some ruts after a rain, particularly during the summer. Near the southern edge of the lake loops you'll come to an intersection (38.66483, −94.89878) where you can either continue and make another southern loop or head back north and west. As the trail heads north and west away from the lake, it can be modified in different ways, thanks to the various trail intersections.

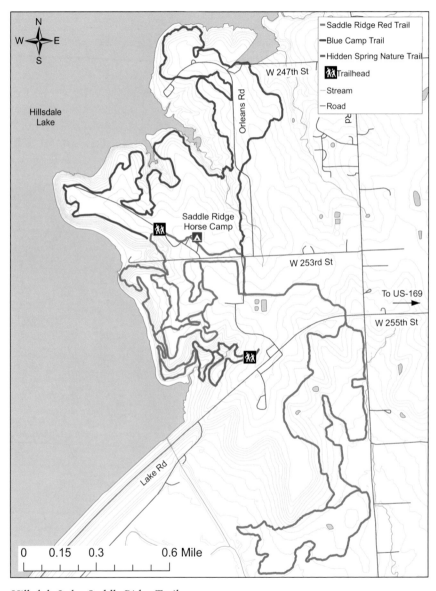

Hillsdale Lake, Saddle Ridge Trails

Eventually, it passes by maintenance buildings and ends up back in the open. You can close the loop here, or you can turn right (east) across a dirt road and take the SE Red Trail's dam loops.

In contrast to the dense forest of the lakeside trails, the loops near the dam are more exposed and have less variation in elevation, although there are enough hills to make it interesting. The loop, which starts (or ends) just south of the Lake Road, is either a 2.8- or a 4.2-mile loop that stays primarily along the edges of the tree line, although it dips in and out of the trees on occasion. You can take the trail to the right or the left and then backtrack along the flatter prairie trail to the west to get back to the equestrian camp. Or you can continue onto the rest of the SE Red Trail to the southwest, which links up with the Outlet Blue Loop.

Directions to the trailhead: From K-7/US-169, turn west onto 255th Street. Drive for 2.6 miles and then turn right (north) onto Harmony Road. Take the first left (west) onto W. 253rd Street. After 0.7 mile, take the park road to the right.

Additional trails: The Red Trail continues for another two loops along the south side of the dam, with similar scenery. It passes by the RC Flying Field and Shooting Range and along some park roads. To the north of the equestrian camp is the Blue Camp Trail, a 5.6-mile loop. The Outlet Blue Loop connects to the Red Trail near the western edge of the Red Trail.

Camping: A horse camp is available at the Saddle Ridge Campground, with utility and primitive campsites. Camping is also available at about 170 additional sites in the Russell Crites area.

KAW RIVER STATE PARK

When it opened to the public in 2010, Kaw River State Park gained the distinction of being the newest state park in Kansas and the only one located in a truly urban setting. Although the metropolitan image of the capital city of Topeka is not often associated with an opportunity for a real wilderness experience, the 76 acres of hardwood forest tucked next to the Kansas River provide a convenient place to get away from the bustle of the city. The area remained undeveloped because it was once part of the extensive campus of the Menninger Clinic — at one time, one of the premier psychiatric facilities in the nation. When the clinic relocated to Houston in 2003, part of the campus was donated to the state of Kansas, leading to the creation of the current state park.

From the park, paddlers can launch into the Kansas River. For those on land, there are trails of varying difficulty, from twisting single-track paths to a wide, gentle hiking trail leading toward the river. In Kansas, native woodlands are most often found hugging the contours of streams and rivers, and the deep woods lining the wide expanse of the Kansas River contain some of the finest forests the state has to offer. Kaw River is one of the most heavily wooded state parks in Kansas, so enjoy the shade as you explore the trail network winding through the towering oaks, and plan to visit in autumn to experience the explosion of fall colors.

Because of the easy access and proximity to Topeka, this area is very popular with hikers, trail runners, and single-track enthusiasts.

Contact: Kaw River State Park, 300 SW Wanamaker Road, Topeka, KS 66606; 785-273-6740.

Hours: 6 a.m. to 11 p.m.

Cost: Free.

FEATURED TRAIL: MAIN DOUBLE-TRACK TRAIL

Trail access: Hike or bike.

Distance: 0.75 mile, one-way.

The park's trails aren't individually named or marked, but one of the best routes to follow is the main double-track trail. It can be accessed from the KDWPT Region 2 Office. The trailhead (39.06355, –95.76040) is not marked either, but it can be found east of the Region 2 office building. From this point, the trail heads north from the parking lot into a thickly wooded area. The main double-track trail is recommended because it is easy to navigate and provides a wide, smooth surface suitable for hiking or biking. The trail descends from the hilltop and then bears east through a mix of tall hardwoods. The sturdy branches form an extensive canopy that keeps the trail pleasantly shaded even during the hottest summer days. Several side trails branch off from the main route and access additional single-track trails within the park system. Near the eastern end of the main trail you'll find a small pond, which is a peaceful spot to linger before returning to the trailhead. For a longer trail experience, the paved road just east of the pond can be followed north down to the river or crossed to access the MacLennan Park trail system to the east. To head back to the trailhead, you can either retrace your steps along the main route or follow a connecting trail north to explore one of the park's single-track trails. Following the northernmost single-track trail back to the trailhead creates a nice loop.

Directions to the trailhead: From I-70 in Topeka, take exit 356 for Wanamaker Road. Turn right and follow Wanamaker Road north approximately 0.5 mile until it ends at the KDWPT Region 2 Office parking lot by the trailhead.

Additional trails: In the Topeka area, there are also excellent hiking and mountain biking trails at MacLennan Park, directly east of Kaw River State Park; see the featured trail later in this chapter. In addition the 7-mile trail system at Dornwood Park (SE 25th Street and SE Highland Avenue) is being expanded and enhanced through the work of the Kansas Trails Council. For a nearby family-friendly hike, try the 2-mile nature trail at the Kansas Museum of History (6425 SW 6th Avenue).

Camping: The trails at Kaw River State Park are for day use only, and no camping is allowed. The closest campground is located at Lake Shawnee in southeast Topeka (3137 SE 29th Street, Topeka, KS 66505; 785-267-1156).

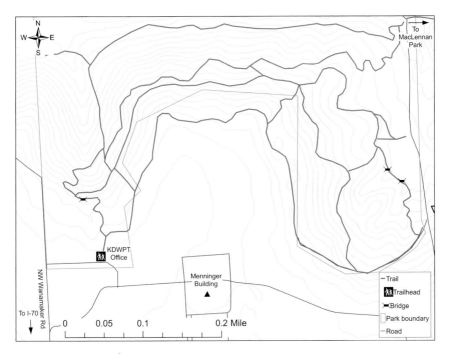

Kaw River State Park

LA CYGNE LAKE–LINN COUNTY PARK

For quiet and solitude less than an hour south of Overland Park, check out La Cygne Lake in Linn County Park. The 2,600-acre lake is named for swans, and you might see some there. You're also likely to see white-tailed deer and wild turkey back in the dense woods of the park. The lake was made as a cooling reservoir for the nearby coal power plant; its smokestacks are visible on parts of the trail. Recreation on the lake is limited to fishing (no swimming, jet-skiing, etc.), which is a particularly popular pastime in winter, since it has a warm-water discharge area; there's also a marina where you can pick up most necessities. The trails here are cleared only twice a year, so they can get overgrown in the summer. Although they're open to hikers as well as those on horseback, they're best suited for horses.
Contact: Linn County Park, 23095 Valley Road, La Cygne, KS 66040; 913-757-6633.
Hours: 24/7.
Cost: $2 a day.

FEATURED TRAIL: SOUTHERN YELLOW AND RED HORSE TRAILS

Trail access: Hike or bridle.
Distance: 4.9-mile loop, 30 miles total.

La Cygne Lake. (Photo by Kristin Conard)

Although there are about 30 miles of trails along the western edge of the lake, the horse camp is at the southern end, and the southern loops take you past the lake, up and down wooded hills, and through short stretches of prairie and wetlands — the highlights of Linn County Park. The Yellow Trail starts at the trailhead along the northern edge of the camp (38.34942, −94.66912) and continues straight along the west side of the road. The trail splits at the road intersection, and you can take it either east or north. Following the loop to the east takes you past open wetlands and prairie along the edge of the lake. Turning north, you pass by the foundation of an old house before the trail heads into the woods. Once in the woods, the trail may become less distinct, so keep an eye out for the yellow blazes painted on the trees. After the loop in the woods, you'll emerge along the edge of a small prairie section, where you can see the towers of the power plant across the lake. After 0.15 mile, the trail goes back into the woods and turns west. At the park road there's a four-way intersection. You can follow the Yellow Trail back down to the horse camp or add on a 1.3-mile loop of the Red Trail.

For the additional loop on the Red Trail, head uphill in either direction from the four-way intersection. For a shorter uphill section, take the trail to the right

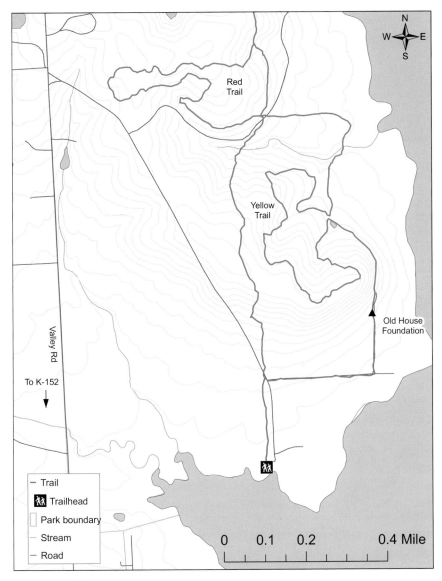

La Cygne Lake

(north) instead of the one to the left (west). The trail along the northern edge of the loop takes you past a barbed wire fence before heading back downhill, broadly parallel to the park roads, and back to the four-way intersection. From there, you can take the Yellow Trail nearly straight south to the horse camp and trailhead for a pleasant change of scenery and some open prairie vistas toward the end of the trail.

Directions to the trailhead: From US-69, turn east onto K-152/E. 2200th Road, then turn left (north) onto Valley Road. After 1.2 miles, take the third right. The pay station is on the right on the park road, and the horse camp and trailhead are at the end of the park road, 1.1 miles from Valley Road.

Additional trails: The Blue Trail follows the contours of the northwestern side of the lake, and it can be accessed from the northern edge of the Red Trail near the RV camping.

Camping: Cabins can be rented, and campsites are available on a first come, first served basis. There are RV hookups for electricity, water, and sewerage at some sites, along with a shower house.

LAWRENCE RIVER TRAILS

The Kansas River is a prominent waterway in northeastern Kansas and is one of the few rivers in the state open to paddling. Formed at the junction of the Smoky Hill and Republican Rivers near Junction City, the Kansas River drains much of the northern part of the state. From this point, the river gradually grows as it continues east and reaches a confluence with the Missouri River along the state border. The trail network built along the north banks of the river in Lawrence provides an excellent opportunity to experience the tranquil, natural beauty of the river. The trail forms a long loop through the majestic hardwoods found between the river and the adjacent flood-control levee. Although most of the trail runs through the woodlands, occasional sections open up into the grassland areas beside the levee, along with several locations that offer spectacular views of the river itself.

Contact: City of Lawrence Parks and Recreation Department, 1141 Massachusetts Street, Lawrence, KS 66044; 785-832-3450.

Hours: Daylight hours.

Cost: Free.

 FEATURED TRAIL: LAWRENCE RIVER TRAIL (TOP BIKE TRAIL)

Trail access: Hike or bike.

Distance: 8.8-mile loop.

To ensure the safety of both hikers and mountain bikers, bikers should ride the loop clockwise, and hikers should go in the opposite direction. There is little overall elevation change, but there are a number of hard rises and steep dips along the way that add variety and difficulty to the route. The entire trail is well marked, and the well-worn dirt and sand path through the wide trail corridor makes for pleasant hiking and fast, fun biking.

If you're biking, start from the marked trailhead (38.97263, −95.21679) and follow the trail into the woods. The first mile is relatively flat and fast, with big trees and some curves and dips. Between miles 1 and 2, the trail dodges in and out of the deep woods into open fields toward the levee. During spring, you may see wild

Lawrence River Trails. (Photo by Jonathan Conard)

strawberries growing along the edge of the woods. Continue west through some roller-coaster dips and twists before starting to angle north. Near the north end of the loop, the trail crosses two bridges before looping back and passing a junction with a side trail (38.98195, –95.16416) that leads down to the river for some great views. After pausing to take in the scenery, return to the main trail and head south to complete the return section of the loop. Before reaching mile marker 6, there's an optional short loop that passes through some sandy and shrubby patches as it winds down toward the river before rejoining the primary trail just past the spot where it branched off from the main route. The last 3 miles of the trail are close to the river's edge and offer some of the route's best views.

Directions to the trailhead: The trails are on the north side of the Kansas River. From I-70, take exit 204 to US-24/US-59E, turn south onto 2nd Street, and continue for 1 mile. Before crossing the river, turn east onto Locust Street and follow this road for 0.9 mile before turning south onto 8th Street. Follow 8th Street south

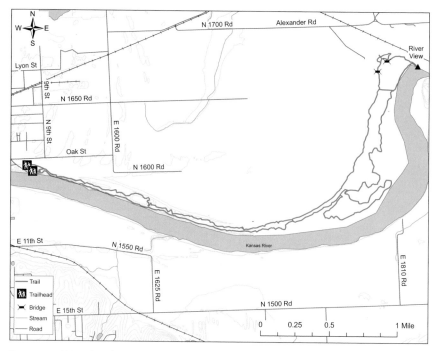

Lawrence River Trails

toward the river, and cross over the levee to reach a parking lot between the levee and the river. If you're coming from the south, take US-59N and continue north over the Kansas River bridge, turn east onto Elm Street, and continue for 0.9 mile before turning south onto 8th Street and crossing the levee to reach the trailhead parking lot.

Additional trails: For a longer trail, the 10-mile Levee Trail can be easily accessed from the Lawrence River Trails. There's not much shade, but the wide, crushed limestone trail along the smooth top provides a good surface for running, walking, or biking. For a short family-friendly hike in Lawrence, explore the trails winding through the 80 natural acres at scenic Prairie Park; see the featured trail later in this chapter.

Camping: Given its urban location, there are no campsites near the trail. For a wide variety of tent and utility camping options, Clinton State Park to the west of Lawrence is a good choice (798 N. 1415 Road, Lawrence, KS 66049; 785-842-8562).

MacLennan Park

This unique park is situated next to the Cedar Crest mansion in Topeka, home to the governor of Kansas. You can enjoy the governor's expansive "public backyard" by visiting the hiking and biking trails at MacLennan Park. It's thought that a branch of the Oregon Trail leading to the Smith's Ferry crossing of the Kansas River passed through the present-day park area. The deep grooves carved into the ground south of the governor's residence were apparently left by these early wagon trains. Later, Frank MacLennan, who owned the *Topeka State Journal* and built the Cedar Crest residence in 1928, purchased the 244-acre tract of land. In 1955 the house and the surrounding estate were "bequeathed to the state of Kansas the real estate and the improvements located thereon and known as Cedar Crest to be used by the state of Kansas for a forest park to be known as MacLennan Park, except for the improvements thereon and the twenty (20) [acres] of land surrounding same, which also bequeathed to the state of Kansas to be used as an executive mansion by the governor of the state of Kansas."

Presently, the area offers a variety of options for hikers and bikers, from the wide, manicured Cedar Crest Trail to the fast, narrow single-track routes that drop sharply toward the Kansas River through deep woods. The 2.7-mile Cedar Crest Trail crosses a large open meadow in the front of the governor's residence and is

MacLennan Park. (Photo by Jonathan Conard)

popular with casual walkers; it also passes several public fishing ponds and an ice-skating pond. The heavily wooded northern and western parts of the park have a more remote feel and offer a connected network of single-track routes curving through majestic oaks and hickories.

Contact: MacLennan Park, SW Fairlawn and Cedar Crest Drive, Topeka, KS 66606.

Hours: 6 a.m. to 11 p.m.

Cost: Free.

 ## FEATURED TRAIL: RED TRAIL (TOP BIKE TRAIL)

Trail access: Hike or bike.

Distance: 1.8-mile loop.

Of all the routes in MacLennan Park, the Red Trail has the most authentic backcountry feel. It is sufficiently removed from the interstate that it's easy to forget you're still in the midst of the capital city. To access the Red Trail from the parking lot by the Cedar Crest residence, take a quick right on a fork along a connecting trail that leads north into the hardwood forest. From the connecting trail, stay right at the first trail junction (39.06753, –95.74976) and also at the next fork. From this point, the Red Trail weaves east through a series of sharp switchbacks before turning north and dropping down toward the Kansas River. A cutoff trail to the left leads back toward the trailhead and offers a nice glimpse of the Kansas River as the route ascends toward the trailhead. However, continue west to enjoy a major highlight of the trail: a carefully crafted terrain park built from natural materials, complete with plenty of bumps and jumps (39.06804, –95.75027). After the terrain park, the Red Trail flattens out as it turns west and parallels a tall bluff along the river's edge. For those who want to log some additional trail miles, the western edge of the Red Trail offers a connecting trail that accesses the Kaw River State Park trails across the road to the west. The Red Trail continues west before looping back to the east and ascending to the trailhead. The packed-dirt trail is well marked by red blazes on trees along the route.

Directions to the trailhead: From I-70 in Topeka, take exit 357A to Fairlawn Road. Turn north onto Fairlawn Road and drive for 0.4 mile; take the first left, which is SW Cedar Crest Road, and follow it until it ends at the parking lot by the governor's residence.

Additional trails: Other trails in MacLennan Park include the Blue Trail (1.8 miles) and the Green Trail (0.7 mile) on the west side of the park. These are fast single-track trails that cross over the Cedar Crest Trail several times as they wind through cedar woodlands and past several small ponds. They have some great scenery and varied terrain. For a tamer trail experience, try the wide Cedar Crest Trail, which is surfaced with crushed limestone and loops along the outer edge of the mowed grass of the governor's "front lawn."

To the west of MacLennan Park, it is possible to connect with the trails at Kaw

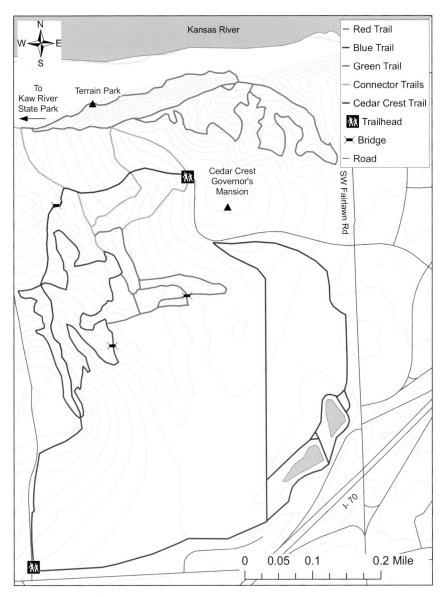

MacLennan Park

River State Park. Dornwood Park (SE 25th Street and SE Highland Avenue) has additional hiking and mountain biking trails. Topeka is also the northern terminus of the Landon Trail, a rail trail that runs south out of the city (see chapter 9). The trailhead can be accessed just east of the *Brown v. Board of Education* Historic Site (1515 SE Monroe Street).

Camping: No camping is allowed; the closest campground is located at Lake Shawnee, in southeastern Topeka. Lake Shawnee has tent and RV campsites (3137 SE 29th Street, Topeka, KS 66505; 785-267-1156).

MELVERN LAKE–EISENHOWER STATE PARK

Along the north shore of Melvern Lake is Eisenhower State Park (formerly Melvern Lake State Park). The park was renamed in 1990 to honor the state's only president (so far), Dwight D. Eisenhower. With a swimming beach; equestrian, hiking, and biking trails; sand volleyball; basketball courts; horseshoe pits; a playground; disc golf; an archery target trail; a kids' fishing pond; and, of course, the lake itself, Eisenhower State Park is a popular destination on the eastern edge of the Flint Hills. The on-site state park office has natural history displays, including some live reptiles and amphibians. You can rent kayaks and canoes from Ike's General Store, and two boat ramps provide access to the lake, where you can fish or just cruise around the 6,930 acres of water.

Monicka Remboldt out for a ride on the Crooked Knee Horse Trails. (Photo by Kristin Conard)

Contact: Eisenhower State Park, 29810 S. Fairlawn Road, Osage City, KS 66523; 785-528-4102.
Hours: 24/7.
Cost: State park fee.

FEATURED TRAIL: CROOKED KNEE HORSE TRAILS–ORANGE LOOP (TOP BRIDLE TRAIL)

Trail access: Hike or bridle.
Distance: 5.8-mile loop, 17 miles total.

Competitive trail rides are sometimes held at the Crooked Knee Horse Trails in Eisenhower State Park, and day-use horse trailer parking is available at the trailhead. The well-marked trails are mostly mowed grass, and they are kept in good condition. Just as importantly, the trails traverse enough hills to keep things interesting, and they offer views of the lake as well as a mix of open prairie vistas and shady woodlands. By making use of both the shorter Orange Loop (5.8 miles) and the longer Blue Loop (10 miles), with yellow connecting trails, you can have a new experience each time. Both the Blue Loop and the Orange Loop start north of the Cowboy Horse Camp (38.52668, –95.75667). After heading north for a few hundred feet, the trails split. The Blue Loop continues north, and the Orange Loop turns left (west). About 250 feet onto the Orange Loop, you'll reach the first of the yellow connector trail intersections. Stay on the trail marked with orange. The first portion takes you briefly into the woods, although most of the trail is across open prairie. In the woods, you'll pass the 0.5 mile marker (all mile and half-mile markers are indicated by orange signposts). Shortly after that, you'll reach another yellow connector trail. The Orange Loop continues north, heading out of the trees and uphill through open prairie that, in spring and summer, should be dotted with blooming wildflowers. Take comfort in knowing that what goes up must come down, and enjoy the leisurely downhill trek back toward the trees after mile marker 1. You'll reach the western edge of one of the yellow connector trails around mile marker 1.5, where you can prepare for another gradual uphill climb to mile marker 2. The trail parallels Wanamaker Road for 0.2 mile. As you start bearing left (southeast) across the prairie and along the south side of the Orange Loop, you'll have some nice views of the lake in the distance, particularly around mile marker 3 (38.51418, –95.75704). From here, you'll start winding back toward the trailhead along the tree line. Between mile markers 3 and 3.5 and mile markers 4.5 and 5, you'll pass yellow connector intersections that link the Orange Loop to the Blue Loop. About 90 feet after mile marker 5, the Orange and Blue Loops join together, and the trail heads downhill through the trees to mile marker 5.5, where there's a yellow connector intersection. After one final uphill push, you're at the trailhead.

Directions to the trailhead: From US-75, turn south onto K-278W/W. 293rd Street. After 3 miles, turn left (south) onto South Fairlawn Road. You'll pass the

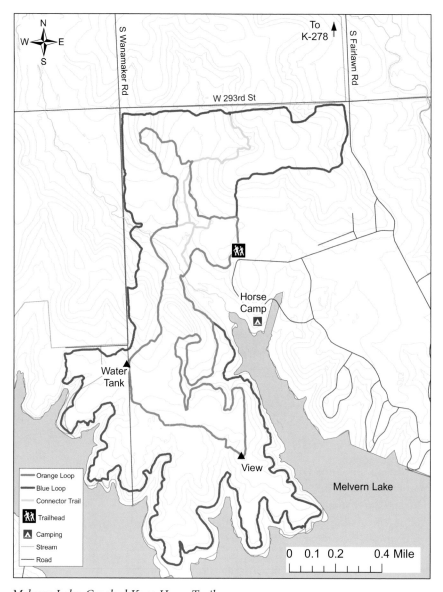

Melvern Lake, Crooked Knee Horse Trails

state park office and take the first right after 0.5 mile. The trailhead is on the right (north).

Additional trails: The Blue Loop of the Crooked Knee Horse Trail is 10 miles and meanders along the edge of the lake and north of the Orange Loop.

The Five Star Campground has a trail with archery targets that combines with another nearby trail for a 5-mile hike or bike trail called the Five Star Trail or Ike's

Trail. West Point Campground boasts the area's newest trail: a 1.5-mile one-way trail for motorized scooters (50cc and under).

Camping: There's equestrian camping at the North Loop of the West Point Campground, and the Cowboy Horse Camp offers primitive camping with tie poles.

MELVERN LAKE–OUTLET PARK

Outlet Park is east of the large dam at Melvern Lake. The dam itself is 9,650 feet long and nearly 118 feet above the Marais des Cygnes River Valley. The Kanza Indians inhabited the valley through the early 1800s, and a Sac and Fox Indian reservation was briefly established in the area in the 1860s. Although access for hiking, biking, and picnicking in nonreservable sites is free in US Army Corps of Engineers parks, there are seasonal fees associated with camping, boat launching, and beach use. Outlet Park has several picnic sites, as well as a larger pavilion that can be reserved for groups. The swimming beach has a shower house, and there's a softball field and two playgrounds; for fishermen, there's a stocked fishing pond and a dock with a fish cleaning station.

The Marais des Cygnes River is nearby. It got its name, which means Marsh of the Swans, from French trappers who visited the area and found it full of wildlife. During spring and fall migrations, Melvern Lake attracts snow geese and ducks. Great blue herons and wood ducks can be found at the lake during the summer, and bald eagles use the area in the winter.

Contact: Melvern Lake Project Office–US Army Corps of Engineers, 31051 Melvern Lake Parkway, Melvern, KS 66510; 785-549-3318.

Hours: 24/7.

Cost: Free.

FEATURED TRAIL: MARAIS DES CYGNES RIVER NATURE TRAIL (TOP FAMILY-FRIENDLY TRAIL)

Trail access: Hike or bike.

Distance: 1.8-mile loop.

The trailhead for the nature trail (38.51832, –95.70805) is located close to a playground. The paved trail passes the playground and restrooms, and after about 500 feet, you'll reach a four-way intersection. If you go left (west) and follow the signs for the primitive trail, you'll be on a smooth gravel trail around a narrow pond for 0.6 mile. At the third small bridge crossing the trail becomes paved again, and there's another intersection. If you bear left, you'll follow a loop with benches and interpretive signage along the way. To the east of the trail, and visible from it, is an oxbow lake. An oxbow (U-shaped) lake is formed when a bend in the river channel becomes cut off and changes from a river ecosystem to something closer to a lake ecosystem, supporting different types of birds and wildlife. As the trail loop closes, you'll head south to the four-way intersection near the trailhead.

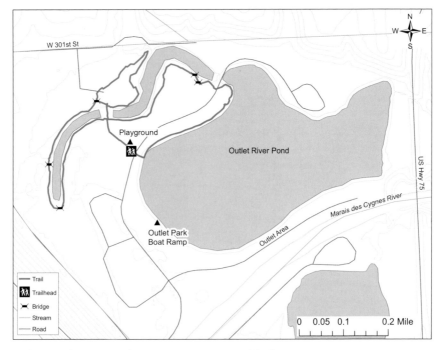

Melvern Lake, Marais des Cygnes River Nature Trail

If you're ready to stop, you can go back to the trailhead. If not, you can continue east along the other side of the oxbow lake on a fine gravel trail that follows the edge of the lake and crosses over two small wooden bridges before crossing the park road. The gravel trail parallels the sidewalk, which circles most of the Outlet River Pond, turns right (northwest) along the western portion of the pond, crosses the park road, and ends at the trailhead.

Directions to the trailhead: From US-50, take exit 155 to US-75 toward Lyndon/Burlington. After 6.4 miles, take the K-31S exit toward Melvern and bear right (northeast) toward the Outlet Area. The trailhead and parking are on the left (west).

Additional trails: Between Coeur d'Alene Park and Arrow Rock Park on the southern side of Outlet Park is a 4-mile one-way trail called the Tallgrass Heritage Trail.

Camping: Each of the camps around the lake has campsites, and Outlet Park and Eisenhower State Park have shower houses.

OREGON TRAIL NATURE PARK

On the southern edge of the 19-acre Oregon Trail Nature Park is the historic Oregon Trail. Three nature trails loop through the small park, and the showcase of the site is the silo with a mural painted by local artist Cynthia Martin, depicting

Oregon Trail Nature Park. (Photo by Mark Conard)

immigrants on the Oregon Trail, wildlife along the trail, and a Native American bison hunt. The park is within the Jeffrey Energy Center Wildlife Area and close to the Jeffrey Energy Center Lake. Jeffrey Energy Center is the state's largest coal power plant. In 1987 what is now Westar Energy partnered with the KDWPT to manage its four separate wildlife areas. Two are open to hunting and fishing, one is closed as a refuge, and the fourth is the Oregon Trail Nature Park.

Contact: Oregon Trail Nature Park, Highway 24, Oregon Trail Road, St. Marys, KS 66536; 785-437-2356. Jeffrey Wildlife Area Office, 7960 State Lake Road, Manhattan, KS 66502; 785-456-6149.
Hours: Daylight hours.
Cost: Free.

FEATURED TRAIL: SEA OF GRASS TRAIL AND POND TRAIL (TOP HISTORICAL TRAIL)

Trail access: Hike.
Distance: 1-mile loop.

In *My Antonia*, Willa Cather equates the grass to the sea: "As I looked about me I felt that the grass was the country, as the water is the sea. . . . And there was so much motion in it; the whole country seemed, somehow, to be running." To access any of the three short nature trails, pull up to a shelter house and restrooms and park near the painted silo and the trailhead (39.22930, –96.15278). The trails split at a roundabout. If you bear left (north-northwest), you'll cross a wooden bridge and then head uphill for the Sea of Grass Trail. The trail splits again shortly after a right turn past the bridge. Bearing right takes you on the Pond Trail, and bearing left keeps you on the Sea of Grass Trail. The Sea of Grass Trail splits again shortly after this, and you can take the loop either left or right. Bearing left takes you along the base of a hill below the amphitheater. The trail dips into the woodlands for a bit before emerging into prairie. Following the trail uphill, you'll reach its northern edge. If you want a short, strenuous section compensated by views of the Kansas River Valley, take the trail offshoot to the north, up a steep hill. To prevent erosion and to help visitors traverse the hillside more easily, wooden steps have been installed. This is a short section — just 0.1 mile. After this side trip, take the trail back downhill (southwest). This side of the trail goes through more wooded sections, but it's mostly along the prairie, with lots of expansive views and little shade. Near the southern end of the trail, there's a short side trail uphill to the amphitheater, which gives you a chance to see the other side of the valley. From the end of the Sea of Grass Trail, you can link up with the Pond Trail for a 0.2-mile addition to your walk. Make sure to check out all sides of the impressive silo mural before you leave.

Directions to the trailhead: The Oregon Trail Nature Park is between Wamego and St. Marys. From US-24, turn north on Schoeman Road. After 0.6 mile, turn left (northwest) onto Oregon Trail Road and travel 0.4 mile. The trailhead is on the right (northeast).

Additional trails: The closest trails are at the Green Memorial Wildlife Area, about 16 miles southwest off of US-24, or the Mount Mitchell Heritage Prairie, a 50-acre tallgrass prairie preserve with hiking trails that climb sharply to the summit of an overlook with a sweeping view of the Kansas River Valley. The site was originally owned by Captain William Mitchell, who served in the free-state militia

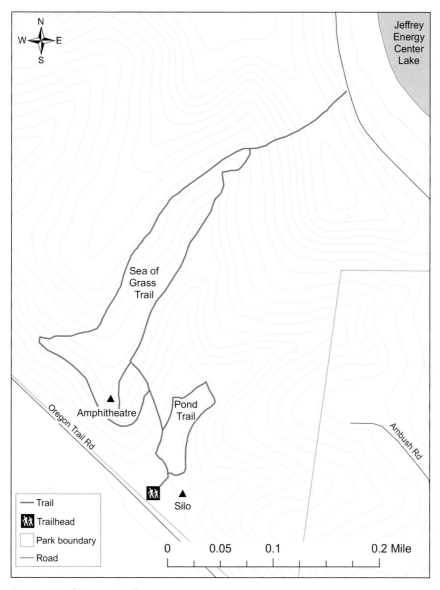

Oregon Trail Nature Park

and maintained a station on the Underground Railroad. The site is located 3.5 miles south of Wamego on K-99; from K-99, turn east onto Mitchell Prairie Lane and drive for 0.5 mile until you reach the trailhead and parking area.

Camping: No camping is allowed at Oregon Trail Nature Park. The closest camping is at Mill Creek Campground and RV Park in Paxico (22470 Campground Road, Paxico, KS 66526; 785-636-5321; millcreek@kansas.net).

PERRY LAKE

Over the past 250 years or so, this area has been transformed from Delaware River Valley to Delaware Indian Reservation to farmland and finally to the current reservoir and park. The 11,150-acre reservoir was built in the 1960s, and it is a wildly popular site for fishing, particularly for bass. There are several day-use and camping areas around the reservoir, with picnic sites and playgrounds. There are also some great trails along the shore and through the oak-hickory woodlands.

Contact: US Army Corps of Engineers–Perry Project Office, 10419 Perry Park Drive, Perry, KS 66073; 785-597-5144; perry.lake@usace.army.mil.

Hours: 24/7.

Cost: Free.

FEATURED TRAIL: PERRY LAKE NATIONAL RECREATION TRAIL (TOP 10 TRAIL)

Trail access: Hike.

Distance: 28-mile loop.

This long, well-maintained and well-marked backpacking trail winds along the shore and through the remote oak-hickory woodlands at Perry Lake. Trail maintenance happens during the late fall and early spring, so spring is an ideal time to tackle this big trail. During summer, you may encounter poison ivy along the trail. You can drive in and leave caches of water along different access points, or you can set up a camp at the halfway point: the campsite near the Old Military Trail trailhead (39.21356, –95.41681). Another option is to make shorter out-and-back hikes. As you walk along the primarily shaded trail, you'll likely see wildlife such as white-tailed deer and wild turkeys; in the winter, you may spot a bald eagle.

The trail has three main trailheads: Slough Creek to the south, Old Military Trail to the north, and Ferguson Road to the southeast. The trail is marked with blue blazes on the trees. The section along Slough Creek is most popular, as it passes several major campsites. Starting at the Slough Creek trailhead at the southern end (39.13719, –95.43389), head north along the lake through the woods for 0.55 mile. There, the trail splits. It was designed to be taken clockwise, so turn left at the intersection. The trail winds up and down along the lake before crossing a bridge at 66th Street, which was an Eagle Scout project in 2006. After another mile, the trail crosses the road that heads down to the Longview Park boat ramp. Shortly after crossing the road, you'll reach the Richard "Mobe" Rucker memorial bench. He was a park ranger who toiled tirelessly on the Perry Lake Trail and helped organize the volunteers who worked on the trails. This bench at Hoover Creek Cove is a good place to stop and take in the views of the lake. It is in a "table rocks" area—places where large rocks are conveniently situated to allow hikers to take a break. Between miles 4 and 5, you may notice some side trails, but stay focused on following the blue blazes, heading for the crossing of Hoover Creek. The packed-dirt trail continues up and down along the lake and crosses a Longview Park road

(39.18758, –95.44084). After another 0.5 mile, you'll cross another Longview Park road and start bearing downhill back toward the shore.

At about mile 7.5 (39.19427, –95.45622), you'll reach the Richard Douthit memorial bench — another spot selected for its views of the lake. Douthit was a trail coordinator from 1991 to 1994. From here, the trail follows the ridges along the shore to the north of a subdivision. As the trail heads back east, you'll cross the

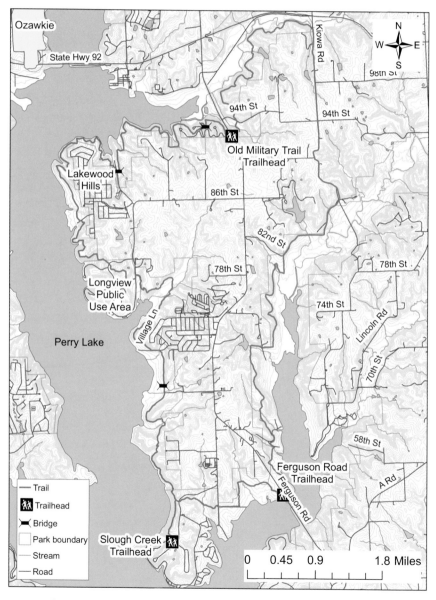

Perry Lake, National Recreation Trail

Old Quarry Bridge, another Eagle Scout project. The trail turns back north, and in another 1.2 miles you'll reach the Dorothy Moore memorial bench at Solitude Point (39.21555, –95.43367), overlooking Little Slough Creek Valley. Moore was a founding member of the Kansas Trails Council, and she was the trail coordinator at Perry Lake from 1994 to 1998. Another 0.4 mile from Solitude Point, past a side trail marked in white blazes that leads to a hikers' campground with a fire ring and a small amphitheater, is the Old Military Trail trailhead (39.21356, –95.41681). At this point, you're halfway through the trail, which crosses Ferguson Road (with parking nearby). The trail follows part of the route used by the military from Fort Leavenworth to Fort Riley — hence its name.

To continue on the more remote, eastern side of the loop, cross over Ferguson Road and the creek. Cross 94th Street and head uphill, with views to the lake to the west. The trail turns north, following a ridge along Little Slough Creek to your left. At 3.5 miles from the Old Military Trail trailhead, head nearly due south for 1.55 miles along Kiowa Road. You'll pass by Lowry School (39.20884, –95.39538) and continue on Kiowa Road until you reach the four-way intersection of Kiowa Road and 82nd Street. Turn right (southwest) onto 82nd Street, along the edge of Camp Jayhawk. When 82nd Street continues west (intersecting with Ferguson Road after 0.6 mile), the trail bears south through the trees (39.19057, –95.40395) and up- and downhills as the final miles unfold. At around 25.5 miles, you'll cross a park road — a reminder that you're close to civilization. One mile later, you'll cross Ferguson Road and pass by the Ferguson trailhead (39.14600, –95.40726). From there, it's 2 miles through the trees back to the Slough Creek trailhead.

Directions to the trailhead: For the Slough Creek and Ferguson trailheads: From US-24, turn north onto County Road 1029/Ferguson Road and continue on Ferguson Road for 5 miles. You'll pass the Ferguson trailhead on the left. To continue to the Slough Creek trailhead, stay on Ferguson Road for another 1.3 miles and turn left (south) onto Slough Creek Road and follow it for 2.1 miles.

FEATURED TRAIL: THUNDER RIDGE TRAIL

Trail access: Hike.
Distance: 2.3-mile loop.

If you stop by the US Army Corps of Engineers office at Perry Lake (10419 Perry Park Drive), you can pick up a Thunder Ridge Trail map. Even though it's not to scale (it's intended for kids to color), it has information about the 30 educational stations along the way. The main trail is marked with white blazes on the trees, and the six side trails down to the camping loops are marked with yellow blazes. The trail starts a few hundred feet south of the Slough Creek Campground entrance (39.14161, –95.43143), and it's marked to be taken clockwise, so head east into the woods. The trail is rocky, so watch your step. It also has some quick ups and downs — a bit like many parts of the much longer Perry Lake National Recreation Trail. Occasionally, the trail passes out of the woods and into the open

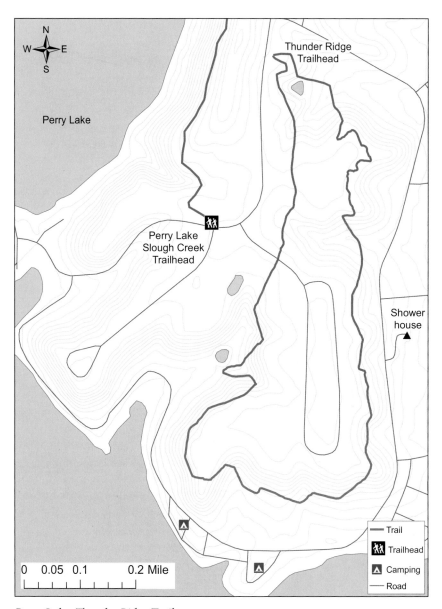

Perry Lake, Thunder Ridge Trail

before heading back into the hardwood forest. It's mostly oak and hickory, but you can also spot elm, ash, and walnut. Listen for the calls and songs of birds such as the American robin and eastern bluebird. The trail makes a loop heading south, and side trails link it to the Slough Creek Campground along the southern edge of the loop. As the trail heads back north, along the western side, there are more

93

open, exposed prairie sections. When you cross the park road, it's 0.4 mile back to the trailhead.

Directions to the trailhead: From US-24, turn north onto County Road 1029/ Ferguson Road and continue on Ferguson Road for 6.3 miles; turn left (south) onto Slough Creek Road and follow it for 1.7 miles. The trailhead is a few hundred feet south of the northern Slough Creek Park camp entrance.

Additional trails: In Perry State Park, on the southwestern side of the lake, there are about 20 miles of popular and very technical bike trails. At Jefferson Point, 25 miles of hiking and bridle trails wind through the upland forest. The Delaware Marsh Trail is a 1.75-mile nature trail along the south side of the dam.

Camping: The US Army Corps of Engineers manages four parks with a mix of primitive camping and electricity and water hookups. Perry State Park has at least four modern cabins. It also has 300 campsites spread over 11 campgrounds, 4 of which have electricity and water hookups. Equestrian camping is available at Wild Horse Campground.

POMONA LAKE

Finished in 1963, the dam at Pomona Lake is more than 100 feet tall; it created 4,000-acre Pomona Lake from 110-Mile and Dragoon Creeks. The lake is known for fishing, and it has four boat ramps and a full-service marina. Located within the Osage Cuestas, it has upland forest with shagbark and bitternut hickory; white, red, and black oak; and some low, long hills and plains. Although it's primarily recreational today, the area has been used for centuries by different groups of people who left their mark. In 1993 the US Army Corps of Engineers–Kansas City District completed a "cultural resource inventory" to catalog any sites or artifacts of archaeological significance. Discoveries included projectile points and historical foundations.

Contact: US Army Corps of Engineers–Pomona Project Office, 5260 Pomona Dam Road, Vassar, KS 66543; 785-453-2201. Pomona State Park, 2290 S. Highway 368, Vassar, KS 66543; 785-828-4933.

Hours: 24/7.

Cost: Free.

FEATURED TRAIL: BLACK HAWK TRAIL

Trail access: Hike or bridle.

Distance: Loop from Cedar Park to 197th Street, 3.5 miles; 21 miles total.

The trail officially starts near 110-Mile Camp (38.67330, –95.58211), but it can be accessed in several different places along the park roads. The Blue Trail follows the government boundary line and is marked with blue reflectors on trees and blue flags. The Orange Trail follows the shoreline and is marked with orange reflectors and orange flags. At times, they overlap and intersect. Yellow flags mark places where you should be especially careful, such as steeper or rockier sections. The Blue Trail is generally in better shape than the Orange Trail, although both can be overgrown in the summer. Trail maintenance is done entirely by volunteers.

From Cedar Park, near the intersection of S. Croco Road and E. 205th Street, the trail picks up heading north (38.69519, −95.61199). The Orange and Blue Trails start together, taking you through open prairie for 0.6 mile before heading into the trees. You'll cross a couple of small streambeds, and the trail weaves in and out of shaded and open areas with blooming wildflowers in the summer. At 0.8 mile in, the Blue and Orange Trails split briefly, joining up again before splitting into a larger loop 400 feet later (38.70541, −95.62019). Taking the Orange Trail to the left (west) leads you (briefly) through the woods along the lake and its rocky shoreline. It then takes you north through the woodlands, made up primarily of black and chinquapin oak and bitternut and shagbark hickory, to the intersection of the Blue and Orange Trails near 197th Street (38.70937, −95.62433). The Blue Trail takes you back toward Cedar Park. You'll pass by an old stone fence, evidence of former homesteads in the area. When you reach the loop intersection (38.70541, −95.62019), you can backtrack to the trailhead at Cedar Park.

Directions to the trailhead: From US-56, turn south onto Maple Street in Overbrook, and follow it for 4 miles (it turns into S. Shawnee Heights Road) to E. 189th Street. Turn right (west) onto E. 189th Street. For the Cedar Park trailhead, turn left (south) onto S. Croco Road and follow it until you get to E. 205th Street. For

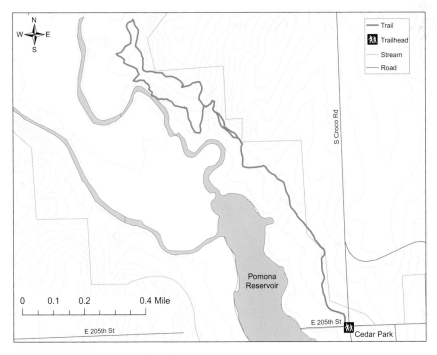

Pomona Lake, Black Hawk Trail

the 110-Mile Park trailhead, turn left (east) onto E. 205th Street; then turn right onto Lake Road 3 and follow it as it becomes E. 209th Street and then S. Pauline Road and dead-ends at the park.

Additional trails: The Black Hawk Trail continues both north and south from Cedar Park, with the Blue and Orange Trails occasionally overlapping and joining to form loops.

At 110-Mile Park there are two shorter nature trails: the Deer Creek Nature Trail and the Witches' Broom Trail. Pomona State Park has a short nature trail across open grassland between Heart Stays Campground and Evening Star Campground and E. 229th Street.

Camping: At 110-Mile Park, seven campsites and horse ties are available. Camping is also available at other US Army Corps of Engineers parks. There are approximately 200 primitive campsites at Pomona State Park on the south side of the lake, and it has 142 RV utility campsites with electricity and water hookups; some also have sewer hookups. In addition, there are four modern, handicapped-accessible cabins.

PRAIRIE PARK NATURE CENTER

Located in southeastern Lawrence is an 80-acre nature preserve that opened in 1999. Take the time to visit the Education Building, where you'll find natural history dioramas with information on the different ecosystems in the area, as well as live animal exhibits featuring birds of prey. Deer, bobcats, and beavers use the area as habitat, and the abundantly blooming wildflowers in spring and summer attract scores of butterflies. The area has even been designated a butterfly habitat by Monarch Watch, an educational outreach and butterfly conservation and research program at the University of Kansas. The trails here crisscross through woodlands along Mary's Lake and through the prairie.

Contact: Prairie Park Nature Center, 2730 Harper Street, Lawrence, KS 66046; 785-832-7980.

Hours: Tuesday to Saturday, 9 a.m. to 5 p.m.; Sunday, 1 to 4 p.m.; closed Monday.

Cost: Free.

FEATURED TRAIL: NATURE TRAIL (TOP WILDLIFE AND WILDFLOWERS TRAIL AND TOP FAMILY-FRIENDLY TRAIL)

Trail access: Hike.

Distance: 1.6 miles total.

If you start along the mowed grass trails heading north from the Education Building (38.93320, –95.21568), you'll pass the western edge of the nature center's prairie grasses. School groups use the area for field trips, so you might run into them while you're out on the trail. The trail heads gently uphill. After 0.12 mile, at the northwestern edge near 27th Street, you'll turn right (east) and skirt the edge

Eastern tiger swallowtail butterfly at Prairie Park Nature Center. (Photo by Kristin Conard)

of the trees. You can head into the trees along the eastern section of the trail, or you can stay on the western, prairie side of the trail. Along the woodland trail, you'll cross a few wooden bridges as you wind through the trees on the packed-dirt path. The woodland trail meets up with the paved trail on the eastern edge of the park before they both head back into the woods and intersect with the prairie trail along a boardwalk across a small wetlands section (38.93169, –95.21431). From the boardwalk, you can head back north through the prairie or continue south for a 0.5-mile loop near the eastern edge of Mary's Lake. Mary's Lake was built in the 1950s. In the 1970s the Lawrence Parks and Recreation Department began to use the site for summer camps. In 1991 the city purchased the lake and began developing the area into the well-maintained park it is now. There is a picnic table along the southeastern edge, near the intersection of the paved trail and the wooded trail. The Mary's Lake loop takes you back to the boardwalk. From there, you can wind through the prairie back to the Education Building.

Directions to the trailhead: From downtown Lawrence, take Massachusetts Street south and turn left (east) onto E. 23rd Street. Take it for 0.7 mile and turn right (south) onto Haskell Avenue. After 0.5 mile, turn left (east) onto E. 27th

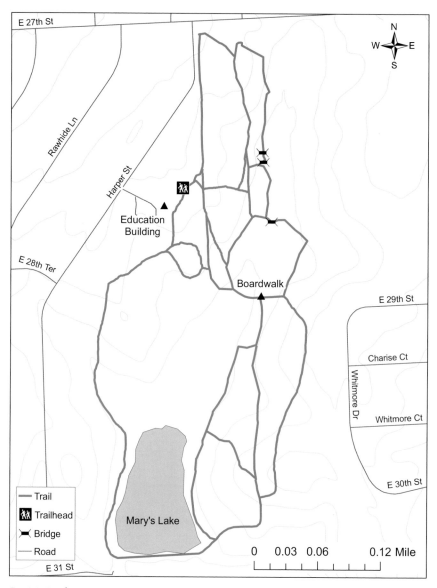

Prairie Park Nature Center

Street, and after 0.4 mile, turn right (south) onto Harper Street. Prairie Park Nature Center is on the left.

Additional trails: Around the southern two-thirds of the nature center is a paved sidewalk. For another top wildlife and wildflowers trail, head to Baker Wetlands, about 2.5 miles southwest off of 35th Street; it has 6 miles of hiking trails.

Camping: No camping is allowed at Prairie Park Nature Center. The closest camping is at Clinton State Park (798 N. 1415 Road, Lawrence, KS 66049; 785-842-8562).

UNIVERSITY OF KANSAS FIELD STATION

The University of Kansas Field Station was established in 1947 as a site for environmental education and long-term ecological field studies. Charles Robinson, Kansas's first governor, originally owned the initial 590 acres of the current site, which were later donated to the university. Distinguished professor and mammalogist E. Raymond Hall secured the property for use as a field station and named Henry S. Fitch its resident naturalist. Fitch continued to live in, work in, and explore the area for more than 50 years while making immeasurable contributions to the fields of herpetology and natural history. The original field station site is now known as the Henry Fitch Natural History Reservation. Additional land acquisitions have increased the field station properties to nearly 1,800 acres. Current

University of Kansas Field Station. (Photo by Jonathan Conard)

research at the field station involves prairie restoration, ecological succession, and medicinal uses of native plants.

Although the field station is focused on ecological research, there are a number of public hiking trails. These trails ascend and descend hilltops and valleys through several separate but contiguous tracts of the property, including the Suzanne Eck McColl Nature Reserve, the Rockefeller Experimental Tract, and the heavily forested Fitch Natural History Reservation. Please respect ongoing research activities and travel only on marked trails in the area.

Contact: Nelson Environmental Study Area, 350 Wild Horse Road, Lawrence, KS 66044; 785-843-8573.

Hours: Daylight hours.

Cost: Free.

FEATURED TRAIL: ROTH TRAIL

Trail access: Hike. No pets allowed on the trail.

Distance: 1.1-mile loop, 5 miles total.

As a biology teacher in Lawrence for 40 years, Stan Roth established a well-deserved reputation as an expert in natural history, and he kindled a passion for the natural world in both his students and his colleagues. The Roth Trail is named in honor of Stan and his wife Janet, who taught so many to understand, appreciate, and respect the northeastern Kansas landscape. The trailhead was designed and constructed by a team of architecture students from the University of Kansas. The eight upright earthen sections of the trailhead itself are punctuated with openings proportioned according to the Fibonacci sequence. These sections were constructed entirely from native soil, which was placed in forms and then compacted with cement and water—a technique known as rammed-earth construction. Spanning the rammed-earth sections is a canopy of steel and cedar beams. The beams are charred as a tribute to the prairie fires that play an integral part in sculpting the native landscape. The unique design of the trailhead has garnered architectural honors, including a 2012 Honor Award for Student Architecture from the Kansas chapter of the American Institute of Architects.

After admiring the trailhead, start north along the Roth Trail. Shortly after the trailhead (39.03874, −95.20701), the Lowland Trail branches to the left and continues through the westernmost portion of the McColl Nature Reserve. At this junction, continue north along the Roth Trail as you start a gradual climb through a mature hardwood forest. The trail switchbacks several times, and you start to gain elevation more rapidly. A fork marks the beginning of the loop portion of the Roth Trail. Following the left fork leads you past the remains of a limestone rock wall (39.04409, −95.20777), a relic from the days before barbed wire and when timber was in limited supply; homesteaders constructed fences of native stone as a labor-intensive but effective means of containing livestock. From the rock wall, the trail slowly begins to loop back toward the east and passes the ruins of a

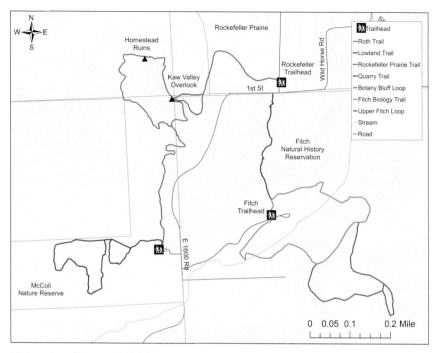

University of Kansas Field Station

homestead (39.04553, –95.20713). The trail continues to ascend until reaching a ridge and skirting the edge of the forest before fully emerging at a majestic overlook from which you can see the Kaw River Valley and the town of Lawrence to the south (39.04406, –95.20592). The structure here was also designed and constructed by a student team from the University of Kansas School of Architecture. From the overlook, you can continue south and descend the ridge to follow the Roth Trail back to the trailhead. From this point, it is also possible to continue east and explore additional trails in the Rockefeller Tract and Fitch Natural History Reservation.

Directions to the trailhead: From the junction of US-59/US-24 and US-24/US-40, go 1.5 miles east on US-24/US-40 to 1600 Road. Turn north onto 1600 Road and continue for 1.1 miles as it angles slightly northwest and reaches a four-way intersection. At the intersection, turn east onto 1900 Road and then turn onto the first road leading back north (1600 Road again). Follow 1600 Road north for an additional 1.7 miles, and look for the parking lot and trailhead for the Roth Trail on the west side of the road.

Additional trails: From the north end of the Roth Trail, explore the 0.4-mile Rockefeller Prairie Trail, which is paved and handicapped accessible. This trail leads to an overlook point where you can enjoy an expansive view south across the Kaw River Valley before continuing through a tract of prairie with a diverse array of native wildflowers and grasses. To the west, the Fitch Biology Trail (0.9 mile) and the Fitch Upper Loop (0.7 mile) cross a towering array of oaks, shagbark hickories, and black walnuts along a thick forested tract named in honor of the aforementioned Henry S. Fitch. Follow the self-guided nature trails along the Fitch Biology Trail and the Fitch Upper Loop, which have informational signs identifying the wide variety of native flora. The Fitch Upper Loop offers great solitude but may be slightly overgrown during the summer.

Camping: No camping is allowed on any of the University of Kansas Field Station property. Clinton State Park, to the west, is the best bet for camping in the vicinity (798 N. 1415 Road, Lawrence, KS 66049; 785-842-8562).

CHAPTER 4

SOUTHEAST KANSAS

These things — the air, the water, the scenery and we who fill these scenes — hold many and many a man to Kansas when money would tempt him away. . . . Here are the still waters, here are the green pastures. Here, the fairest of the world's habitations.

WILLIAM ALLEN WHITE, CIRCA 1912

Great blue heron in Southeast Kansas. Photo by Kristin Conard

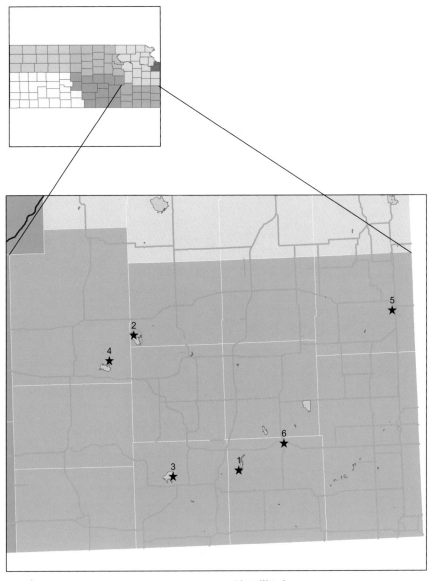

Southeast Kansas

1. Big Hill Lake
2. Cross Timbers State Park
3. Elk City State Park
4. Fall River Lake
5. Gunn Park
6. Tolen Creek Park

Southeast Kansas gets more rain than the rest of the state, which helps the tall-grass prairie, oak-hickory woodland, and oak savannah thrive. The southeast has a variety of physiographic regions. Tucked into the far southeastern corner of the state is a sliver of heavily wooded Ozark Plateau surrounded by an area of Cherokee Lowlands. The region also includes the oak savannahs of the Cross Timbers region and the gently rolling but rocky hills of the Osage Cuestas. Historically, the counties along the state's border with Missouri were mired in unrest and violence before and during the Civil War. In addition, the area has been used extensively for strip mining, and the scars where coal was ripped from the ground are still visible, particularly around Pittsburg. Near West Mineral, you can check out one of the relics from the mining era — an enormous 160-foot electric shovel called Big Brutus. The region's history combined with its varied terrain makes this a fun corner of the state to explore.

BIG HILL LAKE

Technically, the name is Pearson-Skubitz Big Hill Lake, but it's more commonly shortened to Big Hill Lake. The US Army Corps of Engineers manages the 1,240-acre lake near Cherryvale. The lake — which has sandy beaches and is one of the clearest in the state — is a popular spot for fishing, hunting, and boating. The area is hilly and wooded, and it's situated in what is known as the "Little Ozarks."
Contact: US Army Corps of Engineers, PO Box 426, Cherryvale, KS 67335; 620-336-2741.
Hours: 24/7.
Cost: Free.

FEATURED TRAIL: RUTH NIXON NATURE TRAIL

Trail access: Hike.
Distance: 0.9 mile, one-way.
The trail's namesake, Ruth L. Nixon, lived nearby and was a prominent community member and promoter of Big Hill Lake. Because it's a one-way trail, there are two trailheads, and the trail connects the Overlook and Cherryvale Recreation Areas. Along the way are a handful of benches where you can take a break and enjoy the views of the lake. The trail can be taken in either direction — north to south or south to north. The trailhead at the southern end (37.27253, −95.47038) is near the overlook, where you can stop for a great view out over the lake before starting the trail. At the overlook trailhead, an interpretive sign explains some of the history of the area and provides a map of the trail. The trail is rocky, with lots of exposed tree roots, so watch your step. The trail takes you through an area where Paleo-Indian artifacts from 12,000 years ago have been found. More recently, the Osage tribe hunted bison on the prairies and lived along the creeks in the nearby hills. One Osage leader, Pa 'I'n-No-Pa-She (not afraid of long hairs), was

View of Big Hill Lake from the Ruth Nixon Nature Trail. (Photo by Kristin Conard)

known as "Big Hill Joe" to the European settlers in the area. The lake got its name from him.

The trail through the woods is entirely shaded as it runs along the edge of the lake. In some spots, the lake is visible through the trees. Along the way, a few small wooden bridges take the trail over minor tributaries to the lake. Geese and ducks use the lake during migration, and if you're quiet, you might hear a woodpecker or see a white-tailed deer or rabbit along the trail. There are some hills, but there are also plenty of places to stop and rest along the way. Side trails lead west and uphill to the Big Hill Lake camp and campground. At the northern edge of the trail, you'll see a fishing berm along the lake, and the trail turns west and uphill to the Cherryvale Recreation Area trailhead (37.28276, −95.46923).

Directions to the trailhead: For the overlook trailhead: From US-400, take the US-169 ramp to Chanute/Coffeyville and continue on US-169S for 2.4 miles. Turn left (southeast) onto 5700 Road, follow it for 2.1 miles, and then turn left (east) onto E. 5200 Street. After 3.5 miles, turn right (south) onto Cherryvale Parkway and follow it for 0.4 mile to the first left past the US Army Corps of Engineers office. Parking, the trailhead, and the overlook are at the end of the loop.

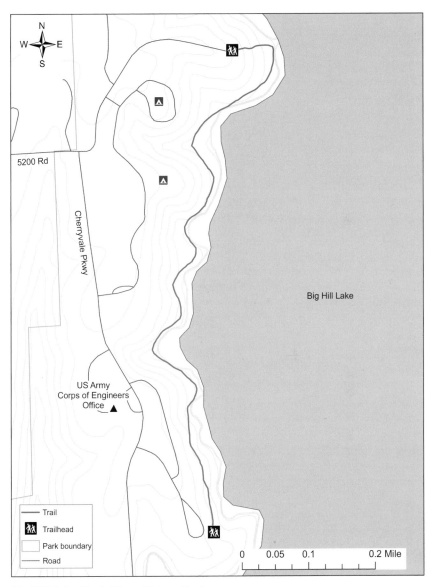

Big Hill Lake, Ruth Nixon Nature Trail

Additional trails: The 17-mile Big Hill Lake Bridle Trail is essentially an H-shaped trail that crosses Rea Bridge and runs along the northern half of the lake. The trail is likely to be overgrown in the summer and may be difficult to follow, especially if you're on foot. However, for the intrepid, you can check out the Kansas Horse Council map and essentially just ride or walk near the perimeter of the lake, keeping an eye out for blue blazes on trees and blue ribbons tied to branches.

Camping: Three campgrounds are available, with 85 campsites. Some electricity hookups are available, as well as flush toilets and showers.

CROSS TIMBERS STATE PARK

Along the 2,800-acre Toronto Reservoir is the 1,075-acre Cross Timbers State Park (formerly Toronto Lake State Park — renamed in 2002) in the hills of the Verdigris River Valley. It's located along the northern edge of the Cross Timbers region, typified by hills covered in oak savannah-grassland and lightly forested primarily with oaks. It has more densely wooded areas along the water, as well as some open prairie. It's essentially part of the boundary between the more heavily wooded east and the nearly treeless Great Plains. Pioneers and explorers referred to the area as the Cross Timbers because a block of trees ran north–south from Kansas down through Oklahoma and into Texas. The trees, such as post oaks and blackjack oaks, were slow-growing and typically scrubby rather than tall and straight. Since they didn't have much value as lumber, they were typically left alone, which means that some of the trees are hundreds of years old. Native Americans of the Osage Nation once used the area for camping and hunting.

Contact: Cross Timbers State Park, 144 Highway 105, Toronto, KS 66777; 620-637-2213.

Hours: 24/7.

Cost: State park fee.

FEATURED TRAIL: ANCIENT OAKS TRAIL

Trail access: Hike.

Distance: 1-mile loop.

In 1982 scientists from the University of Arkansas Tree-Ring Laboratory took core samples from 26 post oaks in this area. Eighteen of those trees were determined to be at least 200 years old, with the oldest dating from 1727. Fourteen of these old-growth oaks can be seen along the Ancient Oaks Trail. Starting from the trailhead off S. Point Road (37.77905, –95.94410), the trail heads downhill along a series of stone steps and winds north through the trees. The trail is marked with blue, and interpretive signs along the way provide information about the trees' ages by noting what historical events were happening when they were just seedlings. Although some of the old-growth and ancient trees are no longer living, others are still thriving. Along the trail, you'll pass some mossy stone ledges, and the western portion of the trail passes close to the river. Along with the old-growth oaks, redbuds grow in this area, which makes it particularly pretty during the spring. Driftwood is strewn between the lake and the trail, and you'll be able to see some of the lake through the trees at the western end of the loop. There's a picnic table if you want to stop and relax or have something to eat before turning north and uphill, back to the trailhead.

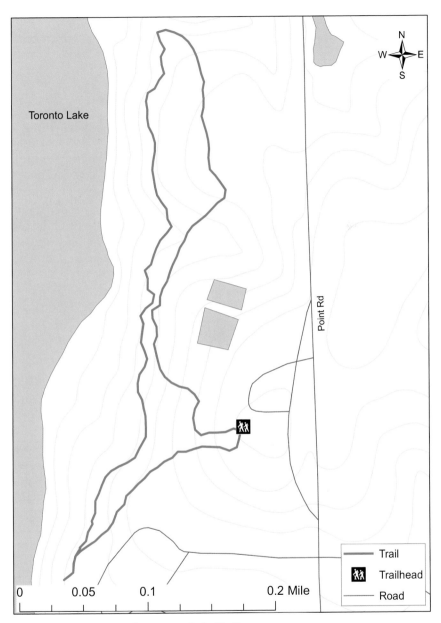

Cross Timbers State Park, Ancient Oaks Trail

Directions to the trailhead: From US-54, turn south onto K-105S. Pass through the town of Toronto and turn left (east) onto K-105S/West Main Street. After 0.5 mile, turn right (south) onto S. Point Road. Follow the road for 1.3 miles and then turn right onto the park road. The trail starts near Toronto Point Permit Station.

FEATURED TRAIL: CHAUTAUQUA HILLS TRAIL

Trail access: Hike or bike.

Distance: Blue Trail, 1.6-mile loop; Yellow Trail, 1.7 miles, one-way; Red West Trail, 2.3-mile loop. Total distance if all three are taken from one trailhead: 11 miles.

The trail has both shady, wooded areas and exposed prairie. The three main sections (Blue Trail, Yellow Trail, and Red West Trail) can be combined to make one long day hike or an overnight hike with backcountry camping; or you can arrange to get a ride from one end of the trail. Another option is to take the Red West or Blue Trail as a shorter loop.

Red West Trail: You can access the Red West loop of the Chautauqua Hills Trail (37.76875, –95.92503) near the end of Coyote Road, as it dead-ends at Toronto Lake. From the parking lot, take the trail to the west; heading south will get you to the lake, but there's no continuation of the trail in that direction. Near the trail-head are several intersecting trails: if you bear left at each intersection, you'll stay on the main trail. Small creeks lead into the lake, and most are likely to be dry. The trail may be a bit overgrown during the summer, and there's likely to be poison ivy, so wear long pants. Once you're in the woods, the Red West loop is well marked with red blazes painted on trees. After about 0.6 mile, you'll reach a trail intersection. You can go either right or left, as both sides of this small loop intersect again. The left side, farthest from the lake, is a bit smoother; the right side goes along the lake and has rockier creek crossings. The trail has some gradual ascents and descents, with clear views of the prairie and farmland to the northeast, along the eastern side of the loop. The western side of the loop offers clearer views of the lake. White-tailed deer live in the Toronto Lake area, especially in the timber, and you're likely to see or startle some. After the two sides of the Red West loop come together, they split again, with both sides of the smaller loop intersecting with the start of the Yellow Trail (37.77854, –95.93097). To finish the Red West Trail, follow the red-blazed trail back along the lake to the beginning.

To continue on the Yellow Trail around the arm of the lake, follow the trail north-northeast across exposed prairie. You'll head back into the timber after about 0.5 mile on the Yellow Trail, and you'll see rocky bluffs above the stream as you continue north. At the northernmost point of the trail, you'll cross a small bridge and then start heading back south (37.79232, –95.92442). Keep an eye out for signs of beaver activity — downed trees that have been gnawed away. About 0.3 mile from the northern bridge, you'll traverse a set of stone steps installed to make your life easier and to prevent erosion. Bikers looking for a thrill can take these steps on wheels. About 0.3 mile past the steps, you'll come to the intersection of the Yellow Trail and the Blue Trail (37.78616, –95.92959). You can continue onto the Blue Trail or turn around on the Yellow Trail and head back to the Red West trailhead.

Blue Trail: The Blue Trail can be taken on its own from the trailhead at the

Near the start of the Blue Trail loop on the Chautauqua Hills Trail. (Photo by Kristin Conard)

Toronto Point Campground (37.77794, –95.93637), or it can be accessed from the Yellow Trail. The Blue Trail has a small loop within it. If you take the trail to the left (east) that's closest to the lake, you'll have some steeper, rocky creek-crossing sections. Both sides of the loop take you through the timber, where there's a chance to see wild turkey, white-tailed deer, quail, or rabbits. The loop section of the Blue Trail comes back together (37.78033, –95.93339) and continues west until you reach a large wooden bridge. The end of the trail is a couple hundred feet uphill to the trailhead (37.77794, –95.93637).

Directions to the trailhead: For the Red West trailhead: From US-54, turn south onto K-105S. Pass through the town of Toronto and turn left (east) onto K-105S/ West Main Street. After 1.9 miles, turn right (southwest) onto Coyote Road and follow it for 1.7 miles. The trailhead is marked with a wooden sign on the right (west).

For the Blue trailhead: From US-54, turn south onto K-105S. Pass through the town of Toronto and turn left (east) onto K-105S/West Main Street. After 0.5 mile, turn right (south) onto S. Point Road. Follow that road for 1.5 miles, and then bear left on the park road. The trail starts near the Osage Plains Campground.

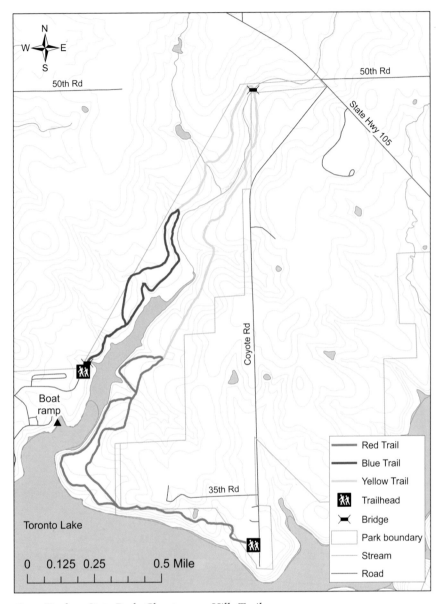

Cross Timbers State Park, Chautauqua Hills Trail

Additional trails: A Red East loop starts north of the Red West loop along Coyote Road. Another Toronto Lake trail is the 1-mile Ancient Oaks Trail (described earlier). Woodson Cove has a 1.25-mile Overlook Trail, and the Holiday Hills area has the 1-mile Blackjack Trail, which connects to the 0.5-mile Oak Ridge Trail.

Camping: Backcountry campsites are listed on the state park map along the Chautauqua Hills Trail, although the sites themselves are little more than small grassy areas that are likely to be overgrown in the summer. Two are accessible from the Yellow Trail, and one is on the Red West Trail loop. Permits are required.

For established campsites, each of the four major areas at the lake offers camping with a mix of utility and primitive sites. The park also has four cabins for rent, one of which is handicapped accessible.

ELK CITY STATE PARK

At this location, the Elk River flows through the hills and steep bluffs of the Osage Cuestas region. The current state park and wildlife area are part of a larger tract of land that was once controlled by the Osage Indians. That area, known as the Osage Diminished Reserve, was the last remnant of land occupied by the tribe in Kansas. The seven bands of the Osage Nation had settlements throughout the area. Chetopa led a band that settled in the area just west of Table Mound and south of the Elk River. And along the north side of the river, near where the current trails pass the river, was a settlement led by Nupawalla. Even though white settlers gradually began to encroach on this area, the Osage controlled the territory until a negotiated treaty resulted in the tribe's removal to land in Oklahoma by 1870. Notable early settlers on this former Osage land included Laura Ingalls Wilder, author of *Little House on the Prairie*, whose family established a homesite west of Independence and slightly south of the current state park.

The Elk River now flows into the Elk City Reservoir, which was completed in 1966 for the purpose of flood control. Surrounding the river is a state park and wildlife area renowned for its trails and towering limestone formations along the bluffs of the river. There are three designated National Recreation Trails in the park, with lengths ranging from 1 to 15 miles.

Contact: Elk City State Park, 4825 Squaw Creek Road, Independence, KS 67301; 620-331-6295.

Hours: 24/7.

Cost: State park fee.

FEATURED TRAIL: ELK RIVER TRAIL (TOP 10 TRAIL)

Trail access: Hike.

Distance: 15 miles, one-way.

The spectacular views and rock formations along this rugged and rocky trail — one of the best in the state — are unmatched in this part of the world. The trail is accessible from three trailheads, but it is marked to be hiked starting at the east trailhead. From the east trailhead, go south across a wide mowed area toward the banks of Gordon Creek, and cross the creek along a plank bridge (37.27971, –95.79987). In high water, the plank bridge may not be safe to cross, but the trail can be accessed by walking east to the nearby park road, crossing the road bridge, and then following a short spur trail that quickly joins the main trail just past

Bluffs along the Elk River Trail. (Photo by Jonathan Conard)

the stream crossing point. The trail then ascends along a route marked with blue blazes.

The trail climbs upward and cuts through a deep corridor in the rock bluffs (37.27886, –95.80020). It continues to ascend sharply and runs through the giant ledges and shelves of a rocky ridge. As the trail passes through these rock formations, it bends to the west and traces the ridgeline of the high bluffs above the lake.

If your legs are tired after the steep climb, there are several spots to rest that offer nice views of the lake, including a particularly scenic vista from a bench dedicated to Dolores Baker, longtime Kansas Trails Council member, at around 2.2 miles (37.26844, –95.81011). After this point, the trail continues to dodge in and out of rocky ravines along the shore of the lake, with some occasional glimpses of the water through the cedar and oak woodlands surrounding the trail. After the 3-mile marker, the trail crosses the faint traces of a two-track road and some open areas that are choice locations for backcountry campsites. Between miles 4 and 6, there are fewer views of the lake as the trail alternates between closed-canopy woodlands and small patches of prairie while crossing several large ravines bisected by small intermittent streams. Use caution when crossing streams along the trail; there are no bridges, and the rocks that must be used as stepping-stones may be slippery.

Before reaching mile 7, the trail edges along the rocky top of a bluff with a nice view of the wide expanse of the Elk River as it gradually transitions into the lake. After this point, the trail bends away from the river while continuing east through woodlands and cutting through some picturesque Pennsylvanian limestone rock formations at 7.75 miles. The trail continues to wind along several ravines with small streams draining into the Elk River before working its way back toward the main river channel and crossing an old park road at 9.5 miles. The trail then intersects with a second park road where a trailhead kiosk is located (37.25959, –95.85971). Some prime primitive camping spots can be found along the trail to the west. This paved road is part of the old Oak Ridge Public Use Area, which is still accessible to the public but is no longer actively maintained by the Corps of Engineers.

The western 5.5 miles of the trail match the overall experience of the first portion, but several highlights deserve particular mention. From the central trailhead in the former Oak Ridge Public Use Area, the trail continues west as it passes a small point slightly off the trail near the 10-mile marker where a rock ledge overhangs a brook (37.25948, –95.86264). This is an excellent spot to stop and soak in the wilderness experience; you can wade amongst the mossy rocks on the streambed, feel the bark of a sycamore growing out of the rock ledge, or just listen to the tumbling water coursing through the rocks. From here, the trail switchbacks up to a table rock lookout along the top of the bluffs (37.25651, –95.85787), where you can view the Elk River flowing toward the reservoir and catch your breath before continuing west.

Between mile markers 12 and 13 is one of the most scenic parts of the western half of the trail. In this section, the trail returns to explore sheer rock ledges and deep fissures among the towering, pockmarked limestone outcroppings. There is also a unique area of falling water that is particularly beautiful when rainfall is sufficient to push multiple rivulets across a circular expanse of the rocky overhang to form an intermittent waterfall (37.26561, –95.87395). The trail crosses directly beneath this water feature and continues to the west before temporarily parting

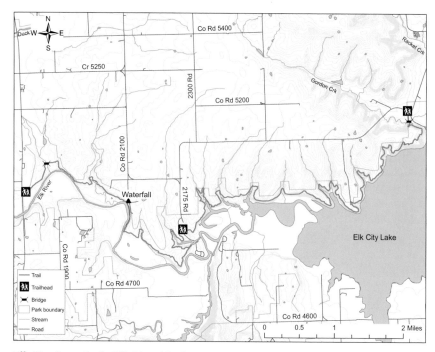

Elk City State Park, Elk River Trail

ways with the Elk River and crossing through some shallow, broad ravines with remnants of rock walls constructed by early settlers in the region. Over the last 2 miles, the trail occasionally returns close to the edge of the river, where the bluffs are less formidable but equally beautiful. Finish the trail by climbing over a stile crossing a barbed wire fence (37.27406, –95.89200), continue straight and cross an old bridge over a small stream, and stay straight on the trail until you reach the western trailhead just off US-160.

Directions to the trailhead: West trailhead (US-160): From Elk City, take US-160 south for 1.7 miles. The trailhead is on the east side of the road with a small gravel parking lot.

Central trailhead (in the former Oak Ridge Public Use Area): From US-160, turn east onto 5200 Road and drive for 1.5 miles. Turn south onto 2100 Road at the T-intersection. Continue for 0.75 mile, where the road bends to the east as it becomes County Road 5000. Continue straight for 0.5 mile and turn south onto 2175 Road, past the dead-end sign as the road bends to the right. Follow this road until you reach a small trailhead on the left with a small gravel parking area.

East trailhead: From the intersection of US-160 and US-75 in Independence, go west on US-160 (Main Street) for 1.7 miles, turn north onto Peter Pan Road, and continue for 2 miles until you reach 4800 Road. Turn west onto 4800 Road, drive for 1.6 miles, and turn north onto Table Mound Road (County Road 3300) before reaching the park office. Follow this road as it bends west and crosses the dam. After crossing the dam, turn left on the first road. The trailhead is located at a small gravel parking lot on the south side of the road.

Camping: Backcountry camping is allowed along the Elk River Trail. Please make sure to pack out all your trash and leave no trace of your visit.

FEATURED TRAIL: TABLE MOUND TRAIL

Trail access: Hike.

Distance: 3 miles, one-way.

The Table Mound Trail is an outstanding one-way trail that treats hikers to a challenging climb through mature woodlands capped by a scramble through steep rock ledges to reach the summit of Table Mound. The trail is maintained with the help of the Kansas Trails Council, and its exceptional quality has earned it the well-deserved designation as a National Recreation Trail. This large hill has long been a notable local landmark. As William Cutler described the area in 1883: "Elevated mounds, with steep declivitous sides, are found in places, rising abruptly out of the midst of a plain, to considerable heights. These are, in some instances, peak shaped, while in others they are capped with an almost level plain, comprising, in some cases, several acres in extent. There are several of these mounds in the county, each of which bears some significant name, such as Table Mound, from its table-like appearance."

To start your ascent up to Table Mound, begin at the lower trailhead along Timber Road (37.25867, –95.77943). The wide, smooth trail starts through a pleasant wooded lane and parallels the reservoir. The trail soon narrows and passes close to the edge of the reservoir, giving hikers a glimpse of the lake before the trail cuts through a heavily wooded area where it dips and climbs through several ravines before crossing a paved park road (37.27296, –95.77686).

After crossing the park road, the trail climbs steadily upward to the edge of the steep limestone bluffs. The towering rock formations along the bluff are stunning, and the trail takes full advantage of the challenging topography as the route weaves through the large rock ledges and fallen boulders. As the trail curves along the contour of the bluff, it reaches a point where hikers have to scramble up a steep corridor through the rocks to ascend to the top of the bluffs (37.28010, –95.77772). After reaching the top, the trail loops back south along the edge of the ridge until it comes to the upper trailhead. It is possible to return along the same route, or you can arrange to be picked up at the parking lot at the upper trailhead. The trail is marked with blue blazes, and hikers are advised to wear sturdy footwear because the terrain is very rocky, especially along the upper part of the route.

Directions to the trailhead: From the intersection of US-160 and US-75 in Independence, go west on US-160 (Main Street) for 1.7 miles, turn north onto Peter Pan Road, and drive for 2 miles until you reach 4800 Road. Turn west onto 4800 Road, continue for 1.6 miles, and enter the state park. Continue straight as the

Table Mound Trail. (Photo by Jonathan Conard)

road enters the park, go past the park office, and turn onto Timber Road to access the lower trailhead for the Table Mound Trail.

Additional trails: The 1-mile Green Thumb Nature Trail shares a trailhead with the Table Mound Trail and makes a short loop through hardwood forest, with several relatively steep but scenic sections. From the parking lot at the top of Memorial Overlook, families may enjoy hiking the Post Oak Self-Guiding Nature Trail

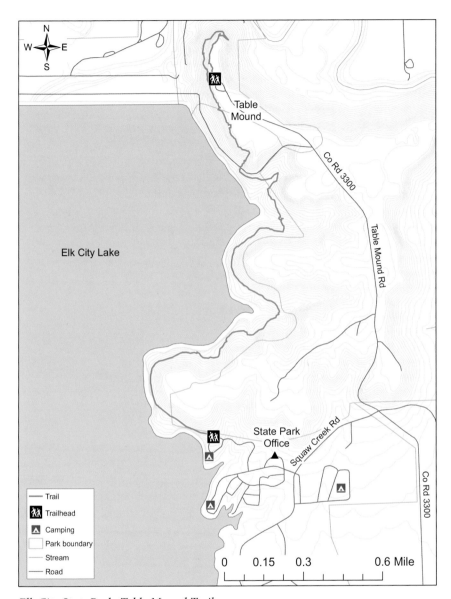

Elk City State Park, Table Mound Trail

(a 0.67-mile loop), which circles through a hardwood forest atop Table Mound. The only trail in the park designated exclusively for mountain bikers is the Eagle Rock Mountain Bike Trail, which is a 4-mile loop through a mix of tree groves and prairie grasses starting just north of the reservoir outlet. All these trails are popular, so if you're willing to trade some scenic value for greater solitude, check out the 2.3-mile Timber Ridge Hiking Trail on the south side of the lake in the Card Creek Area.

Camping: Backcountry camping is allowed on Table Mound Trail in areas south of the road crossing. There are 13 designated primitive campsites located along the Timber Road Campground, which is in a wooded area near the Table Mound and Green Thumb trailheads. Designated wildlife viewing sites are also a unique feature of this campground. Sunset Point Campground provides both primitive and utility sites near the lake.

FALL RIVER STATE PARK

This 980-acre state park along the Fall River Reservoir is a popular spot for canoeing and fishing. Situated between the southern end of the Flint Hills and the Cross Timbers region, the park has a mix of open grasslands and forested areas, with lots of oak trees. The park has six nature trails to explore and two main recreation areas—the Quarry Bay Area on the southeastern side of the reservoir, and the larger Fredonia Bay Area on the southern side of the reservoir. Both areas have camping, playgrounds, and picnic areas. A state park permit is required to enter the park.

Contact: Fall River State Park, 144 Highway 105, Toronto, KS 66777; 620-637-2213.
Hours: 24/7.
Cost: State park fee.

 FEATURED TRAIL: BADGER CREEK NORTH TRAIL (TOP BIKE TRAIL)

Trail access: Hike or bike.
Distance: 3.5-mile loop.

Tucked away in US Army Corps of Engineer property, northeast of Fall River Lake and off of Badger Creek Road, are two mountain bike trails that wind near Badger Creek, along bluffs, and through dense, old-growth oak forest. The Kansas Trails Council and the Corps of Engineers approached the Kansas Singletrack Society to create these bike trails, which were built and developed in 2010; they're maintained by the Kansas Singletrack Society and the Kansas Trails Council. Originally a prairie project was proposed, but because of the rocky soil conditions and the high maintenance required, all timber and wooded trails were constructed. After a hard rain, the trails may be too muddy for a good ride, as they're a mix of packed dirt and rock. The loop trails have lots of dips and turns through the woods, with enough sandstone rocky portions to make them well suited for intermediate and advanced bikers and moderate hikers. The trails are within a hunting area, so it's advisable to wear orange during deer and turkey seasons.

A wooden sign with a map of the trail marks the trailhead for the north trail (37.68844, −96.06267), which can be taken either to the right or to the left. Going right takes you uphill. The shady trail winds through the woods, with pink ribbons tacked to the trees to mark the way. The flowing hillside trail has short ledge sections, rocky streambeds to cross, and large rocks to ride through and

Along the Badger Creek North Trail. (Photo by Kristin Conard)

over. In addition, trees may have fallen across the trail, creating obstacles that are
not overly technical. Near the northern edge of the loop, there are some small
drop-offs along a sandstone ledge. After turning back south, you'll pass some
barbed wire fence sections (if you're riding your bike, slow down). About halfway
through the trail, you'll reach an intersection. You can either cut off the trail and
head back or continue to the right (northwest), following the pink ribbons on the
trees. After some quick ascents with flowing recovery sections, the trail twists and
turns through old-growth post oak, locust, and blackjack oak forest. Crossing over
a small creek bed, the trail turns east. It winds across rocks and up and down hills,
and the second half of the loop roughly parallels the first half for about 0.6 mile.
After a tight switchback, the trail heads down and west and then gradually bears
south and downhill before ending at the trailhead.

Directions to the trailhead: From County Road 20 across the dam, follow signs
for Whitehall Bay Campground. The paved road curves north and east for just
under a mile, and the trailheads are on the right. The north trailhead is about 600
yards past the low water bridge on Badger Creek Road.

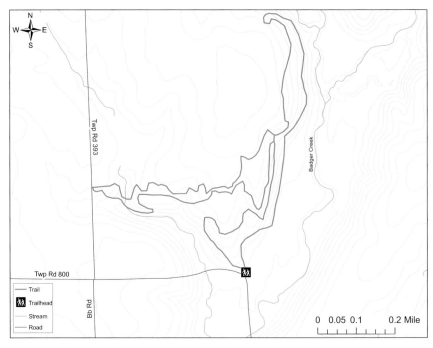

Fall River Lake, Badger Creek North Trail

FEATURED TRAIL: CATCLAW TRAIL

Trail access: Hike or bike.
Distance: 1.8-mile loop.

The Catclaw Trail makes a loop to the southeast of Fall River Lake, and the trailhead is at the northeastern end of the Quarry Bay Area picnic grounds and campsites (37.65870, –96.05387). The trail is a mix of mowed grass and dirt and can get somewhat overgrown during the summer, which may be the trade-off for the brightly colored prairie wildflowers lining the trail in season. Because it's a loop trail, you can go either way — just follow the yellow trail markers. If you take it clockwise, you can end your hike with a rewarding lake view. Heading northeast from the trailhead, the trail goes through a small stand of trees before it clears out into prairie. The trail crosses a small wooden bridge over a creek bed and continues north and east, with alternating shady and exposed stretches, before crossing another wooden bridge. Another few hundred feet from the bridge crossing is the intersection of the Catclaw Trail and the Bluestem Trail (37.66490, –96.05328). Bear north and east to continue on Catclaw Trail; alternatively, you can add another 0.6 mile to your hike by heading west from the intersection onto the Bluestem Trail. About 500 feet from the Catclaw and Bluestem intersection, you'll arrive at the trailhead for the Bluestem Trail (37.66490, –96.05328) and a

View of Fall River Lake from the Catclaw Trail. (Photo by Kristin Conard)

small bridge. The Bluestem Trail runs from the north end of the Quarry Bay Area, making a loop through the prairie and rejoining the Catclaw Trail (37.66585, −96.05043).

At the northern intersection with the Bluestem Trail, the Catclaw Trail crosses a small wooden bridge over an often dry streambed and heads east and south up a small ridge. As you head up the ridge, the underlying sandstone that makes up the rolling hills of the park becomes more obvious underfoot. During the summer, keep an eye out for turkey vultures circling overhead as they ride the wind currents. Along the ridge, signposts marked in yellow clearly indicate the trail, and there are views of the lake on one side and the prairie on the other. The trail runs along the park road, and the trailhead for the Post Oak Trail is across the road near the maintenance building (37.65668, −96.05090).

Directions to the trailhead: From Highway 400, turn north at Z50 Road. If you continue straight on Z50, you'll reach the Fredonia Bay section of the park. For Quarry Bay, stay on Z50 for 1.5 miles and then turn east (right) onto Cummins Road. Cummins Road bears left after about 1.5 miles, where it turns into County Road 20 and crosses the Fall River Reservoir dam. The self-pay station, bathrooms, and Quarry Bay Campground are on the left.

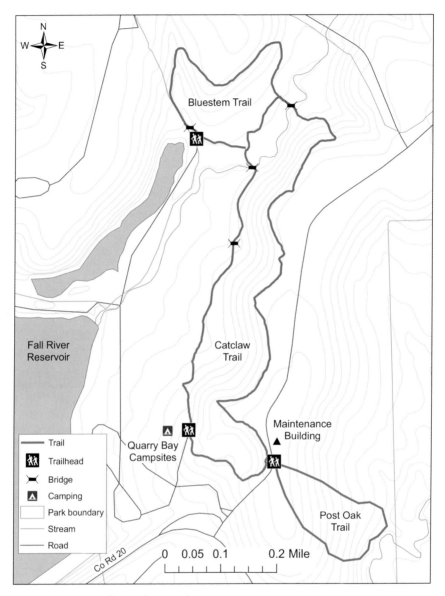

Fall River State Park, Catclaw Trail

Additional trails: You can access the south mountain bike trail from Badger Creek Road. Fall River State Park has a total of six nature trails, all of which are open to hikers and bikers; they are all about 1 mile long, except for the 0.1-mile handicapped-accessible Overlook Trail in Quarry Bay. The Bluestem Trail (0.75 mile) is nearly entirely exposed prairie with little shade; it starts and ends at the north end of Quarry Bay and intersects with the Catclaw Trail. The Post Oak Trail loop (0.75 mile) is also close to the Catclaw Trail, along part of Craig Creek. The trailhead is near the maintenance building and across the paved park road. For those on the Fredonia Bay side of the lake near the Casner Creek Campground, the 1.5-mile Casner Creek Trail takes you through wooded areas and open prairie. **Camping:** Campsites are available at Quarry Bay, and they include a shower house, bathrooms, and a playground. At Fredonia Bay, the campsites are split into five areas: South Rock Ridge, Gobbler's Knob (handicapped facilities available), Fredonia Bay Campground (handicapped facilities available), Wind Hill, and Casner Creek. The campsites can be reserved, and there are hookups for water and electricity, as well as primitive campsites.

GUNN PARK–FORT SCOTT

In 1910 W. C. Gunn gave Fern Lake and the Steward farm to the City of Fort Scott to make a park. Today, the 155-acre park has picnic shelters, playgrounds, campsites, fishing and canoeing at the lake, and a disc golf course. More recently, a number of mountain bike trails were added. In 2009, inspired by a video of mountain bikers flying downhill, Frank Halsey created a 1-mile loop — without asking the city's permission. In 2010 he got the go-ahead to continue building mountain bike trails through the woods along the Marmaton River. He's committed to keeping the trails clear and maintained and improving them. It's an all-volunteer endeavor, as the city doesn't have the resources to maintain the trails.

In the 1860s Fort Scott was the location of skirmishes between abolitionists and border ruffians over the issue of slavery. There is an actual fort, built and used from 1843 to 1852, that is open to visitors. After the Civil War, Fort Scott became one of the largest cities in the region and one of the largest railroad hubs west of the Mississippi. Trains still run regularly through the town, and the plaintive sounds of the train whistles are frequently heard.

Contact: Gunn Park, 1010 Park Avenue, Fort Scott, KS 66701; Fort Scott City Hall, 620-223-0550.

Hours: 24/7. The park may close during inclement weather.

Cost: Free.

FEATURED TRAIL: NORTH AND SOUTH TRAILS

Trail access: Hike or bike.

Distance: 4.5-mile loop.

A single-track trail runs through the woods and along the river. It's well taken care of, with enough variation in the terrain for intermediate and expert riders to have fun and for beginner riders to embrace a challenge. It's easy to modify the trail with occasional loops and connections with the main roads, so you can increase or decrease the distance. Although the North and South Trails connect, each can be ridden by itself, since they both intersect with park roads.

125

Frank Halsey and Shawn Goans on the Gunn Park trails. (Photo by Kristin Conard)

The trailhead for the North Trail (37.82982, –94.71928) is just east of the entrance gate. As you head onto the North Trail, it is mostly smooth and dirt packed, beneath a canopy of trees. About 200 feet past the entrance, the trail splits, but bearing right or left gets you to the same place, as it's a small loop. You can either head around the loop or continue on. There are east and west tracks as the trail heads north, and both tracks meet up again as the trail approaches an access point from 5th Street (37.83670, –94.72001). The trail tracks west and south along the Marmaton River for about 0.75 mile, and you might see turtles or herons in the river. White-tailed deer also make their home in the woods of Gunn Park. A few steep ups and downs and obstacles make the trail exciting. At the end of the river portion of the trail, you'll cross some wooden bridges with a small loop section near the intersection with Park Avenue. If you keep bearing right, you'll continue along the river for a bit before emerging from the woods and along the park road, past a small spillway on the river. Along the western edge of the park, the trail continues past a shelter house and parking area and into the southern loops, which have more switchbacks and options.

The southern loop was built first, in 2009. By 2011, trail production was in full swing, and two years and a lot of volunteer work later, the 4.5 miles of trail were in place. For much of the southern trail, you can see the park drive.

Along the South Trail, you'll reach a divide (37.82390, –94.72638), with the option of going right or left. If you follow the trail to the right, you'll reach a couple of additional intersections where you can add distance. But if you continue to bear east and south through the woods, all options lead to the same spot. Similar to the

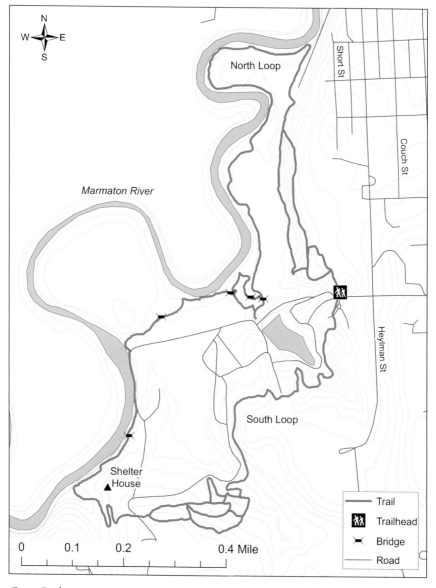

Gunn Park

northern section, some easy obstacles can be found along the way. A few switch-backs mark the spot close to the end of the South Trail, and you'll emerge from the woods a few hundred feet from the trailhead near the park entrance.

Directions to the trailhead: From central Fort Scott, at the US-54 and K-7/US-69 intersection, head south and turn right (west) onto E. 6th Street. Turn left (south) after 3 blocks onto S. National Avenue. After 2 blocks (past the Lyons Twin Mansions), turn right (west) onto 8th Street and take it for 0.5 mile. Turn left (south) onto Burke Street and take the first right (west) onto Park Avenue, which will take you into the park. The trailhead is just before the gated entrance on the right.

Additional trails: In nearby Pittsburg, the 23rd Street Bike Park has a series of intersecting trails through the woods, as well as a pump track. Also in Pittsburg is Wilderness Park, with 4 miles of trails through wetlands, grasslands, and forest.

Forty miles west of Fort Scott, in Iola, plans are under way (as of 2014) to create the Lehigh Portland Rail Trail, thanks to a Kansas Health Foundation grant awarded to Allen County. It will include a portion of the trail near the Southwind Rail Trail, along with a series of mountain bike trails.

Camping: Fourteen campsites are available at the park, with water and electricity hookups. The cost is $8 per night.

TOLEN CREEK PARK

Just off the intersection of US-400 and US-59, near the Walmart and the Stock-yards Travel Plaza, is Tolen Creek Park. It's not necessarily the most obvious place for a hike or a bike ride, but the flat, wide trails promise a pleasant outing. The trails, particularly the northern loop, are exposed, with little or no shade. However, the northern loop is accessible to most strollers and wheelchairs.

Contact: Tolen Creek Park, 1400 Cattle Drive, Parsons, KS 67357; 620-421-7020.
Hours: Daylight hours.
Cost: Free.

FEATURED TRAIL: TOLEN CREEK PARK TRAILS

Trail access: Hike or bike.
Distance: Southern loop, 0.9 mile; northern loop, 1 mile.

There are two loops at Tolen Creek — one south of US-400 and one north of US-400. The trailhead for both (37.36354, –95.25575) is near the 1890s stone house and the fishing pond. The stone house has been preserved for more than 100 years, and for the past several years, the Southeast Kansas Farm History Center has held an annual farm heritage celebration that includes tours of the stone house. The area is also used by a local archery club for competitions and practices; for everyone's safety, signs clearly indicate when the archers are on-site and the trails are closed to others. From the parking area at the trailhead, the southern loop can be taken to the right or left around the fishing pond and into the nearby

Tolen Creek trails. (Photo by Kristin Conard)

wooded area. The wide, flat trail crosses a handful of bridges and paved areas. About halfway around the loop, you'll cross an open grassy field before meeting up with the gravel path that heads back west to the trailhead.

To keep going for another mile, head north from the trailhead beneath the US-400 underpass (37.36577, −95.25336). This part of the trail is paved, but you'll reach the graveled section of the northern loop at the bridge across Tolen Creek. The northern loop splits and can be taken clockwise or counterclockwise. If you take the trail counterclockwise after the bridge, you'll reach another intersection that can also be taken in either direction. These eastern sections of the loop take you along the tree line with a swath of prairie grasses and wildflowers. The eastern side of the northern loop closes at another bridge across Tolen Creek (37.36891, −95.25266). If you took the far eastern loop, you can cut back to the highway underpass from the bridge, or you can continue along the western side of the northern loop that skirts the other side of the tree line along the creek.

Directions to the trailhead: From US-400, take the US-59 ramp for Parsons. Drive for 0.3 mile past the Stockyards Plaza and take the first left (east) after Harding Road.

Tolen Creek Park

Additional trails: Big Hill Lake is 15 miles west on US-400, and it has a nature trail and a bridle trail.

Camping: The closest camping is at Neosho State Fishing Lake–Lake McKinley (3645 Scott Road, Parsons, KS 67357).

CHAPTER 5

NORTH-CENTRAL KANSAS

This country presents a very fine appearance, than which I have not seen a better in all our Spain nor Italy nor a part of France, nor, indeed, in the other countries, where I have traveled in His Majesty's service, for it is not a very rough country, but is made up of hillocks and plains, and very fine appearing rivers and streams, which certainly satisfied me and made me sure that it will be very fruitful in all sorts of products.

JUAN JARAMILLO, CAPTAIN OF THE CORONADO EXPEDITION

Konza Prairie. Photo by Judd Patterson

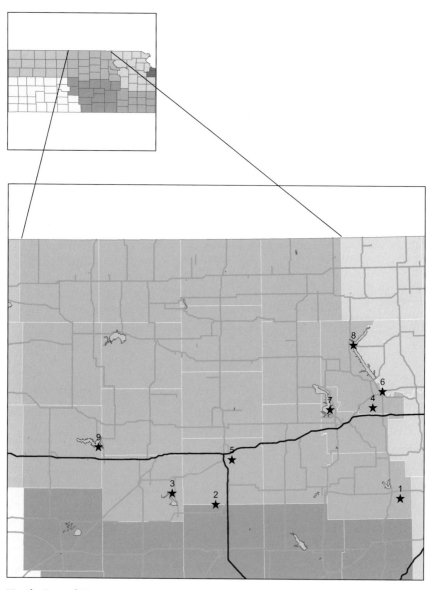

North-Central Kansas

1. Allegawaho Memorial Heritage Park
2. Coronado Heights
3. Kanopolis Lake
4. Konza Prairie
5. Lakewood Park
6. Manhattan River Trails
7. Milford State Park
8. Tuttle Creek State Park
9. Wilson Lake and Wilson State Park

Francisco Vasquez de Coronado visited north-central Kansas in 1541. He was looking for the seven cities of gold, but it is thought that around the hill that now bears his name (Coronado Heights), he gave up and returned to Mexico. While there may not be gold in the hills of north-central Kansas, there is still plenty to appreciate. Plains Indians used the area for hunting, as the prairie supported huge herds of American bison. Even today, bison can be found on the Konza Prairie.

North-central Kansas is made up predominantly of two physiographic regions: the Flint Hills to the east and the Smoky Hills to the west. Out on the trails, you'll find a combination of hills and rolling mixed-grass prairie, along with some pockets of wooded areas, particularly near rivers and lakes. The Smoky Hills combine Greenhorn limestone bluffs and Dakota sandstone hills. In addition, there's a curious collection of tourist attractions, such as the tastiest, tiniest burgers at the Cozy Inn in Salina; the World's Largest Ball of Twine in Cawker City; the Garden of Eden in Lucas; and Little Sweden, otherwise known as Lindsborg.

ALLEGAWAHO MEMORIAL HERITAGE PARK

The name *Kansas* is derived from the Kanza (Kaw) tribe that once controlled a broad expanse of land along the Kansas River Valley. In 1846 the Kaw were relocated to a reservation that includes the present site of Allegawaho Memorial Heritage Park. The park's 1.9-mile trail climbs through rolling hills of tallgrass prairie, where hikers can pause to marvel at the expansive vistas across the Flint Hills before descending through primeval woodlands along Little John Creek. The Kaw inhabited this area until 1874, when the tribe was ousted by the federal government and sent to live on a smaller reservation in Indian Territory. The village site within the park contains ruins of the stone huts built by the government for Kaw families. In 2000 the Kaw Nation repurchased the 158-acre parcel of land as part of its efforts to reclaim its cultural history.

Contact: Allegawaho Memorial Heritage Park, Dunlap Road and X Avenue, Council Grove, Kansas 66846; 620-767-5140.

Hours: 24/7.

Cost: Free.

FEATURED TRAIL: KANZA TRAIL (TOP HISTORICAL TRAIL)

Trail access: Hike.

Distance: 1.9-mile loop.

The Kanza Trail connects hikers with history as it winds through sites inhabited by the Kaw tribe between 1846 and 1874. The trailhead (38.62743, –96.43166) is located north of the Flint Hills Nature Trail and the limestone ruins of the federal agency building formerly used at the reservation. From the point where the trail intersects the gravel road, start the loop by hiking east along a mowed path

Allegawaho Memorial Heritage Park. (Photo by Jonathan Conard)

through the big bluestem and switchgrass blanketing the upland prairie hills. Shortly after the trailhead, stop to appreciate the bronze plaque depicting the tribal seal of the Kaw Nation, with an engraved prayer along the outer edge of the circle. From this point, you can see a 40-foot limestone obelisk rising sharply out of the prairie, north of the trail. This monument was erected as a memorial to an unknown Kaw warrior whose remains were discovered by local Boy Scouts on a campout in 1924 along nearby Little John Creek. The landowner at the time, Frank Haucke, was instrumental in ensuring that the remains were respectfully exhumed and later ceremonially laid to rest under the monument. The Kaw Nation requests that visitors respect the burial site and approach no closer than the trail. The trail continues north around the monument and pushes upward along a steep incline toward a promontory marking the highest point in the park. After completing the steep climb, you'll want to rest for a few minutes on the stone bench at the summit (38.63535, –96.42679), where you can reflect on the grand view below. From here, you have a 360-degree vantage point of the Neosho River Valley and the majestic Flint Hills. The trail descends quickly from the promontory point and crosses the gravel road as it turns west to enter the woodlands along Little John Creek. The woodlands hugging the contours of the intermittent creek are thick with cottonwoods and giant bur oaks whose gnarled branches shaded the creek bed even before the arrival of the Kaw.

The trail bends south along Little John Creek, and you'll cross a small bridge before passing the ruins of three stone cabins (38.63582, –96.43058). The one-room cabins were built from limestone quarried on-site, and they were intended to house Kaw families. However, the Kaw preferred to live communally in traditional villages, and the cabins were used mostly for horses or other livestock before falling into disrepair. The trail continues south past the cabins along Little John Creek to a point marked by traditional Kaw bead patterns and engraved with the names of sixteen clans (38.62866, –96.43317). After a moment of reflection, continue on the trail, looping back east to the starting point along the gravel road.

Directions to the trailhead: From US-56 just east of downtown Council Grove, turn south on Fifth Street for 2 blocks and then turn east onto Walnut for 1 block. Walnut bends southeast and turns into Dunlap Road. Continue on Dunlap Road for approximately 3.5 miles before turning left onto X Avenue. Follow X Avenue east for 0.4 mile, and turn north onto Road 525. Drive north on Road 525 to the old Kaw agency building, which is visible west of the road. Continue heading north of the agency building until you reach the trailhead.

Additional trails: The Flint Hills Nature Trail is a rail trail along the Missouri Pacific Railway that runs from Herington to Osawatomie. A section of the trail passes just south of the Kanza Trail and can be taken 3.5 miles west to Council Grove.

The Pioneer Nature Trail is a 1.24-mile nature trail at Council Grove Lake that has been designated a National Recreation Trail. It stays mostly within woodlands but includes a loop that takes hikers past wallows from the days when bison roamed freely throughout the state. The trailhead is just west of the US Army Corps of Engineers office.

Camping: Camping is allowed on-site, and campsites are available at Council Grove Reservoir, which is located west of Council Grove along US-177. Richey Cove offers good primitive tent sites and a designated swimming area (US Army Corps of Engineers, 945 Lake Road, Council Grove, KS 66846; 620-767-5195).

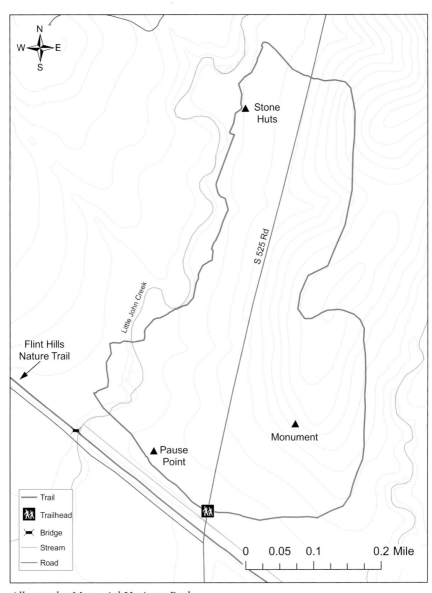

Allegawaho Memorial Heritage Park

CORONADO HEIGHTS

Rising abruptly out of the broad expanse of the Smoky Hill River Valley, Coronado Heights is an impressive overlook that offers views of the surrounding countryside. The prominent hill is the tallest in a series of buttes near the eastern edge of the Smoky Hills and is capped by Dakota sandstone, which has allowed it to

Coronado Heights. (Photo by Scott Bean)

resist the forces of erosion over the years. The summit features a castle-like sandstone structure built by the Works Progress Administration (WPA) in 1936. Take the stairs leading to the roof of the castle for majestic views of the surrounding valley and other nearby buttes. Make sure to look for Soldier Cap Mound to the northwest, which was named for its resemblance to the headgear of Civil War soldiers. The stone picnic tables nearby provide a perfect spot for lunch after reaching the summit.

Coronado Heights is named for explorer Francisco Vasquez de Coronado, who led a Spanish expedition north from Mexico in search of the fabled seven cities of Cibola, which were thought to contain great wealth. Although there is no evidence that Coronado ever stood atop the hill that bears his name, archaeological finds suggest that this region of central Kansas marks the point where Coronado came to the disappointing realization that the cities did not exist, and the expedition turned back.

Contact: Lindsborg Chamber of Commerce, 785-227-3706.
Hours: 8 a.m. to 11 p.m.
Cost: Free.

FEATURED TRAIL: OLSSON TRAIL

Trail access: Hike or bike.

Distance: 1 mile, one-way.

Although it is possible to drive to the summit of Coronado Heights, hiking or biking to the top is a much more rewarding experience. The area may be one of the oldest hiking destinations in the state. Early residents of Lindsborg frequented the hill for picnics and other social gatherings. In the 1920s the original footpath leading to the top of the hill was named the Olsson Trail in honor of the Reverend Olof Olsson, leader of the small group of Swedish immigrants that founded the town of Lindsborg. The current trail system has been greatly expanded from the original footpath. Although the labyrinth of single-track trails encircling Coronado Heights is not marked, the trails are typically easy to follow, and the sharp switchbacks and rocky terrain provide a good challenge to hikers and mountain bikers.

The packed-dirt trail network starts near the base of Coronado Heights. There is no marked trailhead, but the easiest spot to access the trail is as it crosses the paved road a short distance past the entrance gate (38.61011, –97.70358). From here, the trail can be followed on the left side of the road as it bears northwest to ascend in a route that loops the western face of the hill. Several connected trails along the eastern slope can also be explored as they twist and turn toward the summit. Trails on both the eastern and western sides are rocky in places and include numerous switchbacks and sharp turns as they ascend. From either side, the views are panoramic, and the trails pass through a variety of terrain, ranging from open prairie to closed cedar woodlands. At the summit, be sure to explore the castle (38.61336, –97.70319) as you enjoy the views from the top.

Directions to the trailhead: From K-4, turn north on 13th Avenue/S. Coronado Avenue and continue for 2.9 miles before turning left (west) onto W. Coronado Heights Road/Winchester Road. The entrance to the Coronado Heights area is the first right after the Smoky Hill Cemetery.

Additional trails: The trailhead for the 13-mile Meadowlark rail trail is located in the Old Mill Park in Lindsborg. This trail, which is currently under construction, will run south from the trailhead at Lindsborg to McPherson. The newly constructed 2-mile Pioneer Trail that winds through scenic Marquette is another option for a short hike or bike ride through this area.

Camping: No camping is allowed on Coronado Heights, but the nearby town of Lindsborg offers primitive camping at the Old Mill Campground located near the Old Mill Museum (120 Mill Street, Lindsborg, KS 67456; 785-227-3595). The museum showcases a fully restored grain mill built in 1898 along the banks of the Smoky Hill River.

Coronado Heights

KANOPOLIS STATE PARK

Nestled deep in the Smoky Hills, Kanopolis State Park has the distinction of being Kansas's first state park. The region has a rich history of trails, including the Smoky Hill Trail, which ran along the Smoky Hill River corridor and provided a route for travelers rushing to the gold fields of Colorado in 1859 and 1860. Although the

139

Buffalo Tracks Canyon at Kanopolis State Park. (Photo by David Welfelt)

Smoky Hill Trail provided a more direct route than other popular trails, including the Santa Fe Trail and the Platte River route, it was not always easy to follow, and the lack of firewood and inability to replenish provisions made the route a challenging one for early travelers.

Today, the Smoky Hill River supplies the Kanopolis Reservoir, and the state park surrounding the reservoir boasts over 15,000 acres, including a well-developed trail network with more than 27 miles of hike, bike, and bridle trails. The Horsethief Canyon area within Kanopolis State Park features some of the best scenery in the area and includes trails that climb through Dakota sandstone bluffs and steep canyons, with scenic overlooks of the nearby reservoir.

Contact: Kanopolis State Park, 200 Horsethief Road, Marquette, KS 67464; 785-546-2565.

Hours: 24/7.

Cost: State park fee.

FEATURED TRAIL: HORSETHIEF CANYON TRAIL (TOP BRIDLE TRAIL AND TOP 10 TRAIL)

Trail access: Hike, bike, or bridle.
Distance: 5.5-mile loop.

All day-use visitors can access the Horsethief Canyon Trail starting at the trailhead. Equestrians who are camping in the park can also access the trail system from the Rockin' K Horse Campground via the Rockin' K Trail, which originates at the campground and intersects with the Horsethief Canyon Trail. Hikers have the option of starting at the Buffalo Track trailhead and following the self-guided interpretive trail northeast along Bison Creek, past a cutoff trail leading west, and through the canyon until they reach a natural cave carved into the Dakota sandstone bluff by erosion (38.67724, –97.99337). At this point, the Buffalo Track Trail joins the Horsethief Canyon Trail as it climbs out of the canyon and turns northwest.

Starting from the Horsethief trailhead, the trail starts north and slowly climbs into the rolling hills and bluffs of Horsethief Canyon until it intersects with the Buffalo Track Trail. After the junction with the Buffalo Track Trail, the Horsethief Canyon Trail meanders through a network of canyons with expansive views of Kanopolis Lake, towering sandstone bluffs, and red sandstone hoodoos that look surreal in the prairie landscape. Look for the metal gate at the trail junction that marks the westernmost point of the hike.

At this point, the Horsethief Canyon Trail intersects with the Prairie Trail, which continues north and west into the Smoky Hills Wildlife Area. To continue on the Horsethief Canyon Trail, turn southeast at this junction, and you'll soon arrive at Sentinel Rock (38.6748, –98.0023). A brief side hike takes you to the top of this massive sandstone formation, which commands an impressive view of the lake and surrounding canyons. Continuing past Sentinel Rock toward the trailhead, you'll negotiate a series of low water crossings along the bottom of several ravines. Use caution when navigating these crossings, as the water can be several feet deep, depending on recent rainfall. Hikers looking to avoid wet feet can take advantage of several sturdy beaver dams that may make the crossing easier.

Directions to trailhead: From Salina, take K-140W for 20.4 miles to K-141 and turn left (south) onto K-141. Drive for 10 miles, turn right (west) onto Venango Road, and stay right onto Horsethief Road. Continue north through the park to the marked trailhead and parking area.

Additional trails: The Horsethief Canyon Trail connects with the Prairie Trail (5 miles), which accesses scenic Red Rock Canyon. The trail network continues deep into the Smoky Hills Wildlife Area via the Alum Creek Trail (8.3-mile loop). The Prairie Trail and Alum Creek Trail are closed from November 1 to January 31 for hunting season.

For mountain bikers, the Split Boulder Trail is a 1.63-mile ride that begins near

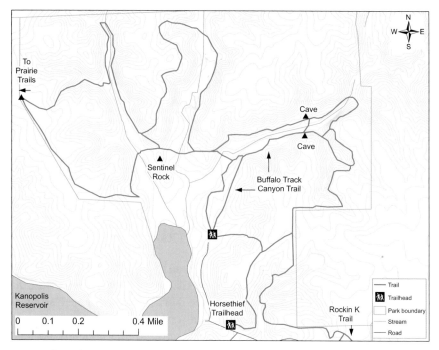

Kanopolis Lake

Eagle Point Campground and passes boulders as it loops along the shoreline of Kanopolis Lake.

Camping: The Eagle Point and Rockwall Campgrounds in Kanopolis State Park are close to the trailhead and offer prime locations for secluded tent camping with great views of the lake.

KONZA PRAIRIE

The Konza Prairie showcases the grandeur of the tallgrass prairie of the Flint Hills — some of the last great stands of tallgrass prairie in the world. The prairie of the Flint Hills was spared from the plow due to the thick layer of limestone and flint near the soil's surface. Much of the upland prairie in the Flint Hills is currently used for pasture, and parts of the Konza Prairie are grazed by a resident herd of bison.

Like much of the Flint Hills, the Konza Prairie has a rugged topography, and the views from the bluffs and ridges along the trails are outstanding. The area is rich in wildlife, with an abundance of white-tailed deer and wild turkeys, especially along the gallery forest areas of Kings Creek. The upland prairie is also home to the greater prairie chicken, whose unique dances and booming mating calls are performed on courtship grounds known as leks during the spring. In addition to

Fall color at Konza Prairie. (Photo by Mark Conard)

the abundant wildlife, purple coneflowers and a variety of other wildflowers put on a showy display in late spring.

The Konza Prairie features three hiking loops that share the same trailhead. The trails range in length from 2.8 to 6.1 miles. All the loops include some uphill climbs, with great scenic vistas of pristine tallgrass prairie. The self-guided interpretive Nature Trail loop includes trail markers whose numbers correspond to the information contained in the brochures available at the trailhead.

Contact: Konza Prairie Biological Station, c/o Kansas State University, Division of Biology, 116 Ackert Hall, Manhattan, KS 66506; 785-587-0441.

Hours: Daylight hours.

Cost: A trail maintenance fee of $2 is appreciated.

FEATURED TRAIL: KINGS CREEK LOOP (TOP 10 TRAIL)

Trail access: Hike. No dogs allowed.
Distance: 4.7-mile loop.

Beginning at the trailhead (39.10672, −96.60896), you'll cross two narrow footbridges over Kings Creek. After a short walk through the gallery forest and along the creek bottom, the trail forks. Either fork can be taken to complete the loop, but taking the trail to the left allows you to follow the guided interpretive signage in sequence. Following the fork to the left, the trail quickly climbs up a steep bluff, with great views of the surrounding prairie landscape. From the ridge along this prairie upland, look south to see the original stone barn and ranch house of the 10,000-acre Dewey Ranch, which was homesteaded by C. P. Dewey and his son Chauncey beginning in 1872. The limestone buildings are currently used as research facilities for scientists from Kansas State University who are conducting a variety of ecological research projects throughout the Konza Prairie. To the northeast, you may be able to see Manhattan in the distance.

Continuing along the ridge, the trail leads past a small radio tower (39.11099, −96.59572) and reaches a trail junction. At this point, the 2.8-mile Nature Trail turns right and loops back toward the trailhead, while the Kings Creek Loop continues east along the upland ridge before reaching a junction with the Godwin Hill Loop. Turn right at this junction to continue along the 4.7-mile Kings Creek Loop, or stay straight for the 6.1-mile Godwin Hill Loop. The Kings Creek Loop turns south here and starts to descend from the upland prairie as the trail passes through patches of sumac that turn a stunningly bright red in the fall. This part of the trail delineates the boundary between two research areas on Konza Prairie that are burned at different frequencies: the area east of the trail is burned once every 20 years, while the area west of the trail is burned annually. These contrasting burn frequencies clearly demonstrate the role of fire in suppressing the encroachment of trees and shaping the vegetation of the prairie.

As you continue to descend from the ridge, turn back west at the next junction, and the trail parallels Kings Creek. The gallery forest along Kings Creek provides a shaded path through a majestic expanse of bur and chinquapin oak trees before reaching the ruins of the Hokanson homestead (39.10372, −96.59516), built by Swedish settlers in 1878. After the homestead, the trail continues west along Kings Creek back toward the trailhead.

Directions to the trailhead: From I-70, take exit 307 to McDowell Creek Road. Turn north on McDowell Creek Road and continue for 4.8 miles. On the right side of the road is a sign for the Konza Prairie Biological Station; turn right on this gravel road and continue for 0.8 mile to the trailhead on the left.

Additional trails: The 2.8-mile Nature Trail Loop passes through both lowland gallery forest and upland prairie, with good views along the ridges. Numbered trail markers throughout the route correspond to information in the brochure

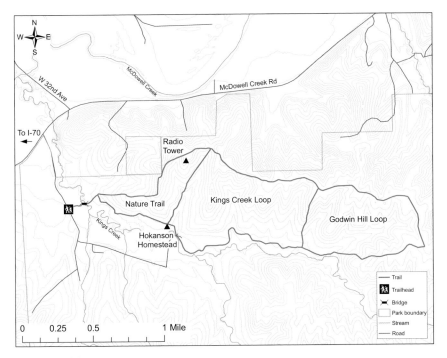

Konza Prairie

available at the trailhead, which is filled with facts about the prairie flora and fauna.

The 6.1-mile Godwin Hill Loop is the longest loop in the trail network and allows hikers to go even deeper into the tallgrass prairie uplands.

Camping: No camping is allowed on Konza Prairie. The closest available campground is north of Manhattan in the River Pond area of Tuttle Creek State Park (5800 A River Pond Road, Manhattan, KS 66502; 785-539-7941).

LAKEWOOD PARK–SALINA

Lakewood Park includes a fishing lake surrounded by a maturing cottonwood forest that is owned and managed by the City of Salina. The 99-acre property is centered on the lake, which was originally a sand pit operated by the Putnam Sand Company. After the company ceased operations, the lake was repurposed for use as a natural area within the city's park system. The many short trails in the park pass through shaded woodlands by the lake and skirt an area of restored prairie replete with wildflowers during the early summer. After exploring the trails, spend some time at the Discovery Center building to learn more about the natural habitats and creatures of this unique urban wildlife sanctuary.

Harris's sparrow at Lakewood Park. (Photo by Judd Patterson)

Contact: Lakewood Discovery Center and Natural Area, PO Box 736, Salina, KS 67402; 785-826-7335.
Hours: Daylight hours.
Cost: Free.

FEATURED TRAIL: COTTONWOOD TRAIL

Trail access: Hike.
Distance: 1-mile loop.

All the trails at the park are connected, so it's easy to combine multiple trails and create a custom hike. The wide trails at Lakewood Park are well maintained and surfaced with a thick layer of wood chips. Trail maps are posted on signs at nearly every major junction, so it's easy to stay oriented as you wander through the connected loops of the nature trails.

We recommend including the Cottonwood Trail as part of your route. It can be accessed either by the Discovery Center parking lot or at a parking lot on the east end of the lake (38.84408, –97.58418). This trail loops around the outer part of a

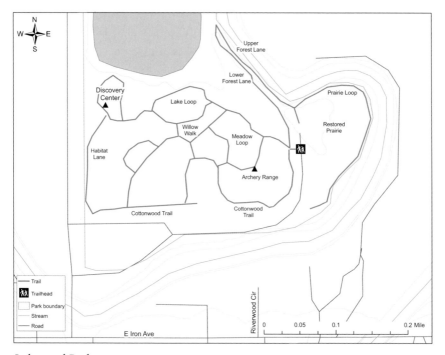

Lakewood Park

large, low-lying basin created as the lake has slowly receded due to sedimentation. Young cottonwoods and willows have eagerly filled the void, and over time, these trees will mature and develop into a stable forest community. As you hike the Cottonwood Trail, it's easy to see this process of gradual change, known as secondary succession. The mix of young forest with more mature woodland along the outer rim of the basin also constitutes a unique blend of habitat types that supports a wonderful diversity of wildlife and songbirds. Watch and listen for woodpeckers in the large dead cottonwood snags scattered throughout the basin.

Directions to the trailhead: From I-70, take exit 253 and go south on Ohio Road for 2.8 miles until you reach Iron Avenue. Turn east onto Iron Avenue and travel for 0.2 mile before turning left (north) onto the entry road to Lakewood Park. Cross a bridge spanning the old Smoky Hill River channel before taking the first road to the right (east). Follow this road until it ends in a parking lot by the east trailhead for the Lakewood Park trail system.

Additional trails: Salina has a variety of hiking and biking paths. Notable trails in the city include the Indian Rock Nature Trail, which ascends to the outcropping known locally as Indian Rock. This 0.75-mile interpretive trail is located at Indian Rock Park (1500 Gypsum Avenue), which can be reached by traveling 2 blocks south on Indiana Avenue from the south entrance to Lakewood Park. The Salina Levee Trail is a flat, crushed limestone trail that is popular with runners and cyclists. The northernmost trailhead is located at Bill Burke Park (1501 E. Craw-ford). From here, the trail runs roughly parallel to the Smoky Hill River channel and continues south for 3.1 miles atop the flood-control levee.

Camping: No camping is allowed at Lakewood Park. The closest camping, com-plete with pool, cabins, and RV and primitive sites, is at the Salina KOA near I-70 (1109 W. Diamond Drive, Salina, KS 67401; 800-562-3126, 785-827-3182).

MANHATTAN RIVER TRAILS

Along the northern edge of the Flint Hills, the trails along the river in this college town (Go Wildcats!) are within the Kansas River Basin. The shale and limestone bedrock is 270 million to 300 million years old. The Kansas River (also known as the Kaw) was named for the native Kanza people who once lived in the area, and it first appeared on a map in 1718. The Kansas River's largest tributary is the Big Blue River (the English translation of the Kanza people's name for this river is Great Blue Earth River), and the Manhattan River Trails run along the confluence of these two rivers. The rivers were a major part of the area's development, and they're still popular places for recreation. In addition to the running and biking trails, you can take a canoe or kayak out on the rivers.

Contact: Manhattan Convention and Visitors Bureau, 501 Poyntz Avenue, Man-hattan, KS 66502; Big Poppi Bikes, 1126 Moro Street, Manhattan, KS 66502; 785-537-3737.

Hours: Daylight hours.

Cost: Free.

 ## FEATURED TRAIL: RIVER TRAIL (TOP BIKE TRAIL)

Trail access: Hike or bike.

Distance: 5.9-mile loop.

The hard-packed single track along the Big Blue River and the Kansas River — complete with a terrain park and a few technical terrain sections — is popular with local cyclists and trail runners. The trail is accessible from the nearby levee system in a couple of places, but the main trailhead is just off US-24 (39.19145, –96.53761). Take the sidewalk to the right (southeast), and cross beneath the large railroad bridge over the river. The trail turns to hard-packed dirt, and it splits. Bearing right takes you closer to the river and on more of a straight but bumpy trail to start. Keep an eye out for tree roots as you ride through the woods. Near the confluence of the Big Blue and Kansas Rivers, the trail turns south and west. You'll come to a drainage ditch from the water treatment center. After a recent rainfall, you'll want to ride around this obstacle to avoid being swept into the river. If it's dry, you can go for a steep up-and-down ride through to the other side. Shortly after the ditch, you'll see the terrain park to your right. It has some jumps and other obstacles you can play on before proceeding along the river. The loop

Ride the mud in Manhattan. (Photo by Kristin Conard)

meets again, and you can either head back to the trailhead or continue on a single trail along the edge of the dam. A side trail links up to the dam and the Linear Trail, while the river trail continues close to the river. This flat section can be ridden fast, and you'll encounter another loop option just before you cross beneath the K-18 bridge, where you might see an itinerant's campsite near the river. You can take the loop to the right or left. Beneath the bridge, you'll head back into the woods and encounter some technical sections as you wind through the trees. The loop turns back at the intersection with another connector to the Linear Trail. Heading back toward the trailhead, you'll reach yet another connector up to the Linear Trail. Passing back beneath the K-18 bridge, you'll link up with the one-way section of trail. If you bear left at the intersection with the first loop, you'll be on the second half of the first loop. Passing by the ditch on the way back, the trail continues with quick dips and climbs and some tight turns before it meets up with the paved sidewalk beneath the railroad bridge and the trailhead.

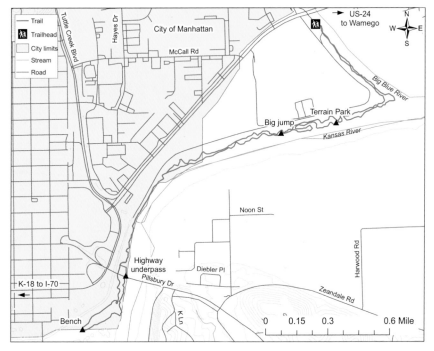

Manhattan River Trail

Directions to the trailhead: From US-24E, take the last right before crossing over the Big Blue River. It's an unnamed road to a parking lot at the trailhead for both the Linear Trail and the River Trail.

Additional trails: The 9-mile Linear Trail is a paved, urban trail that circles nearly the entire city, from Northeast Community Park to Anderson Avenue near Frank Anneberg Park. North of Manhattan are the Fancy Creek Trails at Tuttle Creek State Park.

Camping: The closest camping is at Tuttle Creek State Park (5800 A River Pond Road, Manhattan, KS 66502; 785-539-7941).

MILFORD STATE PARK

With over 16,000 acres of surface water, Milford Lake is the largest reservoir in the state of Kansas. It was built in the late 1960s, although the area around the lake was used for thousands of years by the Paleo-Indians and Native Americans. Along with some good hiking trails, the area features excellent fishing and boating opportunities and a large yacht club. Nearby is the Milford fish hatchery and the nature center, both of which have nature exhibits.

Contact: Milford State Park Office, 3612 State Park Road, Milford, KS 66514; 785-238-3014.

Hours: 24/7.

Cost: Free.

Milford State Park. (Photo by Scott Bean)

FEATURED TRAIL: EAGLE RIDGE TRAIL

Trail access: Hike, bike, or bridle.
Distance: 5.6-mile loop.

The trail network at Milford State Park includes hikes of varying lengths and difficulty, and one of the best long loops is the 5.6-mile Eagle Ridge Trail. It traverses gently rolling hills of tallgrass prairie and cedar woodlands along the west shore of the lake. The hike includes some gentle sustained inclines along a well-maintained mowed trail.

Start your hike at the Eagle Ridge trailhead (39.10026, –96.90711) located on the east shore of the lake and north of the dam. Heading east leads you along areas of open prairie interspersed with woodlands. The trail crosses a lightly used paved park road three times before reaching an intersection with the Old River Bluff Trail. The trail skirts a small crop field that provides a good opportunity to catch a glimpse of white-tailed deer and wild turkeys, especially at dusk and dawn. The Eagle Ridge Trail continues north along the edge of woodland areas until reaching a spur trail leading to the Long Loop segment of the trail. Take this spur if you want to add 1.55 miles to your route. The Long Loop portion of the trail continues north before forming a loop that rejoins the spur trail and takes you back to the main portion of the Eagle Ridge Trail.

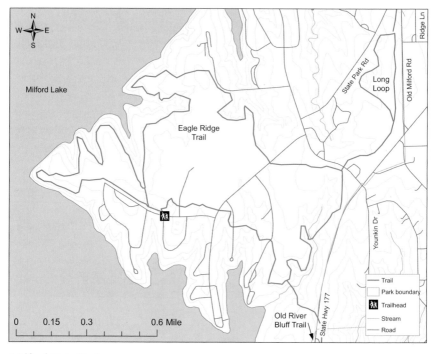

Milford State Park

Past this junction, the trail meanders through cedar woodlands and a series of gentle inclines as it continues west, near the edge of the lake. The western part of the trail closely follows the lakeshore and winds in and out of coves with some big views of the lake (39.108799, −96.904198). During the winter, watch for bald eagles in these coves along the shore. You can take a shortcut trail back to the trailhead if you want to cut 1.5 miles off the hike, but it's worth continuing through the final section for a nice view of the shoreline as you finish the trail.

Directions to the trailhead: From I-70, take exit 295 and follow US-77 north 8 miles to the junction with K-57. Turn left onto K-57S, travel for 1.2 miles, and turn right onto State Park Road.

Additional trails: There are some shorter hiking trails in the park, including the Crystal Trail (2.1 miles) and the Waterfall Trail (0.6 mile). The Old River Bluff Trail (1.5 miles) links the trail network in Milford State Park to the 4.8-mile multiuse (hike, bike, equestrian) Riverwalk Trail, which parallels the Republican River as it runs east from the outlet below Milford Dam to Fort Riley.

Camping: Plenty of campsites can be found along the lake, in seven different campgrounds. Along with primitive and utility sites, cabins are available.

TUTTLE CREEK STATE PARK

Tuttle Creek is the second-largest reservoir in Kansas. It stretches north along the Big Blue River corridor for more than 15 miles from the dam near the city of Manhattan. The 1,200-acre state park surrounding the lake is divided into four units, with multiuse trails found in two of them: Fancy Creek and Randolph. The Fancy Creek unit is located on the northwestern shore of the lake, near the town of Randolph. The Randolph unit is directly east across the lake, on the northeastern shoreline.

Tuttle Creek State Park encompasses terrain that is typical of the Flint Hills region, with rolling hills of tallgrass prairie interspersed with woodland areas along streams and ravines. Although tallgrass prairie is the dominant natural vegetation throughout the Flint Hills, the area around Fancy Creek has extensive stands of eastern red cedar, which gives trail users the opportunity to travel through dense woodlands along the route. The relatively rugged topography of the area adds interest and a degree of challenge.

Contact: Tuttle Creek State Park, 5800 A River Pond Road, Manhattan, KS 66502; 785-539-7941.

Hours: 24/7.

Cost: State park fee.

FEATURED TRAIL: FANCY CREEK TRAIL

Trail access: Hike or bike.

Distance: 4.6-mile loop.

Fancy Creek Trail at Tuttle Creek State Park. (Photo by Jonathan Conard)

The Fancy Creek area features a 4.6-mile loop that is particularly popular with mountain bikers. The constantly changing topography, sharp switchbacks, and intermittent sections of rocky trail present a worthy challenge. The trail may be wet and hard to traverse during the spring, but it typically takes only a couple of days to dry after a big rain.

The loop trail is marked to be taken counterclockwise, but it can be traveled in either direction. Just watch carefully for other riders or hikers who may be going the opposite way. Starting south from the trailhead (39.436895, –96.73249) leads you through a lightly forested area that includes one of the few opportunities to catch an open view of Tuttle Creek Reservoir as it extends to the south (39.43433, –96.73328). The trail starts to turn west and briefly becomes open grassland as you cross the entrance road to the state park; it then continues west into another stand of cedars. You'll pass an intersection for an additional loop (Fancier Loop) that can be taken to the southwest.

As the main trail continues west, it goes through stands of eastern red cedar interspersed with more open meadows. This section of the trail also passes the remnants of a weathered rock wall that was likely built by the area's first settlers (39.43524, –96.73625). Until barbed wire became commonly available, handmade stone fences were used throughout the Flint Hills to contain livestock or protect crop fields. The building of such fences was even encouraged by Kansas law, which awarded an annual bounty of $2 per 40 rods (660 feet) of stone wall or hedgerow fencing that was constructed and maintained. Although limestone is locally abundant and readily available, it took substantial craftsmanship and effort to build these stone structures.

After the rock wall, the trail winds north, and the next notable feature is a scattered array of unusual limestone formations (39.43935, –96.74016). The trail crosses a park road and then continues north and northeast. Upon reaching the northernmost point of the trail, it turns back to the southeast and crosses the park road one more time on a relatively straight track back toward the trailhead.

Directions to trailhead: If you're coming from the west on I-70, take US-77 north 41 miles to the town of Randolph. Turn right (east) onto K-16/Green-Randolph Road and continue east for 1.6 miles until you reach the state park entrance on the north side of the road. Turn left (north) onto 8800 Road, travel for 0.4 mile, and turn right toward a small parking area where the trail begins.

To get to Randolph from eastern Kansas on I-70, take K-177 north 8.5 miles to Manhattan; then take the off-ramp for Fort Riley Boulevard/Tuttle Creek Boulevard. Turn left onto Fort Riley Boulevard, which becomes Tuttle Creek Boulevard/US-24W. Follow Tuttle Creek Boulevard/US-24W for 15 miles, until it merges with US-77N. Take US-77N for 9.2 miles to reach Randolph.

Additional trails: Along with the excellent trail for mountain biking and hiking in the Fancy Creek area, Tuttle Creek is known for a great selection of bridle trails built and maintained by the Flint Hills Trail Riders Association.

The North Randolph Trail, in the Randolph unit of Tuttle Creek State Park, is a 14.75-mile multiuse trail that is especially popular with equestrians. It features hilly terrain and a view of the longest bridge in Kansas, spanning Tuttle Creek along the Green-Randolph Road.

The Carnahan Creek Horse Trail, located in Carnahan Creek Park (on the east side of the Tuttle Creek Reservoir), is managed by Pottawatomie County. It includes a 5-mile loop, with overlooks of the reservoir and views of the surrounding

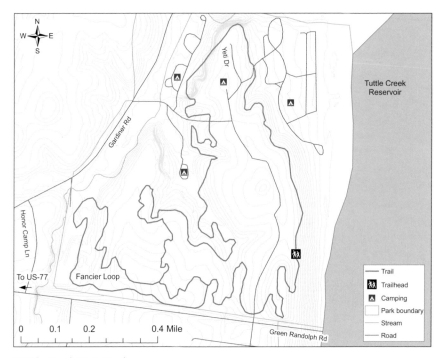

Tuttle Creek State Park

Flint Hills. Trail access is limited to equestrians and hikers. No user fee is required. **Camping:** There are multiple sites for tent camping and for electrical hookups in the Fancy Creek area.

WILSON LAKE

Wilson Lake has the distinction of being one of the clearest lakes in the state. The reservoir, built in 1964 along the Saline River, has an excellent network of hiking and mountain biking trails. The lake is located in the Smoky Hills, in a part of the state known as "post rock country" because of the miles of rock posts dotting the knolls and valleys of the mixed-grass prairie. As this part of Kansas was settled, the striking lack of trees led to the widespread use of limestone posts for fences. These unique and sturdy posts, hewn from extensive deposits of Greenhorn limestone dating from the Cretaceous period, were quarried by the early settlers and commonly used for barbed wire fencing beginning in the 1880s. When Wilson Lake was created, the US Army Corps of Engineers salvaged many of these limestone fence posts and incorporated them into park buildings and structures.

Wilson Lake includes five separate park areas—three managed by the Army Corps of Engineers, and two by the Kansas Department of Wildlife, Parks, and Tourism. Lucas Park, along the north shore of Wilson Lake, includes the 305-acre

Rocktown Natural Area, which has been registered by the Kansas Biological Survey as a Natural and Scientific Area.

Contact: Wilson Lake, US Army Corps of Engineers, 4860 Outlet Boulevard, Sylvan Grove, KS 67481; 785-658-2551.

Hours: 24/7.

Cost: Free.

FEATURED TRAIL: ROCKTOWN TRAIL

Trail access: Hike.

Distance: 2.6-mile loop.

This trail through the western section of Lucas Park includes access to a secluded lake cove and some open prairie vistas. The trail gets its name from the 15- to 30-foot-tall Dakota sandstone rock formations, evoking a city skyline. Pack

Rocktown Trail at Wilson Lake. (Photo by Jonathan Conard)

plenty of water during the summer, since the trail has no shade, and watch for a variety of small lizard species, including the exquisite collared lizard, darting across trails or basking on exposed rock surfaces.

The mowed grass trail starts at the marked trailhead in the parking area (38.94971, –98.53382). It takes you into the prairie grasses and yucca plants common in the Lucas Park area. The trail continues west for 0.25 mile before reaching a branch. Since this branch is the beginning of the loop portion of the trail, you can go either left or right. If you follow the branch to the right, you gain elevation as the trail heads toward a small Dakota sandstone canyon with pleasant overlooks of the lake. Along this section of the trail, a regal row of limestone post rocks runs perpendicular to the trail, stretching into the open prairie.

Along the edge of the canyon, the trail gradually descends to the edge of Wilson Lake, with views of distant red rock formations on the opposite shore. As the trail approaches the lake, you can take a break in Rocktown Cove (38.94992, –98.54797), which has small sand beaches suitable for swimming or wading. This area also boasts a pair of towering sandstone formations rising out of the lake. After leaving the lakefront, the trail continues to loop back over the open prairie toward the trailhead.

Directions to the trailhead: From I-70, take exit 206 and follow K-232 north 9.1 miles over the dam at Wilson Lake. Turn left (southwest) at the turnoff to Lucas

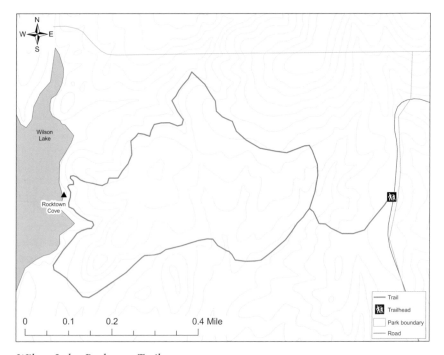

Wilson Lake, Rocktown Trail

Park and follow 203rd Street for 1.4 miles until you reach a T-intersection. Turn left (south) at this intersection, and stay on this road for 1.7 miles past the Corps of Engineers entry booth. Keep right until you reach the small parking area at the trailhead on the right side of the road.

WILSON STATE PARK

On the south side of Wilson Lake is Wilson State Park. In 1966, just two years after the lake was created, it was known only as the Hell Creek Area. The park was expanded in 1984 with the Otoe Area. There are cabins and camping, and the lake is known for its smallmouth and striped bass. Wilson State Park also has one of the state's best mountain biking trails, along with a few nature trails near the campgrounds.

Contact: Wilson State Park, #3 State Park Road, Sylvan Grove, KS 67481; 785-658-2465.

Hours: 24/7.

Cost: State park fee.

FEATURED TRAIL: SWITCHGRASS MOUNTAIN BIKE TRAIL–HELL CREEK LOOP (TOP BIKE TRAIL AND TOP 10 TRAIL)

Trail access: Hike or bike.

Distance: 6-mile loop.

The Switchgrass Trail is a Kansas mountain biker's dream, with over 21 miles of trails winding through the steep hills and valleys of the Hell Creek Area of Wilson State Park. The trails are divided into three separate loops: the Golden Belt Loop, the Marina Loop, and the Hell Creek Loop. In addition, there is a 6-mile EZ Loop that features terrain suitable for novice riders or those who enjoy a less technical riding experience. The Switchgrass Trail was designed especially for mountain biking, but hikers will also appreciate the scenic vistas and challenging ascents. All the loops are outstanding, and the trail was designated an "epic" trail by the International Mountain Biking Association in 2012 — a prestigious honor given only to trails that provide an exemplary riding experience.

The entire Switchgrass Trail is first-rate, but if you have to choose a single loop, take the Hell Creek Loop. It is rated "moderate" in difficulty for mountain bikers and includes intermittent rocks, plenty of elevation change, steep drop-offs, and sharp turns. Those who relish a challenging trail with expansive views along a pristine route are sure to enjoy this loop.

The Hell Creek Loop can be accessed from a gravel parking area on the west side of the bridge over Hell Creek Cove (38.91937, −98.49113). From the parking area, drop down and follow the connector trail to the trail nearest the lake and turn east (right). From here, you'll start the Hell Creek Loop. The packed-dirt trail is well maintained, with mile markers carved into limestone blocks, and it has

159

Switchgrass Trail at Wilson State Park. (Photo by Jonathan Conard)

well-placed and clearly labeled connector trails between portions of the loops. The trail begins by hugging the lakeshore as it passes precariously close to steep drop-offs along the sandstone cliffs abutting the reservoir. The trail soon leaves the lake and winds up and down along the contours of the steep canyons cut through the Hell Creek Area. At mile marker 13, you have the option of taking the connector trail labeled "J" or continuing along the main trail. If you continue on the main trail for another 0.5 mile, you'll pass a separate spur trail that branches off to the left toward a gravel road that accesses the lake. Bear right at this junction to stay on the main trail, and prepare for a steady climb as you pass mile marker 14 and start ascending the canyon ridge, where the trail follows the rim and begins to bear north as it returns to the trailhead.

From this point, you can look back on the miles of trail you have already traveled and appreciate the effort that it has taken to attain the sweeping vistas that greet you at the top of the canyon rim. As you continue to switchback along the

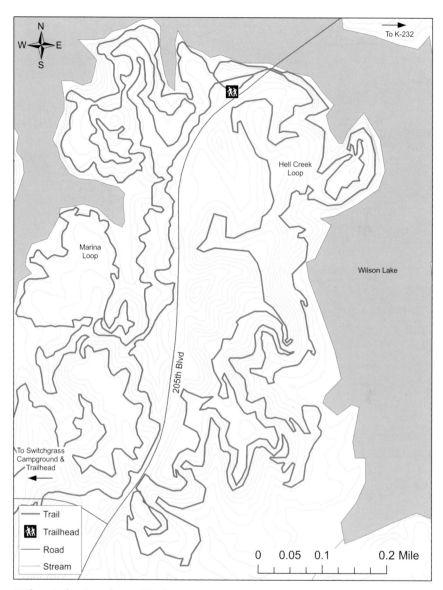

To K-232

Hell Creek
Loop

Marina
Loop

Wilson Lake

205th Blvd

To Switchgrass
Campground &
Trailhead

Trail
Trailhead
Road
Stream

0   0.05   0.1   0.2 Mile

Wilson Lake, Switchgrass Trail

upper part of the canyon, you'll reach the aptly named Lone Tree Hill, with a single tree valiantly standing tall at the crest of the rise. Past Lone Tree Hill, you'll begin to descend along a portion of trail that is slightly smoother and faster as you pass mile marker 16 and return to the parking area.

Directions to the trailhead: From I-70, take exit 206 for K-232 toward Wilson/ Lucas. After driving north for 5.3 miles, turn left (west) toward Hell Creek Bridge. Continue across the bridge, and the trailhead is on the right.

Additional trails: The Prairie Fire Trail, which includes a 2.5-mile loop, is located in the Minooka Park Area along the south shore of Wilson Lake. The trail offers hikers the opportunity to view unique rock formations along the lakeshore. For a quick hike, try the Dakota Trail in the Hell Creek Area of Wilson State Park. This 2-mile loop features scenic views along the interpretive trail.

Camping: The Switchgrass Campground within the Hell Creek Area of the park is closest to the main trailhead for the Switchgrass Trail. It offers primitive and utility campsites.

CHAPTER 6

SOUTH-CENTRAL KANSAS

Prairies make level roadways for the soul to walk, and invite outward, outward to the sky, which invitation is passionate and eloquent beyond describing. Prairies lead into the sky. . . . Big thoughts are nurtured here, with little friction. . . . "No hindrance" would appear a legitimate motto for the stately plains; and the motto is sublime.

WILLIAM A. QUAYLE, *THE PRAIRIE AND THE SEA*

Sunset on the Tallgrass Prairie National Preserve. Photo by Judd Patterson

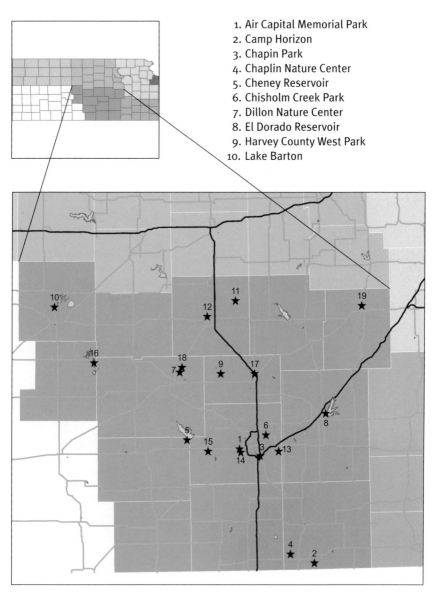

1. Air Capital Memorial Park
2. Camp Horizon
3. Chapin Park
4. Chaplin Nature Center
5. Cheney Reservoir
6. Chisholm Creek Park
7. Dillon Nature Center
8. El Dorado Reservoir
9. Harvey County West Park
10. Lake Barton

South-Central Kansas

11. Maxwell Wildlife Refuge
12. Meadowlark Trail–McPherson/
    Lindsborg
13. Miller's Meadow
14. Pawnee Prairie Park
15. Prairie Sunset Trail
16. Quivira National Wildlife Refuge
17. Sand Creek Trail–Bethel College
18. Sand Hills State Park
19. Tallgrass Prairie National Preserve

South-central Kansas has a variety of physiographic regions. Though primarily encompassing the Arkansas River Lowlands and the Wellington-McPherson Lowlands, the region also catches the edge of the Flint Hills to the east. Much of the land here is used for row-crop agriculture, and the area leads the state in wheat production. The Ninnescah, Arkansas, Little Arkansas, and Walnut Rivers cross the region and, along with the area's wetlands, attract thousands of birds during fall and spring migration.

For off-trail exploring in south-central Kansas, you can visit the state's largest art museum in Wichita, the state's largest city. In Hutchinson, you can head underground to explore Strataca, the Kansas Underground Salt Museum. Hutchinson is also the home of the Kansas State Fair and the Kansas Cosmosphere and Space Center — a world-class space museum.

AIR CAPITAL MEMORIAL PARK

Prior to the opening of Air Capital Memorial Park in 2013, there were few options for single-track enthusiasts in the Wichita area. Through the hard work of the Kansas Singletrack Society, this city park has been transformed into a place where both beginning and advanced mountain bikers can hone their skills. The small 10-acre park, located near Wichita's Midcontinent Airport, once displayed a decommissioned B-47 Stratojet to honor the city's rich aviation tradition and its status as "Air Capital of the World." The aircraft has been removed, and the park has been repurposed for the enjoyment of mountain bikers and hikers. The area includes three loops of varying difficulty, and the rough, wooded terrain is ideal for technical mountain biking.

Contact: Parks and Recreation–City of Wichita, 455 N. Main, 11th Floor, Wichita, KS 67202; 316-268-4361.

Hours: 24/7.

Cost: Free.

FEATURED TRAIL: NORTH, EAST, AND WEST LOOPS

Trail access: Hike or bike.

Distance: 1.8-mile loop.

The newly constructed single-track trail at Air Capital Memorial Park is divided into three short loops totaling 1.8 miles. Each loop is uniquely suited to different ability levels, but the loops can also be combined into one circuit. Starting from the trailhead (37.66615, –97.45449), the North Loop is the friendliest option for beginners who want to take it slow; the fast-flowing trail offers a good chance to warm up before tackling the East and West Loops. The West Loop is the longest of the three and presents some challenging log obstacles, quick descents, and tight turns. To up the ante in terms of technical difficulty, try the East Loop. The "Rock Garden" portion is a virtual minefield of dips and bumps, replete with rocks

Air Capital Memorial Park. (Photo by Randy Van Scyoc)

and concrete slabs. Those seeking a technical challenge will find one around every hairpin turn of the East Loop. Each of the loops is clearly identified by name and well marked with directional arrows. For everyone's safety, bikers should follow the posted directional arrows. Hikers are welcome on the trails, but they should hike the loops in the opposite direction of the posted arrows.

Directions to the trailhead: The trail is located in Wichita, just south of US-54/400, between Maize Road and Tyler Road. If you're coming from the west on US-54/400, take the Maize Road exit and continue straight past Maize Road on the frontage road south of US-54 for 0.3 mile. Turn south (right) onto Seville Street, and make the first turn west (right) onto the park road that leads west to the parking area by the trailhead. If you're coming from the east on US-54/400, take the Tyler Road exit and go south for 0.4 mile before turning west (right) onto W. Harry Street. Follow Harry Street west for 0.5 mile and turn north (right) onto Seville Street. Take Seville Street north until you reach the turn-off to the west (left) onto the park road leading to the trailhead.

166

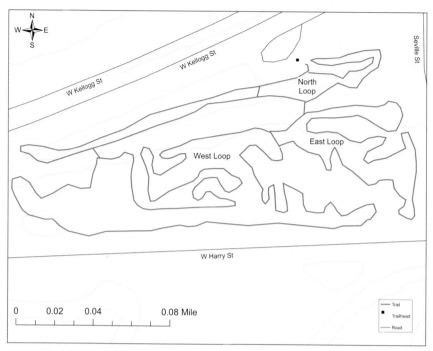

Air Capital Memorial Park

Additional trails: Just south of Air Capital Memorial Park is a separate network of trails winding along Cowskin Creek in Pawnee Prairie Park. Please note that no mountain bikes are allowed in Pawnee Prairie Park, but the area is open to hikers and horses.

Camping: No camping is allowed at Air Capital Memorial Park. Tent camping is available west of Wichita at Lake Afton (24600 W. 39th Street S., Goddard, KS 67052; 316-943-0192). The public observatory at Lake Afton offers museum tours and special programs for viewing the stars and the planets. These programs are held on Friday and Saturday evenings throughout the year (316-978-7827).

CAMP HORIZON–ARKANSAS CITY

Camp Horizon is well known as a popular destination for church camps and retreats, but it is also gaining a reputation for its outstanding trail network, which is the result of a unique collaboration among Camp Horizon, private landowners, and the Kansas Singletrack Society. The property where Camp Horizon is now located was originally the site of the Arkansas City Portland Cement Company, which operated until 1911. The site was privately owned until it was sold to the First Methodist Church of Arkansas City in 1947. Currently, the Great Plains Conference of the United Methodist Church operates the camp, and the natural

167

setting has provided an inspirational and spiritual experience for numerous participants in church camps and retreats. With the development of its trail system, the camp is now open to mountain bikers and hikers as well. Feel free to enjoy the roller-coaster hills and challenging technical terrain of the trails, but keep in mind that hikers and bikers should be mindful and respectful of camp activities and participants.

Contact: Camp Horizon, 20811 Horizon Drive, Arkansas City, KS 67005; 620-442-5533.

Hours: Daylight hours.

Cost: Free.

FEATURED TRAIL: LYLE'S LOOP

Trail access: Hike or bike. No dogs allowed.

Distance: 2.8-mile loop.

This short loop is a gentle introduction to the challenging terrain and scenic beauty that typify the trails at Camp Horizon. The loop starts off with a short but nearly vertical drop-off from the trailhead, but the grade soon moderates and the trail flattens out through some fast terrain in a gentle downhill wooded section. In the first mile, the trail has several switchbacks before you reach a set of massive boulders (37.03605, –96.93113). From here, the single-track trail slowly loses elevation as it continues through a forested area and crosses a primitive double-track road (37.03438, –96.92784). The trail opens up and cuts along a sloping ridge of tallgrass prairie shortly after the mile 2 marker before reaching a marked trail junction that offers the option of returning to the trailhead to complete Lyle's Loop or continuing on 8 miles of additional rugged trails. To return to the trailhead, follow the sign at this junction. The trail bends north and begins to climb steadily back toward the parking area and trailhead. You'll pass by camp facilities, including a campfire ring and a chapel, before reaching the parking lot at the trailhead. This portion of the trail is great for beginning and intermediate mountain bike riders. In addition to opportunities to hone their technical skills, it provides new riders with an enjoyable experience along the more open and faster parts of the trail. The trail corridor is wide enough that there is some margin for error, but keep your speed under control, especially around some of the sharper switchbacks and blind corners.

Directions to the trailhead: From US-166E, continue through Arkansas City onto E. Madison Avenue. As you reach the east side of town, the road becomes 292nd Road/County Road 6. About 2 miles outside of town, the road splits; turn right (south) onto County Road 6/101st Street. After 0.4 mile, turn left (east) to stay on County Road 6/296th Road. After 2 miles, turn right (south) on the first road after Hillcrest Drive. Continue on this road for 0.9 mile. The trailhead is on the left (east).

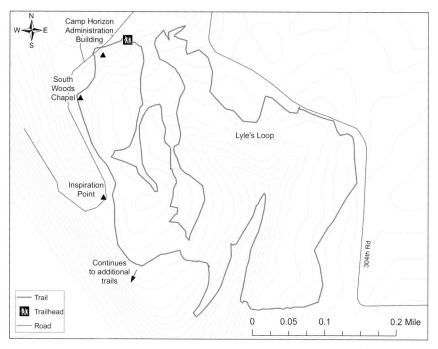

Camp Horizon

Additional trails: If you're an experienced mountain bike rider seeking a challenge, the additional 8 miles of trails at Camp Horizon should be on your must-ride list. If you need a break along the way, check out the old cement factory located near the trail network.

Camping: No camping is allowed at Camp Horizon.

CHAPIN PARK

Until 1954, the 190 acres along a bend in the Arkansas River and west of McConnell Air Force Base was the Chapin hog farm. Then it was a landfill until the 1980s. By 2009, it had been converted into a park. It's also the site of the city's first dog park, opened in 2010. The Arson Canine Ashley Memorial Dog Park is named for the fire department's first canine-unit dog. In addition, there's a model airplane field with a 400-foot concrete runway, and plans are in the works for a skate park.

Contact: Parks and Recreation–City of Wichita, 455 N. Main, 11th Floor, Wichita, KS 67202; 316-268-4361.

Hours: 24/7.

Cost: Free.

FEATURED TRAIL: BIG DITCH RUN, HILLSIDE LOOP, NORTH SLOPE TRAIL, AND WEST SLOPE TRAIL

Trail access: Hike or bike.
Distance: 1.5 miles total.

Entirely exposed, with no shade, the wide gravel trails make a couple of intersecting loops along a small hill near the river. Both the south entrance (37.62728, –97.30881) and the east entrance (37.62808, –97.30576) have trailheads for the gravel paths. Although all portions of the trail connect, each is individually named. From the south entrance near the dog park, you'll start out on the short Hillside Loop, which can be taken by itself for a 0.5-mile loop up and down a small hill; it also connects to the Big Ditch Run and the West Slope Trail. Along the Big Ditch Run, you'll pass the east entrance, across from the model airplane flying field, before turning onto the North Slope Trail, which intersects with the mountain bike trails close to the river. Follow the North Slope Trail gradually uphill, past its intersection with the Hillside Loop, and down the West Slope Trail to check out a view of the river before heading back to the parking area via the paved sidewalk on the south side of the dog park or back along the West Slope Trail and the Hillside Loop.

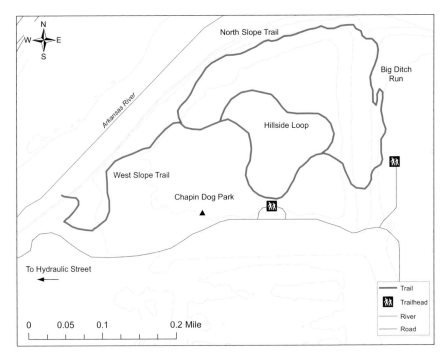

Chapin Park

Directions to the trailhead: From central Wichita, take exit 2 off I-135S for Hydraulic Street. Make the first left (east) off of S. Hydraulic Street after you cross the river. The south entrance is 0.5 mile on the left (north). For the east entrance, continue another 0.2 mile and turn left (north). The entrance is on the left.

Additional trails: Closer to the river, and linked to the northern edge of the walking path, is a small series of mountain biking loops that the city has plans to improve. Continuing west on the paved sidewalk along the south side of the park, you'll link up with the Arkansas River Bike Path, a 10-mile paved trail along both sides of the river that takes you past Wichita icons such as Lawrence-Dumont Stadium and the *Keeper of the Plains* statue.

Camping: No camping is allowed at Chapin Park. The closest tent camping is at Cheney State Park (16000 NE 50th, Cheney, KS 67025; 316-542-3664).

CHAPLIN NATURE CENTER

Encompassing 200 acres bordering the Arkansas River, the Chaplin Nature Center preserves majestic stands of bottomland forest, a pristine spring-fed stream, and open patches of restored prairie. The site was originally homesteaded by relatives of Hazel Chaplin. She sold the site to the Wichita Audubon Society in 1973, which converted it to a natural area. The current nature center includes more than 4 miles of trails that wind through the mature forest and extend out to the edge of the Arkansas River itself. Before starting your hike, learn about the natural history of the area at the visitors' center, housed in a rustic log cabin–style building complete with interactive educational exhibits.

Contact: Chaplin Nature Center, 27814 27th Drive, Arkansas City, KS 67005; 620-442-4133.

Hours: Daylight hours.

Cost: No admission fee is required, but donations to support the nature center are always welcome.

FEATURED TRAIL: RIVER TRAIL (TOP FAMILY-FRIENDLY TRAIL)

Trail access: Hike. No dogs allowed.

Distance: 1.5-mile loop.

The River Trail weaves from the tranquil woods along Spring Creek, a small spring-fed stream lined with tall oaks and walnuts, to the sandy banks of the Arkansas River. Start from behind the visitors' center and descend a multitiered wooden staircase to access the main trail network. At the bottom of the staircase, turn right and follow the trail as it parallels Spring Creek. The shaded trail passes an intersection leading up to the Bluff Trail (37.08617, –97.09689) and turns east. The well-worn path is clearly marked by sturdy limestone trail markers and interpretive signage with natural lore and inspirational wilderness sayings. After crossing Spring Creek on a small wooden bridge (37.08648, –97.09549), the trail turns

Chaplin Nature Center. (Photo by Jonathan Conard)

north and continues under the shaded woodland canopy before intersecting with the Sandbar Trail. For a short side hike, take the Sandbar Trail, which branches off and suddenly emerges from the woods at the wide, sandy banks of the Arkansas River. From here, you can go right up to the water's edge and enjoy a peaceful view of the broad, shallow river as it flows steadily toward the Mississippi.

To return to the River Trail from the Sandbar Trail, you can either turn around and retrace your steps or take another connecting trail farther north along the river. The River Trail continues north before turning back to the west as it passes a bench and continues through the woodlands until it emerges in a small opening amidst a peaceful hardwood grove. Tucked away along the far edge of this grove is a giant wooden chair (37.08958, –97.09815) that allows adults and children alike a chance to climb up and enjoy a unique view of the surrounding forest. The trail emerges briefly from the woodlands and intersects with a mowed maintenance path that borders a restored prairie to the north. After crossing the maintenance path a second time, the trail returns to the woods and takes a concrete crossing over Spring Creek (37.08987, −97.10064). After the concrete crossing, turn southeast along the Wildlife Homes Trail, which leads back to the wooden staircase behind the visitors' center.

Directions to the trailhead: From Arkansas City, turn west on Highway 166 and drive for 3 miles. Turn right (north) on 31st Road and travel for approximately

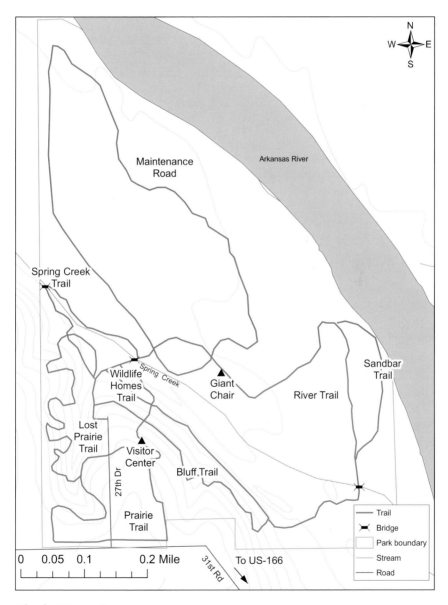

Chaplin Nature Center

2.25 miles until you reach the sign for the nature center. Parking is available, and the trail network can be accessed from behind the visitors' center.

Additional trails: The Bluff Trail (0.7 mile) parallels Spring Creek as it runs southeast of the visitors' center. This trail stays high on the ridge and provides a nice view of the surrounding landscape before intersecting with the River Trail. On the west side of the nature center, the Spring Creek Trail (0.4 mile) is a good option for a shorter loop hike through the shaded woods along Spring Creek. To fully experience the biological diversity of the area, take the Prairie Trail (0.7 mile), which wanders along the edge of a grassland area south of the visitors' center parking lot.

Camping: No camping is allowed at the Chaplin Nature Center.

CHENEY RESERVOIR

The North Fork of the Ninnescah River supplies water for Cheney Reservoir, which in turn supplies the majority of Wichita's drinking water. The Bureau of Reclamation completed the reservoir in 1965, and it is a popular spot for recreational activities, including boating, camping, and hiking. With the only predictable weather in Kansas being a stiff wind, the strong breeze that blows straight across the open waters of Cheney Reservoir makes this one of the best places for sailing in the state. The headquarters of the Ninnescah Sailing Association is located on the shore, and colorful sailboats participate in regattas throughout the year. The reservoir is also popular with birders. Migratory waterfowl, including large flocks of white pelicans and double-crested cormorants, can be seen on the lake. Adjacent to the reservoir, Cheney State Park provides camping facilities and other amenities, while the Cheney Wildlife Area preserves an additional 5,000 acres of land on the north and west sides of the reservoir to protect waterfowl and wildlife.

Contact: Cheney State Park, 16000 NE 50th, Cheney, KS 67025; 316-542-3664.
Hours: 24/7.
Cost: State park fee.

FEATURED TRAIL: WEST TRAIL

Trail access: Hike or bike.
Distance: 5 miles, one-way.

Located along the west side of Cheney Reservoir, this trail starts near the state park office (37.71888, –97.82609) and continues northwest for 5 miles through the park. From the trailhead, head west through an open grassland dotted with eastern red cedars before entering a small woodland. As you pass through the woodland, you'll cross two bridges over gently flowing Geifer Creek. Here, the trail leaves the woods and the scenery opens up as the fast, wide single-track trail cuts through a stretch of grassland before reentering another woodland area. At this point, you'll come to the first fork in the trail, which can be taken in either direction. The right

Cheney State Park. (Photo by Jonathan Conard)

fork allows access to the Smarsh Trailhead (37.72718, –97.84097), while the left fork continues through a more wooded section interspersed with open meadows along the western boundary of the park. Both forks soon rejoin the main trail and continue north toward the Lakeshore Trailhead (37.74421, –97.84745), which is the northernmost access point for the trail network in the park. The trail continuing north from the Lakeshore Trailhead is less frequently used, and it fades from a well-worn dirt path to mowed grass. The trail splits again; the right fork constitutes the Prairie Loop, which soon rejoins the main trail and continues north. This portion of the trail has the best views of the lake, with several locations providing scenic vistas of the open water to the east (37.74644, –97.84878). A short branch of the trail leads east to an access point for a secluded sandy beach where you can wade in the water or lounge on the shore. The final loop on the trail is the Cedar Loop, which passes through a thin stand of eastern red cedars before looping north and merging with the main trail. There is also access to a parking area at

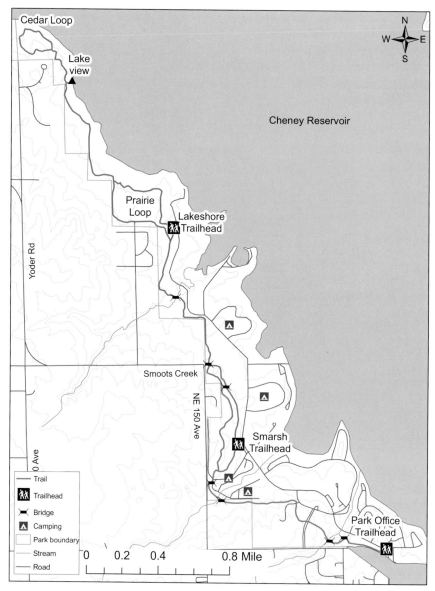

Cheney State Park

the northern end of the trail (37.75923, −97.86308). From here, you can take the trail back to the trailhead or, from the Lakeshore Trailhead, you can return on the paved park road, which will cut some time off the return trip.

Directions to the trailhead: From US-54/400, take the Mt. Vernon exit and go north for 3.5 miles on NE 150 Avenue. Turn right (east) onto NE 50 Street and follow this road for 1 mile until you reach the entrance road to Cheney State Park.

Turn left (north) at the park entrance road. Make the first available right turn, and you will see the KDWPT office on the south side of the road. Park here to access the West Trail's main trailhead, located northwest of the parking lot.

Additional trails: The Geifer Creek Nature Trail (0.13 mile) and the Spring Creek Wildlife Observation Trail (0.75 mile) are good options for a pleasant stroll.

Camping: There are several places to camp near the main trailhead, with choice sites located at the Harding Hill and Geifer Hill camping areas. The Smarsh Creek Campground is farther west of the park office and has electrical hookups as well as a nearby access point for the trail.

CHISHOLM CREEK PARK

One of the largest parks in Wichita, Chisholm Creek Park is an enjoyable place for a leisurely hike amidst some surprisingly diverse habitats, ranging from wetland marshes to restored upland prairies. The Great Plains Nature Center at the main park entrance provides interactive wildlife exhibits and programs that are sure to delight nature lovers of all ages. The boardwalk trail spanning the tranquil marshes scattered throughout the park is an excellent location for sighting all kinds of wildlife — from muskrats to egrets. The trail network offers several different loop options varying in length from 0.5 to 1.7 miles. Although we generally have not included paved trails in this book, the natural setting, diverse habitats, and high quality of the overall experience at Chisholm Creek Park makes this one worthy of mention.

Contact: Great Plains Nature Center, 6232 E. 29th Street N., Wichita, KS 67220; 316-683-5499.

Hours: Daylight hours.

Cost: Free.

FEATURED TRAIL: COTTONWOOD TRAIL (TOP FAMILY-FRIENDLY TRAIL)

Trail access: Hike. No dogs allowed.

Distance: 1.7-mile loop.

The trail network is essentially one large loop, with multiple cutoff trails that constitute a number of smaller, individually named loop trails. The Cottonwood Trail is the longest of the loops in the park and encompasses the greatest diversity of habitat types. To follow the trail counterclockwise from the Great Plains Nature Center (37.73959, −97.26431), start north on the paved trail. Past a cutoff for the Quail Loop, which branches to the west, you'll reach a boardwalk that crosses over a small marsh frequented by snowy egrets and great blue herons. The boardwalk provides the unique experience of being able to walk directly through marshes and wetlands that would otherwise be inaccessible. After the boardwalk section, the trail continues north and passes a cutoff trail for the Heron Loop, which branches to the west. The trail crosses Chisholm Creek, named for Jesse Chisholm. He was

Chisholm Creek Park. (Photo by Jonathan Conard)

a key character in Wichita's early history and is perhaps best known for establishing the Chisholm Trail, which brought Texas cattle 600 miles north to Kansas. The Cottonwood Trail parallels the creek along an area of grassland and passes the cut-off trail for the Bluestem Trail before reaching a small pond, where you might see great blue herons, egrets, or basking turtles. The trail then continues west before entering a wooded area along Chisholm Creek. The trail crosses Chisholm Creek and begins to loop back east toward the trailhead, skirting the edge of several prairie patches bordering the riparian zone of the creek. These "edge habitats," where woodland and prairie meet, are favorite locations for white-tailed deer. The trail passes over one more section of boardwalk, along the marshy wetland on the east side of the park, before returning to the trailhead.

Directions to the trailhead: From K-96, take the exit toward Woodlawn and head south on Woodlawn for 0.5 mile. Turn right (west) onto E. 29th Street N., and take the first right 0.2 mile later. This will take you to the parking area for

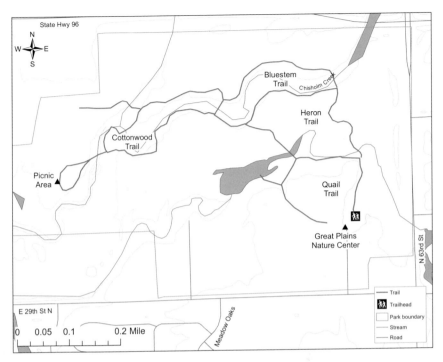

Chisholm Creek Park

the Great Plains Nature Center. The trailhead is at the northern edge of the parking lot.

Additional trails: Several shorter loops are also available at Chisholm Creek Park, including the 0.5-mile Quail Trail, 0.9-mile Heron Trail, and 1.1-mile Bluestem Trail.

Camping: Camping is not allowed at Chisholm Creek Park. Tent camping is available west of Wichita at Lake Afton (24600 W. 39th Street S., Goddard, KS 67052; 316-943-0192). The public observatory at Lake Afton offers museum tours and special programs for viewing the stars and the planets. These programs are held on Friday and Saturday evenings throughout the year (316-978-7827).

DILLON NATURE CENTER

The beauty of the Dillon Nature Center can best be experienced by taking a leisurely stroll along the well-maintained hiking trails, which include several short family-friendly loops. Before starting your hike, visit the Discovery Center; it is an excellent place to learn more about the natural history of the area through interactive exhibits, aquaria, and a science library. At the Discovery Center, the observation deck and picture windows overlooking the pond provide a first glimpse of the area's beauty. The trails encircle the spring-fed pond at the heart of the nature

Pond at Dillon Nature Center. (Photo by Kristin Conard)

center, where you may see lazy painted turtles basking on submerged logs. The pond is stocked for fishing and is surrounded by a mature woodland area that includes a variety of native and exotic tree species. In late spring, an amazing profusion of colorful blooms can be seen in the extensive flower beds planted with annuals; these flowers attract a diverse array of pollinators, including a variety of butterflies. In the fall, there is often brilliant color in the trees. The nature center has been designated a National Urban Wildlife Sanctuary. Children will delight in the Jim Smith Family Playscape, which allows them to explore the natural world in a safe environment. The area was originally owned by the Dillon Stores company, which maintained it as a private recreation spot for employees before donating the land to the City of Hutchinson in 1971.

Contact: Dillon Nature Center, 3002 E. 30th Avenue, Hutchinson, KS 67502; 316-663-7411.

Hours: The nature center and trails open at 8 a.m. on weekdays and 9 a.m. on weekends; they close at sunset.

Cost: No entrance fee is required, although donations are appreciated.

FEATURED TRAIL: WOODARD TRAIL (TOP FAMILY-FRIENDLY TRAIL)

Trail access: Hike.
Distance: 0.86-mile loop.

The Woodard Trail has been designated a National Recreation Trail, which constitutes federal recognition of "exemplary trails of local or regional significance." The trail starts at the Dillon Nature Center entrance (38.08787, –97.87632), near

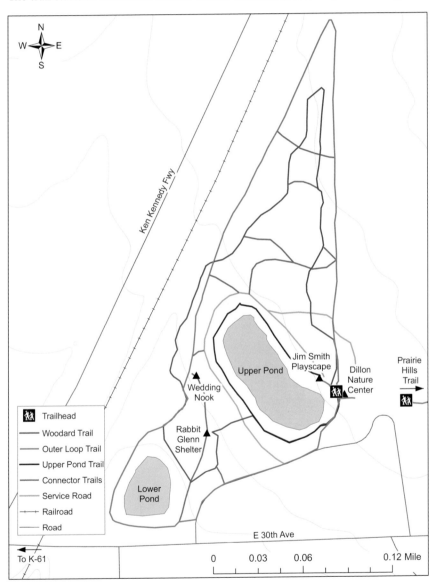

Dillon Nature Center, Woodard Trail

an inspiring, larger-than-life bronze sculpture of a soaring eagle. Follow the blue trail markers as the route meanders through shaded woodlands with a mix of cedars and native hardwoods, which provide shelter for the nearly 200 bird species that have been sighted at the nature center. The trail briefly leaves the woodlands and passes through a small area of restored prairie before continuing around the main pond area. As the trail continues along the edge of the Upper Pond, you have the option of taking the Lower Pond Loop to add a little distance to your hike. The Lower Pond is preserved as a natural area, and it is a nice quiet spot to watch for turtles and frogs on the shaded banks. Shortly after circling the Lower Pond, the Woodard Trail joins the paved loop trail that surrounds the pond as it returns to the visitors' center to complete the hike.

Directions to the trailhead: Take K-61 to Hutchinson and continue until you reach 30th Street. Turn east on 30th Street and continue for half a block to the entrance marked on the north (left) side of the road.

FEATURED TRAIL: PRAIRIE HILLS/WESTAR ENERGY TRAIL

Trail access: Hike.
Distance: 1-mile loop.

Sunrise on the Prairie Hills/Westar Energy Trail. (Photo by Mark Conard)

Dillon Nature Center, Prairie Hills/Westar Energy Trail

On the west side of the Dillon Nature Center parking lot is the trailhead for the Prairie Hills/Westar Energy Trail (38.08780, –97.87544). The exposed, mowed grass trail makes a loop through restored prairie. It's an easy hike, with some gentle hills. The trail crosses a road to the Westar Energy plant north of the trail before it splits into a small loop. Along the south side of the loop, you can access a side trail that takes you to the 9/11 Memorial by the fire station. The memorial was dedicated in June 2012, and it features part of a steel beam from the wreckage of the World Trade Center. Several stone markers and plaques encircle the memorial, and there are benches where you can sit for a moment of reflection before continuing on the trail. Near the eastern edge of the trail is an offshoot that leads to the nearby Prairie Hills Middle School and Lucille Drive. Before you leave, be sure to explore the exhibits at the Dillon Nature Center.

Directions to the trailhead: Take K-61 to Hutchinson and continue until you reach 30th Street. Turn east on 30th Street and continue for half a block to the entrance marked on the north (left) side of the road.

Additional trails: There are several short interconnected trails throughout the Dillon Nature Center, including the Outer Loop Trail (0.86 mile) and the Upper Pond Trail (0.29 mile). The Outer Loop Trail is the longest loop around the nature center pond; it weaves through a mix of wooded areas and restored prairie along the outer edge of the property. The Upper Pond Trail is a paved trail (handicapped accessible) that circles the pond.

Camping: No camping is allowed at the Dillon Nature Center. The closest RV camping is at the Kansas State Fair RV Park (20th and Poplar, Hutchinson, KS 67502; 620-669-3615 or 620-694-6541). It's open for general camping except in the month of September (during the fair). Campsites are also available at Sand Hills State Park.

EL DORADO STATE PARK

The Spanish phrase *El Dorado* translates roughly as "the gilded," and the name was bestowed on a fabled city in South America that was believed to be tremendously rich in gold. There was no gold involved when Captain J. Cracklin named the city of El Dorado, Kansas. He led an expedition from Lawrence in 1857, searching for suitable land to establish a town. When he arrived near the site of the present-day town, the golden hues of the sun shining across the beautiful Walnut River Valley inspired Cracklin to exclaim, "El Dorado!" The only gold ever discovered in El Dorado was "black gold," when the Stapleton #1 well first hit oil in 1915. Since then, the rich oil fields surrounding the town have yielded tremendous amounts of oil.

El Dorado State Park is the largest in Kansas, and it borders one of the newest reservoirs in the state. Established in 1981 by damming the Walnut River, El Dorado Reservoir has more than 8,000 acres of surface water and is a favorite among boaters and anglers. The surrounding state park offers multiple trail options, with a variety of short nature trails in addition to an equestrian trail that winds along the edge of the reservoir in the Boulder Bluff area.

Contact: El Dorado State Park Office, 618 Bluestem Point Road, El Dorado, KS 67042; 316-321-7180.

Hours: 24/7.

Cost: State park fee.

FEATURED TRAIL: BOULDER BLUFF TRAIL

Trail access: Hike, bike, or bridle.

Distance: 12-mile loop.

The Boulder Bluff Trail — the longest in the state park — is a mowed grass trail that loops through open prairie as it parallels the shoreline of the large reservoir. This trail is used primarily as a bridle trail, although hikers and bikers are also welcome. The southernmost trailhead (37.84744, –96.82680) is a good starting point for day users; overnight campers can also access the trail from the campgrounds in the Boulder Bluff area of the state park. If you're starting from the southernmost trailhead, head north and continue along the western edge of the park, parallel to the railroad tracks. Brown carsonite markers indicate the mowed grass route, and metal signs mark each mile. The trail is flat and open for the vast majority of the route, so it is easy to stay oriented. Starting north, the trail splits. You can follow either the eastern or the western branch of the trail as you continue north. The

Boulder Bluff Trail at El Dorado Reservoir. (Photo by Jonathan Conard)

western part of the trail continues to closely parallel the railroad tracks through open grassland, away from the lake. We recommend taking the eastern branch and following the more scenic part of the trail through open tallgrass prairie with interspersed patches of dogwood and other shrubs. The trail passes a junction for an alternate route away from the railroad (37.86118, –96.82644). It then winds back toward the east and north to trace the rocky shoreline of the reservoir, along coves and peninsulas protruding into it. The trail continues north along the edge of the reservoir and passes through several camping areas, including an equestrian camping area and a trailside hitching post (37.88822, –96.80391). Near the Walnut Valley Sailing Club, the trail joins the park road (37.89552, –96.80968) for a short distance before branching back to the east. The northernmost portion of the trail forms a loop that passes through some of the only woodlands along the route and an old rock quarry. From here, the trail loops back to the point where it travels along the park road. You can return to the trailhead by following the western half of the trail near the railroad tracks, or you can retrace your steps along the eastern section of the trail. The eastern part of the trail is recommended, since the western branch is close to the frequently used railroad tracks and lacks scenic lake views. If you want to follow the eastern route but would like a change of scenery, retrace your path south until you reach a cutoff loop marked as an "alternate route away from the railway" (37.87635, –96.81797). This cuts some distance off your return trip and takes you along a broad prairie hilltop with good views of the lake

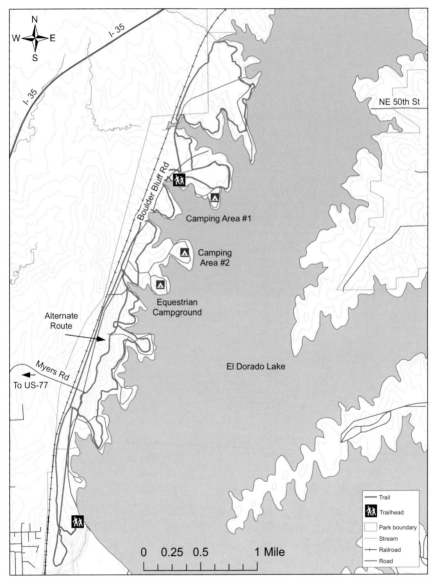

El Dorado State Park, Boulder Bluff Trail

(37.86882, –96.82101). The alternate route soon rejoins the main trail, which can be followed back to the trailhead.

Directions to the trailhead: From the intersection of US-54/US-77 in El Dorado, turn left (north) on US-77 and then turn right (east) on Myers Road. After 1.6 miles, you'll enter the park. Turn right (south) along the paved park road, and continue for 1.1 miles until you reach a parking lot for the trailhead on the west side of the road.

Additional trails: Near the southern trailhead, in the Walnut River area of the state park, there are several shorter trails, including the challenging Double Black Diamond Mountain Bike Trail (2 miles), Teter Nature Trail (0.75 mile), and Walnut Ridge Trail (0.75 mile). These pleasant trails travel through more heavily wooded areas along the Walnut River and Bemis Creek.

Camping: Around the reservoir, the Boulder Bluff, Bluestem Point, Shady Creek, and Walnut River camping areas all have handicapped-accessible facilities. The park has 10 cabins and more than 1,000 campsites, with a mix of primitive and utility sites. Boulder Bluff has an equestrian campground with access to the Boulder Bluff Trail.

HARVEY COUNTY WEST PARK

This 310-acre park was established along the banks of the Arkansas River in the 1930s, providing a favorite location for generations of Harvey County residents to enjoy picnicking, fishing, and swimming in a tranquil natural setting. The park includes a fishing lake, riparian woodlands, and areas of sand prairie that are crisscrossed by hiking and horseback riding trails. The western edge of the park is designated the Sand Hills Natural History Preserve. Its gently rolling hills of sand prairie constitute a unique community of natural vegetation that has stabilized the dunes originally deposited from the wind-blown sand from the nearby riverbed during the late Holocene period.

Contact: Harvey County West Park, 15835 NW 24th Street, Burrton, KS 67020; 316-835-3189.

Hours: 24/7. Trails are closed during deer rifle season.

Cost: The trails are free to hikers but cost $4 per horse/rider.

FEATURED TRAIL: MOWED PATHS

Trail access: Hike or bridle.

Distance: 4 miles total.

The trails at Harvey County West Park offer a variety of options as they wind along the waterside and back into the woodlands characterized by a mix of cedars and shrubs. There are multiple connected trails in the park, so this is one place where you can wander through the trail network and choose whatever interconnecting loops are best suited to your particular time and distance preferences.

Harvey County West Park. (Photo by Amanda Botterweck)

Hikers shouldn't miss the chance to start at the unique suspension footbridge (38.07672, –97.58363) spanning a narrow lake off the Little Arkansas River. The bridge's thick cables and concrete piers are extremely sturdy, yet it's exciting for children and adults alike to carefully edge across the gently swaying footbridge to the opposite shore. Hikers who want to follow the old nature trail, marked by numbered signposts, can turn left at this point and follow the trail counterclockwise as it winds through the woodlands bordering the edge of the small lake for approximately 1 mile. Equestrians or hikers who prefer a longer route can explore the multiuse trails running across the western portion of the park, known as the Sand Hills Natural History Preserve. The mowed trails of this area wind through mixed cedar woodlands and occasional catalpa groves along wide, sandy paths. Other access points are located on the southeastern (38.07313, –97.57871) or northern (38.07936, –96.58562) edge of the trail network.

Directions to the trailhead: From US-50 west of Newton, turn north on Halstead Road, travel for 6 miles, and turn west (left) onto NW 36th Street. After 3.5 miles, turn left onto the park road and follow it south to the ranger station and parking area. Cross the suspension bridge to access the trail network.

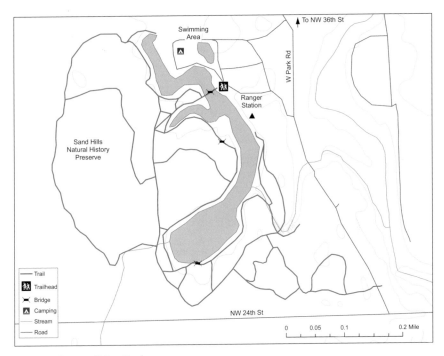

Harvey County West Park

Additional trails: In the eastern part of the county, Harvey County East Park has approximately 5.5 miles of hiking and bridle trails around a 314-acre lake. The trails are free to hikers but cost $4 per horse/rider and are closed during deer rifle season.
Camping: Primitive camping and sites with electricity are available.

LAKE BARTON–GREAT BEND

Even though Lake Barton no longer has a lake, it's still a great recreational site for hikers and mountain bikers. There was once a small lake north of Great Bend, but when the dam was breached, the lake drained. The former lake bed is now encircled by thick cedars and stately cottonwoods, and its center is an open grassland that provides habitat for white-tailed deer and songbirds. If left undisturbed, nature will continue to slowly reclaim the landscape. Experienced mountain bikers will be able to pick up significant speed as they fly through the relatively flat loop trail, while beginners will appreciate the opportunity for an enjoyable ride with few technical obstacles.
Contact: Great Bend Convention and Visitors Bureau, 3007 10th Street, Great Bend, KS 67530; 620-792-2750.
Hours: Daylight hours.
Cost: Free.

Lake Barton. (Photo by Jonathan Conard)

Featured Trail: Lake Barton Trail

Trail access: Hike or bike.
Distance: 2-mile loop.

From the small parking area at the unmarked trailhead (38.44919, –98.77729), a path leads to the loop portion of the trail. The loop can be taken in either direction, for a slightly different twist on the route. If you turn right at the first junction, heading north and following the loop counterclockwise, you'll enter a dense stand of cedars that provides good wind protection and plenty of shade. From here, the dirt single-track trail continues to snake north before bending and revealing a glimpse of the dry lake bed as you emerge from the cedars. Farther to the north lies the dam, which presents riders and hikers with a short but intense climb (38.45429, –98.77891). The trail goes up and down the side of the former dam, and its concrete surface gives mountain bikers a little taste of Moab-like slickrock

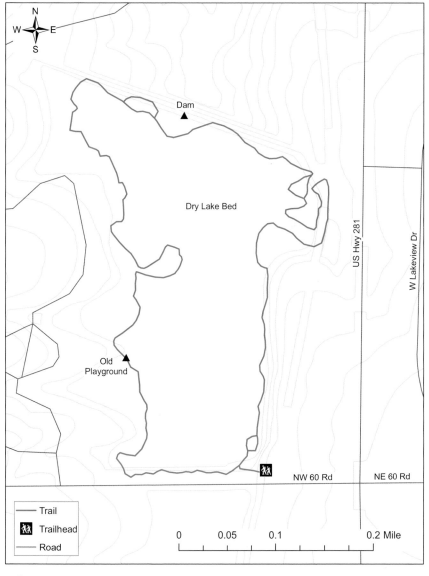

Lake Barton

riding. Past the dam, the trail angles back south as it continues to circle the lake bed. As you continue to loop back toward the trailhead, there's ample indication that this area was once used for other purposes, with abandoned piers and a former playground area (38.45081, –98.77945) slowly becoming overgrown with prairie grasses and shrubs. One former pier has been converted into an elevated log obstacle of sorts, but the safety of crossing the aging structure is questionable. After passing the playground area, the trail goes through a more open mix of cottonwoods and elms as it loops back toward the trailhead to complete the route.

Directions to the trailhead: From the intersection of K-96 and US-281 in Great Bend, go north on US-281 for 5 miles. Turn left (west) onto NW 60th Road and drive for 0.1 mile, where you'll find a small gravel parking lot on the north side of the road.

Additional trails: East of Lake Barton, the Cheyenne Bottoms Wildlife Area is unsurpassed for bird watching and outdoor recreation. Although there are no designated trails, there are miles of gravel roads running along dikes throughout the wetlands complex that can be used by hikers and mountain bikers. The sprawling marshes are one of the premier locations to view birds migrating along the Central Flyway, and the area has been designated a wetland of international importance. For a short hike with the family, try the 0.25-mile George Stumps Nature Trail, located at the Kansas Wetlands Education Center on the southeast side of Cheyenne Bottoms (592 NE K-96, Great Bend, KS 67530; 620-566-1466).

Camping: No camping is allowed at Lake Barton, although there is a primitive campsite located nearby at the Cheyenne Bottoms Wildlife Area (56 NE 40 Road, Great Bend, KS; 620-793-7730). The campsite has no facilities, but it is worth visiting for the bird-watching opportunities. A tremendous variety of migratory waterfowl and shorebirds, including sandhill cranes, frequents the area during the fall and spring. From Lake Barton, go east on NE 60th Road until you reach US-281. From the intersection with US-281, continue east on NE 60th Road for approximately 1.2 miles until you get to the turn-off for the campsite on the south side of the road.

MAXWELL WILDLIFE REFUGE–MCPHERSON STATE FISHING LAKE

Getting up close and personal with free-ranging bison is an unforgettable experience. There are a few places where you can observe bison in Kansas: the Sandsage Bison Range near Garden City, the Konza Prairie south of Manhattan, and the Tallgrass Prairie Preserve in the heart of the Flint Hills. However, one of the best places to see these shaggy beasts is at the Maxwell Wildlife Refuge, just north of Canton. The refuge was acquired by the state of Kansas in 1943 through a generous donation from the estate of Henry Maxwell. Maxwell, the son of one of the early settlers of McPherson County, wanted to preserve the native prairie, complete with bison, for the enjoyment of future generations. Due to his foresight and generosity, present-day visitors can experience the area much as it was in the early

American bison. (Photo by Judd Patterson)

1800s. The Maxwell Wildlife Refuge currently maintains a herd of around 200 bison and 50 elk, making this the only public area in the state where you can observe both species. On the way to the trailhead, take a leisurely drive through the bison enclosure, where you can see the massive bulls and the cow and calf groups grazing on the mixed-grass prairie hills. It's also worthwhile to take a few minutes to climb to the top of the wildlife observation tower, which offers a panoramic view of almost the entire refuge. Please note that visitors are required to stay on designated roads and cannot leave their vehicles when passing through the bison enclosure.

Contact: Maxwell Wildlife Refuge, 2577 Pueblo Road, Canton, KS 67428; 620-628-4592.

Hours: Daylight hours.

Cost: Free.

FEATURED TRAIL: GYPSUM CREEK NATURE TRAIL

Trail access: Hike.

Distance: 0.5 mile, one-way.

From the trailhead (38.47183, –97.47142), located near the edge of the campsites on the west side of McPherson State Fishing Lake, the trail runs south through a wooded area along Gypsum Creek. There are two boardwalk bridges that pass over small waterways feeding into the main creek. The trail forks soon after crossing the bridges. Taking the right branch leads you along a loop that quickly rejoins the other fork as you continue south. After rejoining the main trail, watch for signs of beaver activity as you continue along the packed-dirt trail until you reach the banks of Gypsum Creek. At this point, the trail ends, and the gently flowing creek is an idyllic spot to relax for a few minutes before returning to the trailhead. Note that although there appears to be a trail that continues on the other side of the creek, this path is no longer maintained and quickly fades away.

Directions to the trailhead: From the south, take US-56 and turn north onto 27th Avenue. Drive for 1 mile through Canton and then continue for 6 more miles. Turn left (west) onto Pueblo Road and drive for 2.2 miles. Turn left (southwest) at the first road past the Maxwell Wildlife Refuge Tour Center, and follow the park road for 0.9 mile until it ends in a loop.

Additional trails: The Sunflower–Santa Fe Trail is a 33-mile rail-trail project that will eventually run from McPherson to Marion. You can access the currently completed 2-mile section of trail in the town of Galva, south of the Maxwell Wildlife Refuge.

Camping: McPherson State Fishing Lake has primitive campsites and picnic facilities in wooded campgrounds on the western edge of the lake.

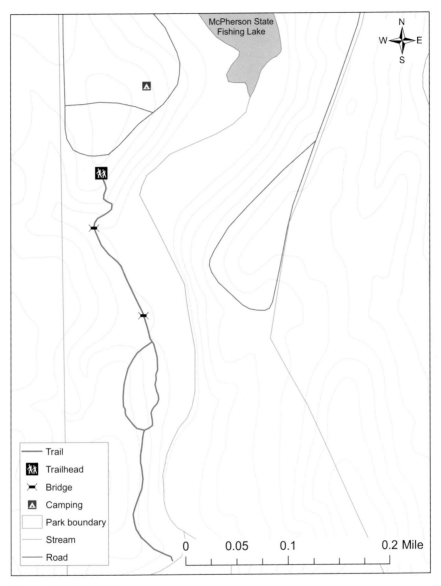

McPherson State
Fishing Lake

Trail
Trailhead
Bridge
Camping
Park boundary
Stream
Road

0   0.05   0.1   0.2 Mile

Maxwell Wildlife Refuge

MEADOWLARK TRAIL–MCPHERSON/LINDSBORG

The former Union Pacific Railroad running from McPherson to Lindsborg is in the process of being converted into a rail trail by the Central Kansas Conservancy. Work on the trail began in 1996. So far, a 4-mile section of trail from McPherson north to Pawnee Road and a 3-mile section from Lindsborg south to Shawnee Road are currently open. The terrain along the trail varies from the gently rolling

Katie and Melissa Conard on the Meadowlark Trail. (Photo by Jonathan Conard)

hills of open farmland north of McPherson to the wooded banks of the Smoky Hill River south of Lindsborg.

Contact: Central Kansas Conservancy Inc., PO Box 322, McPherson, KS 67460.
Hours: Daylight hours.
Cost: Free.

FEATURED TRAIL: MEADOWLARK TRAIL — McPHERSON TO PAWNEE ROAD

Trail access: Hike, bike, or bridle.
Distance: 4 miles, one-way.

From the trailhead in McPherson (38.39125, –97.67613), the trail heads due north along a wide crushed-limestone path. It goes through pastoral fields of golden wheat and large expanses of open farmland, with a few trees scattered along the way. The Meadowlark Trail is very well marked and easy to follow, with wooden signs indicating the names of each intersecting dirt road and distance

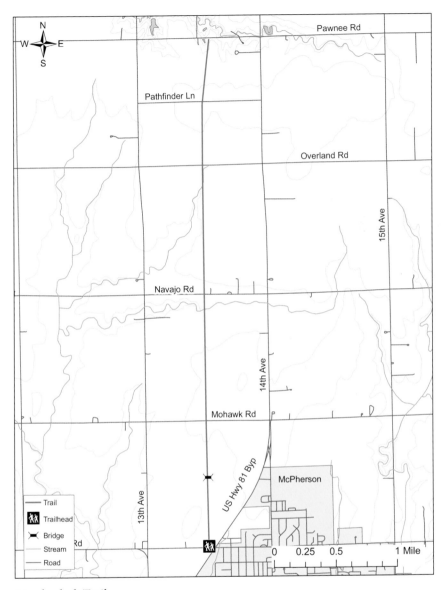

Meadowlark Trail

markers every 0.5 mile. As you enjoy the wide-open views of the countryside, listen for the sweet song of the trail's namesake. At 3.5 miles, the trail passes a grain elevator, which used to be served by the rail line and now stands as a clear landmark in the otherwise flat landscape. The expansive horizon and big sky are showcased throughout the route. Past the grain elevator, the trail continues north and ends at the intersection with Pawnee Road. The trail is exposed along the entire route from McPherson to Pawnee Road, with little protection from the elements.

Directions to the trailhead: Take US-56 to the west edge of McPherson, turn north on old US-81, and drive for 1.6 miles. Turn west onto Moccasin Road. After 0.1 mile, pull off into a small parking area to access the trail to the north.

Additional trails: The 3-mile stretch of the Meadowlark Trail that goes south from Lindsborg to Shawnee Road is shorter but more scenic, as it passes through a wooded corridor with vantage points that overlook the Smoky Hill River. To reach this part of the trail from Lindsborg, follow 1st Street south until it crosses the Smoky Hill River; the trail starts south of the Old Mill Campground. The northernmost end of the Meadowlark Trail adjoins the paved Valkommen ("welcome" in Swedish) Trail, which takes a scenic path through the beautiful city of Lindsborg. A short drive past Lindsborg to the north allows you to access a scenic trail leading through prairie grasses and sandstone outcroppings to an impressive overlook at the top of Coronado Heights.

Camping: No camping is allowed on the trail, although campsites are available in Lindsborg at the Old Mill Campground near the Old Mill Museum, which showcases a fully restored grain mill built in 1898 along the banks of the Smoky Hill River (120 Mill Street, Lindsborg, KS 67456; 785-227-3595).

MILLER'S MEADOW–WICHITA

Miller's Meadow has the distinction of being on private property. The owners have developed a first-rate trail and graciously allow public access for mountain bikers and hikers. When Steve Miller purchased property on the southeast edge of Wichita more than a decade ago, his brother Tim saw an opportunity to develop a mountain biking trail from scratch. With few viable options for off-road biking in the Wichita area, the property's open meadows and woodland patches provided the perfect location for a trail. Tim enlisted help from friends and local mountain biking enthusiasts to undertake the daunting task of carving out more than 4 miles of trail through the hedgerows and woodlands. The result is a fast single-track trail that has become one of the most popular mountain biking destinations in Wichita. Since this is private property, please be especially respectful, and be aware that agricultural, hunting, or other activities may occur at any time.

Contact: Tim Miller, 316-519-4322.

Hours: 24/7.

Cost: Free.

FEATURED TRAIL: MILLER'S MEADOW LOOP

Trail access: Hike or bike.

Distance: 4.5-mile loop.

The trail is marked to be ridden in opposite directions on alternating days, so follow the instructions on the sign at the trailhead to determine which way to go. If you're taking the loop clockwise from the trailhead (37.65006, –97.17518), the

Miller's Meadow Loop. (Photo by Jonathan Conard)

trail heads southwest through a grassy area along the edge of a woodland in a flat and fast section of trail. It then turns due south along an old windbreak of Osage orange trees next to an open crop field. The trail bends sharply east and continues to parallel the hedgerow before making a U-turn and returning west along a narrow path cut through the center of the small row of Osage orange trees. The trail turns north along the edge of the property and continues through the woodland area. This initial section of the trail can be ridden relatively quickly, as there are few sharp turns and limited changes in elevation. The trail briefly leaves the woodlands and loops around an open meadow, where white blooms of yarrow punctuate the grassland, providing a pleasant scene in the early summer. After passing through the meadow and reentering the woodlands along the northwestern edge of the property, the trail's level of difficulty increases as multiple switchbacks cut sharply back and forth across a small intermittent creek and adjoining woodlands.

199

Miller's Meadow

The switchbacks continue to cut across the streambed as you wind your way back toward the trailhead through the shaded woodlands.

Directions to the trailhead: From US-54/400 in Wichita, turn south on S. 143rd Street E./Springdale Drive and continue south for 2 miles until you reach Pawnee Street. Turn right (west) on Pawnee Street and continue for 0.2 mile until you reach a gravel parking area on the south side of the road.

Additional trails: Other trails in the Wichita area include Chisholm Creek Park, Pawnee Prairie Park, and Air Capital Memorial Park (see the featured trails elsewhere in this chapter).

Camping: No camping is allowed at Miller's Meadow. The nearest camping facilities are at Santa Fe Lake (11367 SW Shore Drive, Augusta, KS 67010; 316-775-9926). This small lake is 2 miles north of US-54 on Santa Fe Lake Road and has both primitive and utility campsites.

PAWNEE PRAIRIE PARK

Pawnee Prairie Park encompasses 400+ acres of prairie and riparian woodlands along Cowskin Creek in west Wichita. The park was named for the Native American tribe that ranged throughout present-day Nebraska and Kansas. The name of the creek can be traced back to the early history of the Chisholm Trail, which was used to drive cattle from Texas north across Indian Territory to the railways in Kansas. Texas longhorns that died during these cattle drives were skinned, and the hides were left to dry along the banks of the creek — hence the name Cowskin Creek.

The dense riparian vegetation along the winding creek makes it a good spot to observe a variety of songbirds, particularly during the summer. While on the trail, you may glimpse a red-eyed vireo or even a pileated woodpecker among the forest canopy along the creek banks. Pawnee Prairie Park is one of the largest natural areas within the city limits of Wichita, and its trails are much loved by horse riders, trail runners, and hikers. The marked trails include a paved nature trail and a horse trail named in honor of Marsh and Irene Plumlee, who were instrumental in developing the area for the enjoyment of equestrians.

Contact: Pawnee Prairie Park, 2625 S. Tyler Road, Wichita, KS 67215; 316-683-5499.

Hours: Daylight hours.

Cost: Free.

Riding at Pawnee Prairie Park. (Photo by Jonathan Conard)

FEATURED TRAIL: PLUMLEE HORSE TRAIL

Trail access: Hike or bridle.
Distance: 4.7-mile loop.

The bridle trail starts west from the trailhead by the parking lot through an open grassland before entering a mix of cottonwoods and elms along the banks of Cowskin Creek. The trail turns north at the intersection with a paved concrete

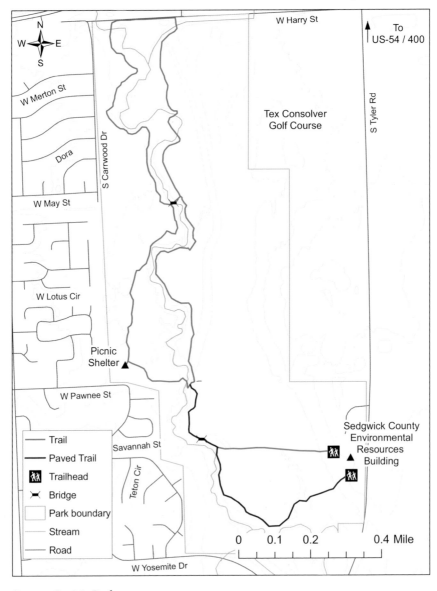

Pawnee Prairie Park

nature trail and continues along the west side of the creek. Several cutoff trails can be taken to the west to cross the creek, but the main trail continues north through woodlands with a thick understory and a mix of cottonwood, black walnut, hackberry, box elder, and honey locust. Watch for poison ivy along the creek, especially if you venture off onto any of the small, unmarked social trails that intermittently crisscross the main trail. The main trail leads you to the northern end of the park near Harry Street. From this point, you can cut back west and pick up the trail as it crosses Cowskin Creek and bends south. The trail continues south along the west edge of the creek and passes through a thick forest of eastern red cedar. As the trail continues south, another trail to the west leads to a picnic shelter and an access point along Pawnee Road. To return to the main trailhead, cross back over the creek and retrace your steps to the east.

Directions to the trailhead: From US-54/400 on the west side of Wichita, exit south on Tyler Road and continue south for 2 miles. The paved parking lot and the building for the Sedgwick County Department of Environmental Resources is on the right (west) side of Tyler Road.

Additional trails: Just north of Pawnee Prairie Park, Air Capital Memorial Park has trails for hiking and mountain biking. Other noteworthy trails in the Wichita area include Miller's Meadow and the 2.5 miles of paved nature trails at Chisholm Creek Park adjacent to the Great Plains Nature Center.

Camping: The nearest location for tent camping is west of Wichita at Lake Afton (24600 W. 39th Street S., Goddard, KS 67052; 316-943-0192). The public observatory at Lake Afton offers museum tours and special programs for viewing the stars and the planets. These programs are held on Friday and Saturday evenings throughout the year (316-978-7827).

PRAIRIE SUNSET TRAIL

The nonprofit Prairie Travelers organization was created to support the building of interconnected trails along preserved rail corridors. Its members are the caretakers and maintainers of the Prairie Sunset Trail, which was once part of the Central Kansas Railway, a 900-mile short-line railroad that transported much of the Kansas wheat harvest. The trail was opened in July 2007, and extends east from Goddard to S. Hoover Road in west Wichita, totaling 15 miles.

Contact: Prairie Travelers, 316-685-4545; prairietravelers.org; prairietravelers@yahoo.com.

Hours: Daylight hours.

Cost: Free.

FEATURED TRAIL: PRAIRIE SUNSET TRAIL—GARDEN PLAIN TO GODDARD

Trail access: Hike, bike, or bridle.

Distance: 8 miles, one-way.

Cecile Kellenbarger Memorial Bridge on the Prairie Sunset Trail. (Photo by Joyce Conard)

The Prairie Sunset Trail runs from Goddard to Garden Plain, with eventual plans to add another 4 miles to Wichita. The one-way trail between 295th Street W. and 167th Street W. can be taken in either direction. Traveling from west to east, there's an overall descent in terms of elevation, although it's a relatively flat trail; traveling from east to west, the elevation changes are gradual. At its western edge in Garden Plain, the trail starts just south of the intersection of S. 295th Street W. and W. Santa Fe Street (37.65633, −97.67953). The covered bridge near the Garden Plain trailhead is a memorial for Cecile Kellenbarger, a cyclist and longtime trail volunteer. It was dedicated on July 4, 2012, to commemorate her passion for the trails of Kansas.

Within 0.25 mile, you'll be out of town and riding along a lightly tree-lined corridor through farmland. About every mile or so there are wooden benches along the wide gravel trail, where you can stop and rest before continuing. The trail alternates between shady and open sections, and in the latter you'll be treated to classic views of Kansas farmland. About 2.75 miles into the trail, you'll head through a small underpass. After a 5.5-mile trek through the countryside, you'll reach the western edge of Goddard. At S. Walnut Street, you'll find yourself on a sidewalk

Prairie Sunset Trail

going through Linear Park. The park has exercise equipment, bathrooms, picnic tables, and a storm shelter — all the emergency necessities. Cross Main Street and continue along E. Santa Fe Street, which crosses S. Goddard Street, and you'll be back on the gravel rail trail for 2 more miles at 167th Street W.

Directions to the trailhead: For the Garden Plain trailhead: From US-54, take the K-163 exit toward Garden Plain/295th Street W. and head south for 1 mile. The trailhead is on the left (east), shortly after the intersection of 295th Street W. and W. Santa Fe Street.

For the trailhead east of Goddard: If you're coming from the north, take K-14/96, turn south on 167th Street W., and continue for 11.5 miles. The trailhead is on the right (west). From the east, take US-54W and turn left (south) onto S. 167th Street W. The trailhead is about 0.4 mile from US-54W.

Additional trails: Nearby Cheney State Park, 12 miles northwest of Garden Plain, features the Geifer Creek Nature Trail (0.13 mile) and the Spring Creek Wildlife Observation Trail (0.75 mile), as well as the 5-mile West Trail for hiking and biking (see the featured trail earlier in this chapter).

Camping: No camping is allowed along the trail; the closest camping is at Cheney State Park (16000 NE 50th, Cheney, KS 67025; 316-542-3664).

QUIVIRA NATIONAL WILDLIFE REFUGE

Quivira National Wildlife Refuge consists of salt marshes and numerous wetlands interspersed with mixed-grass prairie, providing critical habitat for migratory waterfowl. The shallow marshes scattered throughout the refuge have high salinity levels due to the underground saltwater deposits' proximity to the surface. These marshes support unusual plant assemblages that are not often found in Kansas, including salt grass and seepweed along the edges of the wetlands.

In addition to the numerous small wetlands and marshes throughout the refuge, there are two major marshes: Big Salt Marsh, along the north side of the refuge, and Little Salt Marsh, farther south near refuge headquarters. These wetlands are used by a diverse assortment of ducks, geese, and shorebirds as they migrate along the Central Flyway from their northern breeding grounds to their more southerly wintering areas. The refuge provides critical habitat for these migratory species, including the endangered whooping crane. The marshes also provide

Sunset at Quivira National Wildlife Refuge. (Photo by Mark Conard)

habitat for a number of mammal species, including muskrats and beavers. Wildlife is abundant throughout the 22,135 acres of the refuge. It has a large population of white-tailed deer, and they are commonly seen near the woodland areas.

Contact: Quivira National Wildlife Refuge, 1434 NE 80th Avenue, Stafford, KS 67578; 620-486-2393.

Hours: From 1.5 hours before sunrise to 1.5 hours after sunset.

Cost: Free.

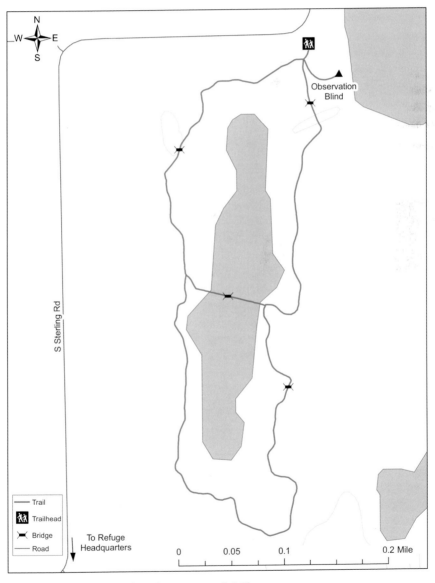

Quivira National Wildlife Refuge, Migrant's Mile

FEATURED TRAIL: MIGRANT'S MILE (TOP FAMILY-FRIENDLY TRAIL)

Trail access: Hike.
Distance: 1.25-mile loop.

Migrant's Mile consists of two loops that circle a wetland marsh embedded in a woodland grove. The trail offers hikers a chance to fully experience the unique sights, sounds, and earthy smells of a wetland marsh, and because there is little topographic variation, it's an easy hike for families. The trail runs south from the trailhead (38.14369, –98.49153) and quickly reaches a four-way junction. The left path is a 75-yard spur that leads to a wildlife viewing blind overlooking a small lake frequented by geese and ducks. The two loops of the trail can be hiked by going either straight or to the right at this four-way junction. If you turn right, the trail winds through a shaded woodland with a mix of cottonwood, honey locust, and elm trees—a favorite spot of white-tailed deer. The trail emerges from the woodland and opens up with a view of the wetland marsh.

Along the edge of this marsh, you'll reach another trail junction. Go straight to continue on the short loop of the trail, which crosses a long wooden footbridge (38.14033, –98.49306) bisecting the marsh before winding back toward the trailhead. Take a right at this junction to hike the long loop, which crosses a boardwalk over a small waterway and continues through open prairie and cedar woodlands before turning north to loop back toward the trailhead.

Directions to the trailhead: From Stafford, go east for 5 miles on US-50 and turn left (north) onto NE 130th Avenue. Follow this road north for 7 miles and turn right (east) onto NE 70th Street/4th Street. After going 1 mile east, turn north (left) onto NE 140th Avenue. Continue north on 140th Avenue through Quivira National Wildlife Refuge for approximately 6.4 miles. After the road bends to the east, there's a gravel pullout by the trailhead on the right.

FEATURED TRAIL: LITTLE SALT MARSH TRAIL (TOP WILDLIFE AND WILDFLOWERS TRAIL)

Trail access: Hike.
Distance: 1 mile.

The trail starts at the Kids' Fishing Pond at the southern end of Quivira National Wildlife Refuge. It curves gently along the edge of the fishing pond before continuing toward Little Salt Marsh to the northwest. After passing the fishing pond, the trail crosses through some former woodlands, where an extensive effort to restore native prairie has succeeded. Prescribed burning is critical to maintain prairie areas, and evidence of frequent fires can be seen on the trunks of the trees that remain in the area.

The trail soon enters open prairie, with an expansive view of Little Salt Marsh. This salt marsh is little in name only, and the impressive expanse of shallow water is often packed with flocks of ducks, geese, and sandhill cranes, especially during

Birds at Little Salt Marsh, Quivira National Wildlife Refuge. (Photo by Mark Conard)

the fall and spring migrations. The trail continues to a Y-junction: the left fork leads to a wildlife viewing blind (38.07995, –98.49282) on the edge of the marsh, and the right fork leads to an observation tower (38.07923, –98.4921), complete with a spotting scope and panoramic views of the wetlands.

Directions to the trailhead: From Stafford, go east 5 miles on US-50 and turn left (north) onto NE 130th Avenue. Follow this road north for 7 miles and turn right (east) onto NE 70th Street/4th Street. After traveling 1 mile east, turn north (left) onto NE 140th Avenue, and continue on this road for 1.1 miles until you see a turn-off and a sign for the Kids' Fishing Pond to your left.

Additional trails: The North Lake Trail, on the north side of the refuge, is a short 0.5-mile hike along a mowed grass path to secluded North Lake. Note that this trail is within a public hunting area.

Birdhouse Boulevard Trail starts from the parking lot of the visitors' center on the south side of Quivira. This 0.25-mile loop crosses through an open prairie

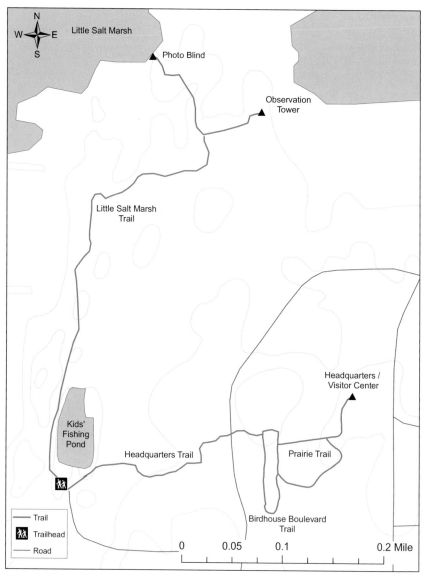

Quivira National Wildlife Refuge, Little Salt Marsh Trail

before looping through a cedar woodland. You can also access the Little Salt Marsh trailhead via a short trail that branches off toward the Kids' Fishing Pond.

Camping: No camping is allowed at Quivira National Wildlife Refuge. Sterling Lake, located 15 miles east of the refuge, is one of the closest campgrounds. It offers electrical hookups and primitive camping beside a small lake in the town of Sterling (E. Van Buren, Sterling, KS 67579; 620-278-3423).

SAND CREEK TRAIL–BETHEL COLLEGE

When the Atchison, Topeka, and Santa Fe Railroad extended to Newton in 1871, the town replaced Abilene as the main shipping point for cattle driven north from Texas. The arrival of the railroad brought a tremendous and immediate cowboy influence to the town, and the area had a wild and woolly reputation in those days. When the railhead extended to Wichita and Dodge City, the cattle trade moved as well, and Newton gradually lost its status as the "wickedest little city in the West."

In 1886 Mennonite immigrants founded North Newton and established Bethel College in 1887, making it the oldest Mennonite school in the country. A strong Mennonite influence remains. Notable contributions included the introduction of Turkey Red winter wheat to the area, which helped establish Kansas's reputation as the breadbasket of America. Whereas the cattle trails from the early days of Newton are preserved only in memory, the Sand Creek Trail on the Bethel College campus provides an opportunity to hike in an area rich in history.

Contact: Bethel College, PO Box 179, North Newton, KS 67117; 316-283-7965.
Hours: Daylight hours.
Cost: Free.

FEATURED TRAIL: SAND CREEK TRAIL

Trail access: Hike or bike.
Distance: 2.1-mile loop.

The trailhead for the Sand Creek Trail is located at Memorial Grove on the eastern edge of the Bethel College campus (38.07549, –97.34077). Memorial Grove was established in 2003 to provide a place for contemplation, worship, and quiet reflection in a natural setting. The area is popular with both students and community residents, who frequently gather on the benches under the gazebo and around the limestone fire pit in the center of the grove. From Memorial Grove, the trail starts west, parallel to the Kidron-Martin Canal, which was built in 1925 to channel water into the Sand Creek drainage in an effort to alleviate flooding from nearby Kidron Creek. The trail turns north and parallels the meandering route of Sand Creek. It is well maintained with a wood-chip surface, and markers identify tree species along the way. The section of trail along Sand Creek is the most scenic, passing through the peaceful shade of elms and hackberries within sight of the creek. Continue straight at the trail junction as you leave the riparian woodlands and turn west along a section of trail paralleling the highway. The trail turns south and passes through what is known as Arbor Lane, a double row of trees planted in 2006 to showcase 18 different species along the main entrance to the community of North Newton. Upon reaching the Mennonite Central Committee building, the trail turns back east, and you can take the straight path to complete a small loop that returns you to the first segment of the trail. After completing the loop section, turn south to return to the trailhead at Memorial Grove.

Sand Creek Trail in North Newton. (Photo by David Welfelt)

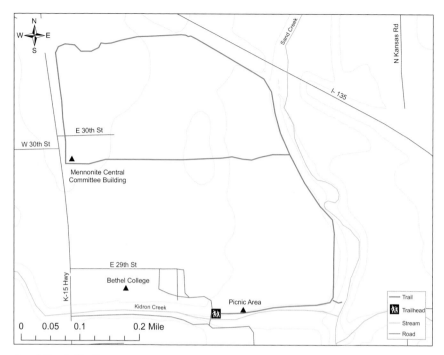

Sand Creek Trail

Directions to the trailhead: From I-35, take exit 34 toward K-15. Take K-15 south and turn east (left) onto 29th Street. Follow this road past the parking lot and tennis courts; it bends to the south and then turns back southeast to the pullout for a parking area by Memorial Grove, where the trailhead is located.

Additional trails: The Sand Creek Trail is the only one in the immediate area; there are multiuse trails at Harvey County West Park and Harvey County East Park.

Camping: No camping is permitted in Memorial Grove or along the trail. The nearest camping is at Athletic Park (700 W. 1st Street, Newton, KS 67114). This 39-acre facility is the recreational hub of the city of Newton. It hosts a variety of community activities and provides amenities such as athletic fields, a band shell, and a public pool.

SAND HILLS STATE PARK

Over countless generations, the nearly constant Kansas wind has shaped the extensive sand deposits from the Arkansas River into a series of distinct dunes. While recounting his travels along the Arkansas River, Zebulon Pike noted, "These vast plains of the western hemisphere, may become in time equally celebrated as the sandy deserts of Africa, for I saw in my route, in various places, tracts of many

Autumn at Sand Hills State Park. (Photo by Mark Conard)

leagues, where the wind had thrown up the sand, in all the fanciful forms of the ocean's rolling wave, and on which not a speck of vegetable matter existed." Today, these formerly active and shifting sand dunes in the 1,123-acre state park have been stabilized by the roots of big sandreed, sand bluestem, and sand dropseed — the core components of a unique assemblage of plants in the region's sand prairie landscape. This is one of the few state parks in Kansas that is not associated with a reservoir, and the trails weaving amidst the dunes are the main attraction. The entire area is maintained in a natural state, and there are no developed roads within the park itself. The dunes rise up to 40 feet high, adding considerable topographic variation to an otherwise flat landscape. The flora of the park is dominated by the grasses and shrubs of the sand prairie carpeting the rolling dunes, but there are also opportunities for woodland hiking.

Contact: Sand Hills State Park, c/o Cheney State Park, 16000 NE 50th, Cheney, KS 67025; 316-542-3664.
Hours: 24/7.
Cost: State park fee.

Featured Trail: Prairie Trail

Trail access: Hike, bike, or bridle.
Distance: 1.9-mile loop, 14 miles total.

The park north of Hutchinson includes eight interconnected trails ranging in length from 1 to 4 miles, with a total of 14 miles of hiking and biking trails within the park. To navigate the network of mowed trails, it helps to keep an eye on the trail markers, which clearly indicate each separate route. All the trails are accessible from parking lots located along 56th Avenue on the park's south border and along 69th Avenue on its north border.

The Prairie Trail starts from the trailhead on 56th Street (38.11598, −97.85896). After a short hike north through a woodland patch, the trail opens up into a mix of plum thickets and prairie-covered dunes. Hikers can take a quick side trip on a steep trail that ascends a massive 40-foot dune to an overlook point with a panoramic view of the rest of the park. After descending from the dune overlook, continue north along the trail's left branch. The Prairie Trail goes north past the turn-off point for the Dune Trail, which can be taken to form a shorter 1-mile loop that returns to the trailhead. Continue north along the Prairie Trail until you reach the turnaround point near the northern end of the park. As the trail returns south toward the trailhead, it passes through woodland areas that provide shade and habitat for a variety of songbirds, such as Bell's vireo and the orchard oriole. On either side of the trail, note the numerous broken limbs and downed trees that fell during a fierce ice storm in 2007. As the years pass, fungi and other decomposers will break down these fallen trees, and new seedlings will grow to claim a place amongst the canopy. As the trail continues south, watch for an old windmill and a number of scattered nest boxes built for songbirds. The Prairie Trail rejoins the Dune Trail and continues south before returning to the trailhead.

Directions to the trailhead: The trail can be accessed off of K-61, which runs between Hutchinson and McPherson. From K-61 just north of Hutchinson, exit onto 56th Avenue. Follow this road east for 0.8 miles to the parking area and trailhead on the north side of the road.

Additional trails: The 1-mile Dune Trail is recommended for a family-friendly hike that includes climbing a 40-foot dune with a scenic overlook of the park. The Cottonwood Trail is a 0.5-mile interpretive hiking trail that forms a loop; its many markers indicate points of interest along the way, and a trail guide is available at the kiosk at the 69th Street trailhead.

For horses, the best trails include the popular Rolling Hills Trail, which forms a 3.8-mile loop that can be started from either 56th Street or 69th Street. The

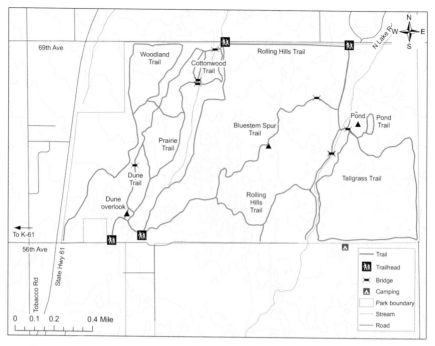

Sand Hills State Park

Bluestem Spur Trail bisects the Rolling Hills Trail and provides an alternate route to complete the loop. The Tallgrass Trail forms a 2.2-mile loop in the southeast corner of the park and connects with the Rolling Hills Trail to add distance to either route. The 2.2-mile Woodland Trail winds through stately cottonwoods along the western edge of the park and along a loop route frequented by equestrians.

Camping: A state park campground equipped with facilities for equestrians is located along the south side of 56th Street, near the east end of Sand Hills State Park. For a unique urban camping experience, try the fairgrounds in nearby Hutchinson, where RV sites are available except during the Kansas State Fair in September (20th and Poplar, Hutchinson, KS 67502; 620-669-3615 or 620-694-6541).

TALLGRASS PRAIRIE NATIONAL PRESERVE

Nowhere is the natural beauty of Kansas more evident than among the sea of grasses blanketing the Flint Hills. In many ways, the prairie *is* Kansas, bringing together the sky, sun, wind, and grass in ways that can't be experienced elsewhere. The vast, unbroken expanses of grasslands that once formed the distinctive tallgrass prairie ecosystem of North America have been diminished tremendously. However, Kansas holds a place of pride as one of the last strongholds of the tallgrass prairie, and at the Tallgrass Prairie National Preserve, you can still walk on miles of trails leading to seemingly endless vistas.

Lower Fox Creek School at Tallgrass Prairie National Preserve. (Photo by Mark Conard)

Periodic fires once swept naturally across the prairie. Today, fire is an important management tool and is used to promote the growth of prairie grasses and destroy any trees that venture too far from the bottomlands near creeks and streams. Grasslands are not complete without large grazers, including the noble bison. Although this part of the tallgrass prairie was spared from the plow due to the underlying limestone and chert of the Flint Hills, the native bison were replaced by herds of cattle that thrived on the prairie grasses. In addition to grazers, the grasslands provide excellent breeding habitat for migratory songbirds. If you hike during the spring and early summer, you may catch a glimpse of a prairie chicken or be serenaded by dickcissels, upland sandpipers, grasshopper sparrows, and meadowlarks.

Contact: Tallgrass Prairie National Preserve Visitor Center, 2480B KS Highway 177, Strong City, KS 66869; 620-273-8494.
Hours: 24/7.
Cost: Free.

FEATURED TRAIL: CRUSHER HILL LOOP

Trail access: Hike. No pets allowed on backcountry hiking trails.
Distance: 3.6-mile loop.

In the southwest section of the preserve, the fairly challenging Crusher Hill Loop offers great open views of the Flint Hills tallgrass prairie. The trail's unusual name is derived from a former rock-crushing operation on this part of the property. Starting behind the large stone barn at the ranch complex, go south on the gravel double-track trail through the West Traps Pasture gate and continue until you reach an intersection about 350 feet past the first gate. At this intersection, the gravel double track continues toward the scenic overlook, and the trail that branches south takes you to the Crusher Hill Loop via the Ranch Legacy Trail, which winds south past an intersection with the Z Bar Spur Trail (38.43053, –96.55820) and next to pens used in ranching operations on the preserve. The trail crosses a small intermittent stream before turning east; it's worth noting that there are no bridges across many of the small streams throughout the preserve, so be prepared to get your feet wet if you're hiking after a recent rain. As you ascend toward the intersection with the Crusher Hill Loop, note the abundance of milkweed plants, which attract a variety of butterfly species, including the rare regal fritillary and the stately monarch butterfly. Turn left to start the Crusher Hill Loop, which descends to a scenic grove of cottonwoods (38.42122, –96.58401) that provides welcome shade and a great spot for a break. Meandering through the grove is a trickling stream filled by clear, cool water from a nearby natural spring. If you look closely, you can see the ruins of an old homestead north of the grove. As you leave the cottonwood grove, the trail ascends sharply as it approaches the intersection with the Ranch Legacy Trail. From here, you can either follow the path back toward the trailhead or head north on the Ranch Legacy Trail, which will take you to the Scenic Overlook Trail, and continue hiking the trail network that stretches north across the preserve.

FEATURED TRAIL: SCENIC OVERLOOK TRAIL (TOP WILDLIFE AND WILDFLOWERS TRAIL AND TOP 10 TRAIL)

Trail access: Hike. No pets allowed on backcountry hiking trails.
Distance: 3.2 miles, one-way.

This route takes you to the highest point in the Tallgrass Prairie National Preserve. From the overlook, miles of unbroken grassland stretch out in all directions, and it's easy to envision how the world appeared to early explorers and settlers as

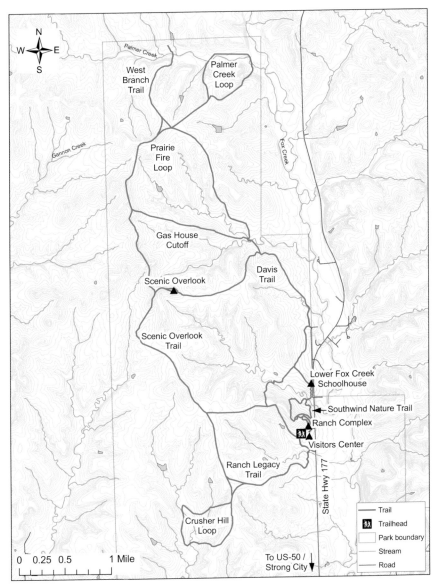

Tallgrass Prairie National Preserve

they passed through the Flint Hills. The hike starts behind the massive limestone barn built by Stephen F. Jones to house livestock and draft horses. From the back of the barn, follow the gravel road into West Traps Pasture. The route is easy to follow, since the limestone gravel surface continues all the way to the top of the overlook point. The trail passes a small pond before intersecting with the Davis Trail (38.43741, –96.56640) and entering Windmill Pasture. Windmill Pasture is

Tallgrass Prairie National Preserve. (Photo by Joyce Conard)

home to a resident bison herd, so watch carefully for these regal beasts; the herd of 20 to 30 may be scattered throughout the 1,100-acre pasture. Feel free to observe the bison, but park officials ask that hikers stay on the trail for their own safety and to avoid disturbing the animals.

As the trail continues, you'll slowly but steadily gain elevation as you pass an intersection to the Ranch Legacy Trail and continue northeast through Windmill Pasture. In addition to bison, this is a good spot to watch for prairie chickens. In the spring, prairie chickens congregate in areas known as leks, where they perform elaborate (and entertaining) breeding rituals complete with "booming" vocalizations, foot drumming, and showy displays from the competitive male suitors.

From Windmill Pasture, the trail ascends into Big Pasture, where you are close to the high point of the hike. The final ascent is a short but steep climb that takes you to an overlook where you can view the preserve's entire sweeping vista (38.45576, −96.58459). From the overlook point, the most direct route to the trailhead is to return the way you came, but you can add variety to your hike by returning via the Davis Trail. To access the Davis Trail, continue east past the scenic overlook point, where you'll descend along a flat ridge to reach the trail. The Davis Trail continues to slowly descend toward Lower Fox Creek and loops back toward the trailhead. It passes within view of the one-room Lower Fox Creek School, which was built from native limestone in 1882. The Schoolhouse Spur Trail can be taken directly to the schoolhouse for further exploration. The Davis Trail crosses several intermittent streams without bridges, which may present a challenge after a rain.

Directions to the trailhead: From US-50 just west of Strong City, turn north onto K-177 and drive for 3.1 miles before turning into the visitors' center parking lot to the west.

Additional trails: From the Scenic Overlook Trail, it's possible to venture farther north into the prairie hills along the Prairie Fire Loop, adding 5.9 miles to your route.

For a shorter trek, children love hiking from the ranch headquarters to the picturesque Lower Fox Creek Schoolhouse. The schoolhouse is located on land donated by Stephen F. Jones and was constructed from native stone by the same architect who built the ranch house and the Chase County courthouse in Cottonwood Falls. The schoolhouse was completed in 1882 and served as the primary school for children in the area until it closed in 1930. If you're starting from ranch headquarters, take the Southwind Nature Trail loop (1.9 miles), which has a short spur leading to the schoolhouse. The trail goes through prairie that can't be grazed, so you can actually experience the tallgrass prairie.

For a change of scenery, try the nature trails on the east side of the preserve. The Fox Creek Nature Trail (6.1-mile loop) and the Bottomland Nature Trail (0.75-mile loop) take visitors along the narrow strip of bottomland forest bordering scenic Fox Creek. Catch-and-release fishing is allowed in sections of Fox Creek, and leashed pets are permitted on these nature trails.

Camping: No camping is allowed in the preserve, but nearby Chase State Fishing Lake is a great option for free primitive camping (1130 Lake Road, Council Grove, KS 66846; 620-767-5900). Be sure to visit the scenic waterfall along the spillway below the dam and explore the 383 acres of Flint Hills prairie surrounding the lake, which is managed as a wildlife area.

CHAPTER 7

NORTHWEST KANSAS

While I know the standard claim is that Yosemite, Niagara Falls, the upper Yellowstone and the like, afford the greatest natural shows, I am not so sure but the Prairies and Plains, while less stunning at first sight, last longer, fill the esthetic sense fuller, precede all the rest, and make North America's characteristic landscape.

WALT WHITMAN

Cedar Bluff Reservoir. Photo by Jonathan Conard

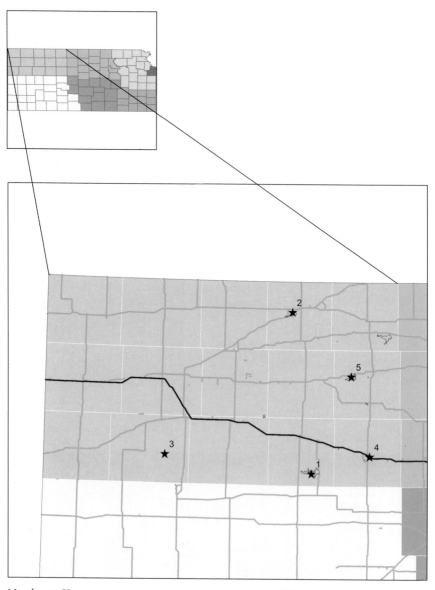

Northwest Kansas

1. Cedar Bluff State Park
2. Prairie Dog State Park
3. Smoky Valley Ranch
4. Sternberg Museum of Natural History
5. Webster Lake

The northwest region of Kansas consists primarily of the High Plains, although it also includes the northern and western reaches of the Smoky Hills. The state's highest point — Mount Sunflower — is located here, in Wallace County near the Colorado border. The region is predominantly open prairie and cropland with long, rolling hills; occasional chalk buttes and bluffs; and woodlands near rivers and lakes. It's also geologically significant as a depository for fossils from the Cretaceous period. What is now fairly flat grassland was, millions of years ago, an inland sea that was home to all sorts of unique creatures. This inland sea and the regions later used by the Paleo-Indians as hunting grounds have resulted in some amazing archeological discoveries.

CEDAR BLUFF STATE PARK

Cedar Bluff State Park is located on the western edge of the Smoky Hills, where the stark limestone outcroppings accentuate the beauty of the rugged bluffs throughout the area. The reservoir was completed in 1951 and provides a variety of outdoor recreational opportunities, including renowned black bass fishing. The current site of Cedar Bluff Reservoir is along the route of the Smoky Hill Trail, which ran west through Kansas toward the gold fields of Colorado. Blufton Station, a stop along the Smoky Hill Trail, was located just north of the current reservoir. The Agave Ridge Nature Trail is located on the south side of the reservoir amidst the towering limestone bluffs and shallow canyons in the secluded Page Creek area.

Contact: Cedar Bluff State Park, 32001 147 Highway, Ellis, KS 67637; 785-726-3212; CedarBluffSP@ksoutdoors.com.

Hours: 24/7.

Cost: State park fee.

FEATURED TRAIL: AGAVE RIDGE NATURE TRAIL (TOP 10 TRAIL)

Trail access: Hike or bike.

Distance: 5-mile loop.

The trail is located along the south shore of the reservoir at the west end of the Page Creek area. The trailhead is marked with a kiosk and has a small parking area (38.77713, –99.78699). The trail system combines a short paved nature trail loop with a more challenging 4.1-mile route that branches off and crosses rugged canyons and scenic limestone bluffs throughout the backcountry of the Page Creek area. Take the paved loop of the Agave Ridge Nature Trail until it branches off and follows a mowed grass path in a southerly direction. The trail crosses an old double-track road and descends gradually into a canyon before reaching a sparse stand of cottonwoods that shade the bed of an intermittent creek. Shortly after

Cedar Bluff Reservoir. (Photo by Jonathan Conard)

crossing a wide wooden bridge (38.76908, –99.79209), you'll reach a fork in the trail. Follow the trail markings and go right at this junction.

The right fork leads you north toward the shoreline of Cedar Bluff Reservoir, where there are expansive views of the lake and surrounding bluffs. The trail ascends across a ridge before reaching the high point of the journey — a scenic overlook complete with a bench atop a tall bluff with panoramic views (38.77838,

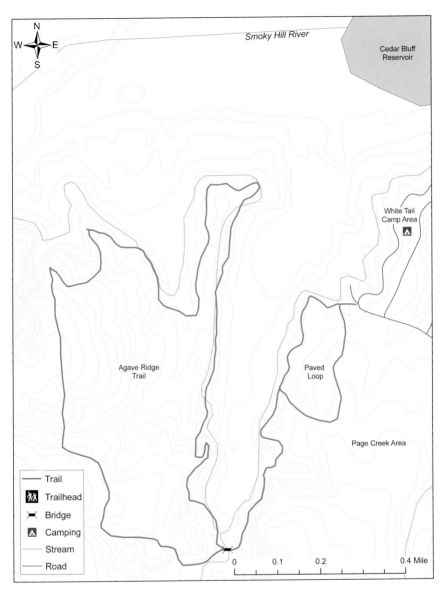

Cedar Bluff State Park

–99.80026). During the early summer, there is a profusion of wildflowers along the route; especially beautiful along this particular section are the vibrant red-orange blooms of Indian blanketflower carpeting the upland ridges. From the overlook point, the trail turns south along an upland ridge before descending again into the canyon below. On this southernmost portion of the trail, you'll have a nice view of the towering limestone formations along the canyon walls to the south. The loop then rejoins the initial segment of trail, which takes you back to the paved nature trail and trailhead.

Directions to the trailhead: From I-70, take exit 135 toward Ogallah and turn south on K-147. Follow K-147 south for 19 miles and turn right (west) onto CC Road and drive for 3.5 miles. Take a right at the fork and follow this road for 1.6 miles before turning left onto a state park road that will take you to the trailhead on the left side of the road.

Additional trails: On the north side of the reservoir near the Blufton area is an unmaintained trail that leads into Threshing Machine Canyon. For a short time, this site was a station stop along the Butterfield Overland Dispatch route, used by stagecoach travelers and traders to head west. Early travelers described the area as picturesque, and it was a popular camping site even after the station was moved 3 miles west to White Rock. The canyon's name is derived from events that transpired in 1867, when a party transporting a threshing machine to Utah was ambushed and massacred by Native Americans. This trail is within the Cedar Bluff Wildlife Area, so check with the park office before visiting, since the area is closed at certain times of the year.

Camping: The Page Creek area on the south shore of Cedar Bluff Reservoir has some of the best primitive campsites in the park, and utility sites are also available. These campsites are typically more secluded than those in the Blufton area. The Whitetail Camp Area and the Comanche Camp Area are some of the closest campgrounds to the trailhead and have multiple campsites available. On the western edge of the reservoir, Cedar Bluff Wildlife Area has free primitive campsites with no facilities.

PRAIRIE DOG STATE PARK

This park along the north shore of the Keith Sebelius Reservoir, near Norton, is distinguished by the large prairie dog statue that greets visitors at the entrance. The 1,150-acre park is made up of shortgrass prairie, and it features an active and growing prairie dog town. Large underground colonies like this one may be hard to find, since black-tailed prairie dogs have been regarded as pests that eat the grass needed by cattle. They are sometimes poisoned or shot. However, here in the state park, the prairie dogs' network of tunnels is protected, and the population of these highly social animals is growing.

Prairie dogs make their homes on the shortgrass prairie because the low vegetation makes it easy for them to see any nearby predators. They are also an important part of the shortgrass prairie ecosystem. As they dig, they stir up the soil, allowing short grasses such as buffalo grass to grow. Their empty burrows are used by other species, including cottontail rabbits and burrowing owls. And prairie dogs are a source of food for the endangered black-footed ferret, which was once thought to be extinct.

Prairie Dog State Park. (Photo by Mark Conard)

Despite the prairie dog town in the park, it was actually named after Prairie Dog Creek, which runs into the reservoir. History buffs can check out the one-room Hillman Schoolhouse, which was built in 1886 in northwestern Norton County and moved to its current location, near the park office, in the 1960s. The renovated adobe house near the Prairie Dog Campground was built by the John Spencer family in the 1890s; it's the only adobe house in Kansas that's still in its original location. And for lake lovers, the 1,000-acre Keith Sebelius Reservoir is open for boating, water-skiing, and fishing.

Contact: Prairie Dog State Park, 13037 State Highway 261, Norton, KS 67654; 785-877-2953.

Hours: 24/7.

Cost: State park fee.

FEATURED TRAIL: STEVE MATHES NATURE TRAIL (TOP FAMILY-FRIENDLY TRAIL)

Trail access: Hike.

Distance: 1.2-mile loop.

Built in 1991 with funding from the National Recreational Trails Funding Act, the Steve Mathes Nature Trail is named for a longtime employee of the Kansas

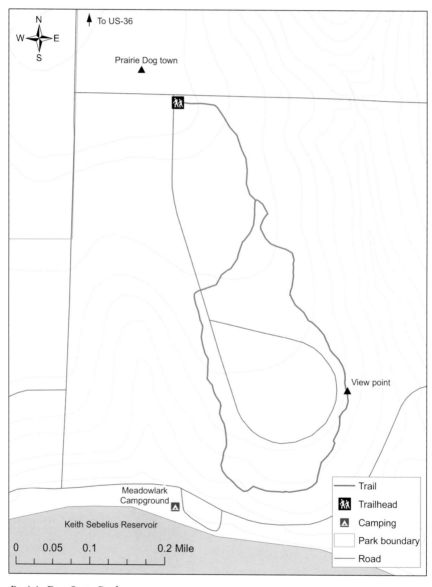

Prairie Dog State Park

state parks system. It is relatively flat and wide, making it ideal for a family hike. The trailhead (39.80905, –99.96235) and a parking area are just south of the prairie dog town. As you arrive at the trailhead, you're likely to hear their high-pitched barks and yips and see a quick flurry of activity as the prairie dogs duck back underground. If you're patient and quiet, they'll eventually emerge and go about their business.

The first 0.25 mile of the easy loop trail is paved, a 2009 improvement to make part of the trail handicapped accessible. At the end of the paved section is a covered bench that offers some shade on the otherwise exposed trail. The trail splits at the bench: you can walk the loop either clockwise or counterclockwise along the wide, packed-dirt trail. There are markers every 0.25 mile and interpretive signs with information about the prairie ecosystem and the flora and fauna. In addition to prairie dogs, keep an eye out for a variety of other wildlife, including mule deer, cottontail rabbits, ring-necked pheasants, bald eagles, and migrating Canada geese. During the spring and summer, wildflowers such as common milkweed are in bloom, and warblers, thrushes, and other songbirds can be heard. On the southern portion of the loop, the reservoir can be seen from the trail. About halfway around the loop is another shaded bench, and just after that is a short spur south to the Meadowlark Campground (39.80119, –99.95976). If you're hiking the trail clockwise, when you cross the paved park road, you have about 0.25 mile left until the loop ends back at the bench, and it's another 0.25 mile on the sidewalk back to the trailhead.

Directions to the trailhead: From Norton, take K-383S/US-36W west out of town for about 4 miles. Turn left (south) on K-261 and continue for just over 1 mile. The park is on the left (east).

Additional trails: Although there are no other nonpaved trails, the park roads make a loop connecting the campsites, offering a leisurely bike ride.

Camping: There are a handful of campgrounds near the lake throughout the park, with primitive and utility sites; water is available from mid-April through mid-October. The park also has four modern cabins and handicapped-accessible camping.

SMOKY VALLEY RANCH

In Logan County, the Nature Conservancy owns and maintains the 16,800-acre Smoky Valley Ranch. Purchased in 1999, it combines both subtle and dramatic landscapes — miles of gently rolling shortgrass prairie combined with impressive chalk bluffs and ravines. It's a large working ranch, not a public park. Land is leased to local ranchers for cattle grazing, and the rough pasture section, which contains the trails, is open to hikers. The Nature Conservancy in Kansas has been working to preserve this area as one of ecological, geological, and cultural significance.

Some unusual and threatened species make their home out on the remote prairie. Prairie dogs were much more common on the prairie before the 1900s, and

American badger at Smoky Valley Ranch. (Photo by Judd Patterson)

so were black-footed ferrets — a prairie dog predator. But with the conversion of much of the native shortgrass prairie to cropland, and with ranchers' prolonged attacks on prairie dogs, the black-footed ferret was left with little to eat and began to die out; it was placed on the federal endangered species list in 1964 and declared extinct in 1979. However, after the 1981 discovery of a small population in Wyoming, and after years of careful monitoring, ten black-footed ferrets were reintroduced to the Smoky Valley Ranch in 2007 by the US Fish and Wildlife Service. This rare nocturnal mammal has once again made a place for itself on the prairies of western Kansas.

Another species on the brink is the green toad. Threatened in Kansas, it can be found in only three Kansas counties, one of which is Logan County. Although the green toad lives within the Smoky Valley Ranch, it can be tricky to spot: despite its bright green and yellow color, it's less than 2 inches long. Count yourself lucky if you observe a green toad or one of the region's other wildlife species, including the lesser prairie chicken, swift fox, and American badger. With a distinctive gait that's a bit like a waddle and a broad, flat body, the badger is a fierce and solitary creature described in Native American folklore as hardworking and protective.

The ranch is also full of history. The area has been used as hunting grounds for thousands of years, including by the Cheyenne and the Arapaho. In 1895, on what would become Smoky Valley Ranch, researchers discovered the first physical evidence that humans were in North America at the end of the last ice age. They found the site of a bison jump, where Paleo-Indians drove bison over a cliff. Bison, of course, were an important source of food and supplies.

Contact: The Nature Conservancy, Kansas Chapter, 700 SW Jackson Street, Suite 804, Topeka, KS 66603; 785-233-4400; Kansas@tnc.org.

Hours: Daylight hours.

Cost: Free.

FEATURED TRAIL: LONG LOOP

Trail access: Hike. No dogs allowed.

Distance: 5.3-mile loop.

The trail names at Smoky Valley Ranch are straightforward and descriptive. The two trails are the Short Loop, at about 1.3 miles, and the Long Loop, at about

Cretaceous formations at Smoky Valley Ranch. (Photo by Kristin Conard)

5.3 miles; both are designed to be hiked counterclockwise, and they're both within the 1,100-acre portion of the ranch called Rough Pasture — an apt name. The trails are narrow and may be uneven; at times, they're easily confused with nearby cattle trails that occasionally cross the main trail. Part of Smoky Valley Ranch is leased to local ranchers for cattle grazing, so there may be cattle in the pasture, but they're not likely to bother you. The same can't be said of the sun and the wind. The trail goes through open pasture that's entirely exposed, so be prepared for the elements. This is a good hike for anyone who likes solitude and wide open spaces.

From the parking lot and the wooden sign at the trailhead for both trails (38.88758, –101.01826), pass through a gate and bear right. Make note of the two trees west of the trailhead. From high points along the trail you'll probably be able to see them, which will help orient you. The trail is a single-track natural path, and 0.25 mile into the hike you'll be treated with a view of some impressive Cretaceous formations (38.88498, –101.01900). During the Cretaceous period, the area that is now Kansas was an inland sea where large marine reptiles, sharks, and giant clams lived. Well-preserved fossil remnants from this period have been unearthed in these chalk badlands.

The trail splits at around 0.75 mile from the beginning (38.88163, –101.01380), with the Short Loop turning back north and west and the Long Loop continuing east and south. The trail follows the gently rolling landscape with some ups and downs in the terrain. Not long after the trail splits, you'll cross a typically dry creek bed (38.87533, –101.00478) on the way to the mile 1 stone marker (all the miles are marked with large stones). Only after a heavy rainfall is there likely to be standing water in the creek bed. Between mile markers 1 and 2, you'll pass a large tree (trees are a big deal in northwestern Kansas) down a small drop-off along the banks of Twelve Mile Creek.

This cliff near Twelve Mile Creek was the site where Charles Wood found the first evidence that humans lived in North America after the last ice age. Wood discovered this Paleo-Indian site in 1895 after a June storm washed away soil along the cliffs near the creek. Some University of Kansas scientists happened to be in the area, and they excavated bones from 10 giant bison and a spear point. This striking archaeological evidence enhanced our understanding of how people spread to North America. However, the discovery was marked by scandal. The spear point was photographed and taken to the University of Kansas museum in Lawrence. Following a lecture about its discovery, the box containing the spear point was passed around the room; the box was later found to be empty, and the spear point has never been returned.

After stone mile marker 2 (38.87383, –100.99933), the trail becomes less distinct as it runs along the cliff edges. Narrow white posts have been placed to help guide you along the small ridges as they curve and wind around the rocky ridge. A farm road runs from 370th Road to a water tank within the Long Loop, and between mile markers 2 and 3, you'll cross this faint farm road a couple of times (38.87581, –100.99483 and 38.87617, –100.99357).

It's easy to get turned around on the trail, where the open vistas contain few landmarks. In addition to the farm road, cattle trails leading to water sources look very similar to the hiking trail itself. Between mile markers 2 and 3, keep the short chalk cliffs to your right (east) until you pass mile marker 3 (38.88043, –100.99122). As you continue through the pasture, your next landmark is an old windmill, with just the cement pit remaining. At 0.25 mile past mile marker 3 (with the cement pit to your right), you'll start heading back west (38.88322, –100.99101). To the north, you may see cattle grazing in nearby pastures. The occasional brown flex trail marker will help guide you to mile marker 4 (38.88530, –101.00277), on the other side of Twelve Mile Creek. In the streambed, even during a dry summer, wildflowers such as white beardtongue may be growing. The trail continues west and north, with a series of small hills along the way. The final stretch back to the trailhead, after the intersection of the Short and Long Loops (38.88477, –101.01460) and mile marker 5 (38.88570, –101.01575), is a gradual uphill climb over the pasture and back to the parking area.

Directions to the trailhead: From Oakley, follow US-40W to the western edge of Monument, Kansas. Turn left (south) on 350th Road and continue for 15 miles. Parking at the trailhead is on the left (east) side of the road.

Additional trails: Along with the Long Loop, there's the approximately 1.3-mile Short Loop.

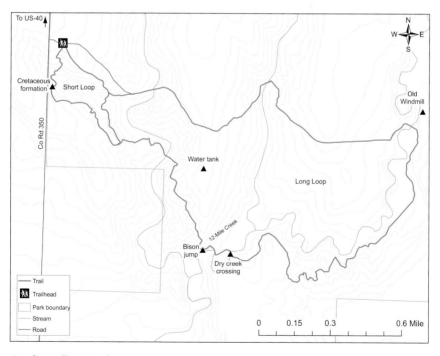

Smoky Valley Ranch

Camping: No camping is allowed at Smoky Valley Ranch. The closest spot for both tent and RV camping is north of the ranch at High Plains Camping (462 US-83, Oakley, KS 67748; 785-672-3538). Another option is to go east to US-83 and head south toward Lake Scott State Park, which offers both tent and RV campsites.

STERNBERG MUSEUM OF NATURAL HISTORY

The geological history of Kansas is rich and varied, and some of the most exciting paleontological finds were deposited when a vast and shallow inland sea cut a swath through the center of North America. During the Cretaceous period, approximately 65 million to 144 million years ago, a jaw-dropping assortment of aquatic beasts thrived in the sea that covered present-day Kansas. As that sea slowly receded, the story of these amazing creatures was preserved in the fossils deposited in the layer of Smoky Hills chalk found throughout northwestern Kansas.

Kansas was a hotbed of fossil-hunting expeditions during the late 1800s, and one of the first serious fossil collectors was Dr. George M. Sternberg. Sternberg was a military doctor assigned to Fort Harker, an outpost in present-day Kanopolis. He procured a prodigious quantity of fossil specimens from the Dakota sandstone formations near Fort Harker and from the Smoky Hills chalk of western Kansas, many of which are currently part of the collection at the Smithsonian Museum. George's younger brother, Charles H. Sternberg, became famous in his own right as a fossil hunter, and Charles's three sons carried on the paleontological tradition. One of those sons, George F. Sternberg, was hired by Fort Hays State University in 1927 as a curator for its museum, and his work formed the basis of one of the premier paleontological collections in the state of Kansas. Today, the rich prehistoric diversity of western Kansas is on display at the Sternberg Museum of Natural History at Fort Hays State University, where visitors can observe a range of fossils and specimens, including the famous fish within a fish. A 2011 addition is a 2-mile network of nature trails for the enjoyment of hikers; these trails go through a 22-acre outdoor classroom with an amphitheater and small ponds west of the museum.

Contact: Sternberg Museum, 3000 Sternberg Drive, Hays, KS 67601; 785-628-4286.
Hours: Daylight hours.
Cost: Free.

FEATURED TRAIL: DR. HOWARD REYNOLDS NATURE TRAILS — PRAIRIE CROSSING AND CHETOLAH TRAILS

Trail access: Hike.
Distance: 1.1-mile loop, 2 miles total.

Immediately west of the Sternberg Museum of Natural History, a small network of footpaths crisscrosses a 22-acre plot of land that is in the process of being

Dr. Howard Reynolds Nature Trails at the Sternberg Museum of Natural History. (Photo by Jonathan Conard)

restored to native vegetation. The nature trails were dedicated in 2011 and are named in honor of Dr. Howard Reynolds, a longtime professor at Fort Hays State University and curator of the herbarium at the Sternberg Museum. The trailhead marker to the west of the Sternberg Museum parking lot is unique: the name of the trail is hewn into an elevated wooden signpost that spans the entrance to the trail system (38.88999, −99.30078). The main trail is the Prairie Crossing Trail, which takes a meandering route along the north side of the area. The trail here is a narrow dirt path that can be overgrown in the early summer, but the signage should help keep you on the trail as you cross an open grassland that is being re-seeded with native prairie plants.

Upon reaching the northwestern edge of the Prairie Crossing Trail, a junction leads down a flight of wooden stairs through a small woodland area called the Cottonwood Cove Loop. The trail is more established here, and the shade provided by cottonwoods and eastern red cedars is a welcome respite. The main trail

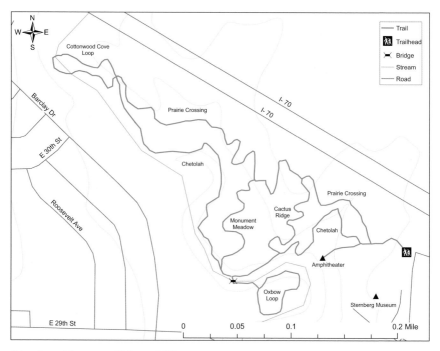

Sternberg Museum of Natural History

back to the trailhead is the Chetolah Trail (the name used by some Plains tribes for the Smoky Hill River). As you return to the trailhead, note the small amphitheater (38.88991, −99.30224) located a short distance down a spur trail near the trailhead. The entire loop is short enough to be hiked in its entirety, but cutoff trails, including Monument Meadow and Cactus Ridge, can be taken to form a shorter loop route, if desired. The winding Cactus Ridge Trail has numerous prickly pear cacti and a diverse assortment of wildflowers along a small ridge.

Directions to the trailhead: From I-70, take exit 161 and go north on Commerce Parkway. Take the first left turn onto E. 27th Street/Airbase Road and go west for 1.2 miles before turning right onto Sternberg Drive. The trailhead is on the northwest side of the parking lot by the museum.

Additional trails: Explore the rest of the trail network by taking additional loops such as the Cottonwood Cove Loop, the Oxbow Loop, and the Cactus Ridge Trail.

Camping: Although there are no camping facilities at the Sternberg Museum, you can drive west from Hays and camp at Cedar Bluff Reservoir (32001 147 Highway, Ellis, KS 67637). Other options include Wilson State Park, which is east of Hays along I-70 (#3 State Park Road, Sylvan Grove, KS 67481; 785-658-2465).

WEBSTER STATE PARK

At the edge of the Solomon River Valley, 880-acre Webster State Park is centered around Webster Reservoir, built in 1958. The 3,700-acre lake has walleye, channel catfish, largemouth bass, and other sport fish. With a combination of prairie expanses and woodlands, the park is home to plenty of wildlife, including white-tailed deer, great blue herons, red-tailed hawks, mule deer, pheasants, bald eagles, and more. During spring and fall, all kinds of birds pass through on the Central Flyway, including white pelicans, American wigeons, marbled godwits, and western grebes. To get a dose of history while you're in the area, stop by the Nicodemus Historical Site. The unincorporated town of Nicodemus, located 10 miles west of the park, was founded in 1877, and it's the last surviving town established by African Americans after the Civil War.

Webster State Park. (Photo by Mark Conard)

CHAPTER 8

SOUTHWEST KANSAS

The high plains at first gave him an overpowering impression of emptiness. Never before had he beheld such a sky — the cosmic vault of blue appeared to occupy a good three fourths of the world, making small and unimportant the scattered farm houses with their meager clumps of ragged trees and inevitable windmills.

But though the vastness at first oppressed him, eventually it distilled in him a sensation of fetterless freedom which he grew to love almost jubilantly.

PAUL I. WELLMAN, *THE WALLS OF JERICHO*

View from Point of Rocks, overlooking the Cimarron River Valley. Photo by Kristin Conard

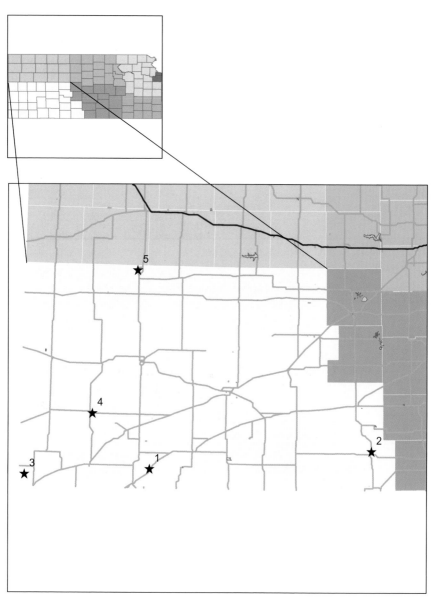

Southwest Kansas

1. Arkalon Park
2. Barber State Fishing Lake
3. Cimarron National Grassland
4. Frazier Park
5. Lake Scott State Park

Southwest Kansas is made up of wide vistas and long, gently rolling hills. It is primarily within the High Plains physiographic region but also includes a small western portion of the Arkansas River Lowlands and the Red Hills. This is one of the driest regions in the state, rivaled only by northwest Kansas. Its predominantly flat and open landscape typifies outsiders' impression of Kansas, thanks in great part to the film *The Wizard of Oz*. To embrace this Hollywood connection, you can visit the Dorothy's House Museum in Liberal. This is also a historically significant region, with Native American ruins, Santa Fe Trail ruts you can actually follow, and a landscape shaped by the dust storms of the 1930s.

ARKALON PARK

At Arkalon, the railroad crosses the Cimarron River, and although the town founded here in the 1880s didn't survive, the area is now a park with interwoven trails along the river, as well as picnic and camping areas. Arkalon Park opened in 1989, and high schools in the area use the trails for cross-country races during the fall. Amidst the dry, mostly treeless expanses of the surrounding farmland, Arkalon is tucked down in the river valley — an oasis of green that even nearby residents are unaware of. The park has two parts — the area to the southwest has small fishing ponds, and the other is near the campground and picnic areas. The more extensive trail system runs between the picnic area and the Cimarron River. To the east from the campground, you can see Mighty Samson of the Cimarron, a railroad bridge built after the 1937 flood washed out the original bridge.
Contact: Arkalon Park, 600 N. Panhandle, Liberal, KS 67901; 316-626-0531.
Hours: 7 a.m. to 10 p.m. from April 1 to October 31.
Cost: Free.

FEATURED TRAIL: NATURE TRAILS

Trail access: Hike.
Distance: 2 miles total.
   Along the river are a series of interconnecting nature trails that start near the campground and explore the area next to the Cimarron River as it winds through this small valley. The trails can be picked up at a number of places. At the northern edge of the campground, you can access both halves of the trails (37.14993, −100.76310). The wide, flat trails are a mix of mowed grass and sand or dirt. You can turn either right or left 450 feet from the trailhead. If you turn right, you'll make a small loop before returning to the intersection for the more extensive trails to the west. These trails follow the banks of the Cimarron River, and they are dotted with benches. At some points, you'll be walking through stands of cattails taller than your head. The trails can be taken as a loop back to the northern trailhead, or you can access the southern end of the campground from the western edge of the trails.

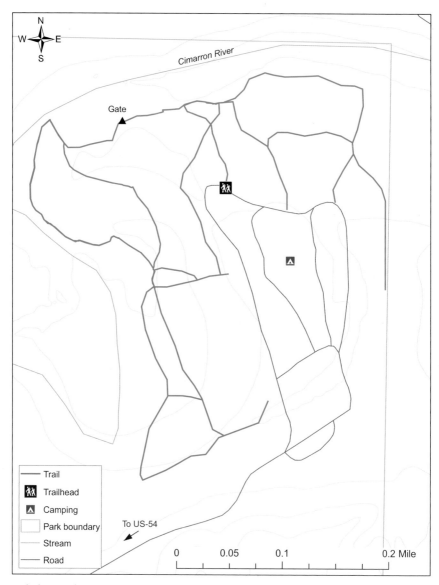

Arkalon Park

Directions to the trailhead: From Liberal, take US-54E for 8.3 miles. Turn left (north) onto R Park Road and drive for approximately 1.5 miles, until the road dead-ends at a T-junction. Turn right into the park, and take the first left into the campground.

Additional trails: You can take a walk around Wriston Marsh, named for local "Pete" Wriston, who first came up with the idea of Arkalon Park. At the entrance gate across the railroad tracks, turn left and follow the road for about 1.65 miles. An approximately 1-mile primitive trail encircles the marsh, and the road goes about halfway around and ends near the boardwalk that crosses the marsh.

Camping: Primitive campsites and sites with hookups are available from April 1 to October 31. There's a bathhouse and an RV dump station, along with picnic areas in the pleasantly shady and secluded camping area.

Barber State Fishing Lake

Barber State Fishing Lake was constructed in 1955 in north Medicine Lodge. It's actually two lakes (the upper and lower lakes) separated by a levee. Medicine Lodge is part of the Gypsum Hills Scenic Byway, and the lake is within the Red Hills physiographic region, so you can expect to see rolling hills and buttes colored red from the iron oxide in the soil. The natural salts and chemicals in the

Barber State Fishing Lake. (Photo by Mark Conard)

247

waters have therapeutic properties. The Plains Indians considered the hills a place of healing — hence the name Medicine Lodge.

Contact: Barber County Conservation District, 800 W. 3rd Avenue, Medicine Lodge, KS 67104; 620-886-5311.

Hours: Daylight hours.

Cost: Free.

FEATURED TRAIL: RED CEDAR NATURE TRAIL

Trail access: Hike.

Distance: 1.5-mile loop.

Encircling the entire 51-acre lower lake, the Red Cedar Nature Trail is an easy, pleasant walk primarily beneath the trees, and it has some nice lake views. The trail was built in the early 1990s, and it's a good way to stretch your legs before or after a fishing trip. The fishing lake is well stocked with channel catfish, carp, walleye, largemouth bass, and bluegill. The wide, wood chip–covered trail can be accessed on either the east or west side of the lake. On the west side, close to the boat ramp (37.29746, –98.58376), the trail heads north. Shortly after crossing the park road, about 0.4 mile from the trailhead, the trail crosses a grass levee (37.30090, –98.58262). There are pleasant views of the lake here, and you might spot some Canada geese. If you want to take your time on the hike, there are benches dotting the trail. Also along the trail is an abundance of eastern red cedar, accounting for its name. Although eastern red cedars are native to Kansas, they are invasive in certain prairie areas and can choke out the native grasses. After crossing a bridge on the north side of the levee, the trail winds back into the trees and heads east and south around the other side of the lake. The trail crosses the dirt roads of the park a few times, allowing easy access to the campgrounds. The wood-chip and dirt portion of the trail ends at the Well Road trailhead on the southeast side of the lake (37.29687, –98.57803). To close the loop, hike the 0.6 mile of road around the southern portion of the lake across the dam.

Directions to the trailhead: From the intersection of Highways 281 and 160, head north on US-281/Iliff Street for 1.5 miles and turn right for the lake. Follow the dirt park road for 0.1 mile. The trailhead is on the north side of the parking lot. If you want to take the scenic route into or out of Medicine Lodge, take US-160 to Coldwater. This 42-mile stretch of east-west highway is the Gypsum Hills Scenic Byway.

Additional trails: The 42-mile Gypsum Hills Scenic Byway is a popular and challenging cycling route. The traffic is light along US-160, but there are no paved shoulders. This is a rugged stretch of countryside the likes of which you won't find anywhere else in Kansas.

Camping: Free primitive camping is available at Barber State Fishing Lake. There are no hookups or showers.

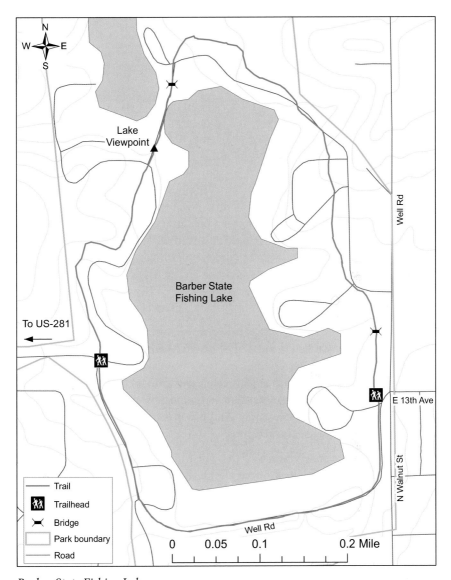

Barber State Fishing Lake

CIMARRON NATIONAL GRASSLAND

In 1941 the Cimarron River in far southwestern Kansas flooded, uncovering a Spanish signature and the year 1541 carved in the sandstone near the base of Point of Rocks, an outcropping overlooking the Cimarron River Valley. It was the signature of Francisco Vasquez de Coronado, who had been looking for the seven cities of gold. (Sadly, the signature is no longer there.) This broad expanse of the plains

249

was used for hunting by multiple Native American tribes, including the Comanche, Kiowa, Plains Apache, and Arapaho.

About 300 years after Coronado visited Point of Rocks, it became a landmark on the Santa Fe Trail, as was the nearby Middle Spring (any place in the High Plains that's a reliable water source is a good landmark to know — even today!). In the mid-1860s to 1880s homesteaders began to stake their claims in the far southwestern corner of Kansas, thanks to the Homestead Act of 1862. With the arrival of the railroad in 1913, the towns of Wilburton, Rolla, and Elkhart sprang up. On the outskirts of these towns, farmers worked the sandy soil, growing everything from wheat to watermelons.

It was that extensive working of the land, combined with an eight-year drought and high temperatures, that made the dust storms of the 1930s so devastating. Precipitation hovered at around 11 inches a year for the decade, and the disastrous impact on those who made their living off the land can't be overstated. Loose topsoil was whipped into dust clouds hundreds of feet high, and the dust found its way into homes through seemingly invisible cracks. The day of the biggest dust storm was later called Black Sunday — April 14, 1935. The 1,000-mile-wide cloud traveled 1,500 miles across the plains, with winds gusting up to 100 miles per hour. The *Liberal News* reported on April 15, 1935:

> A great black bank rolled in out of the northeast, and in a twinkling when it struck Liberal, plunged everything into inky blackness, worse than that on any midnight, when there is at least some starlight and outlines of objects can be seen. When the storm struck it was impossible to see one's hand before his face even two inches away. And it was several minutes before any trace of daylight whatsoever returned.

The government bought some of the worst-hit areas, and by 1939, 107,000 acres had been purchased. It was from all this that the Cimarron National Grassland, officially designated in 1960, was born. Under the guidance of the Soil Conservation Service and the Forest Service, and with years of hard work, the 108,175 acres of the Cimarron National Grassland have been restored to a thriving mix of shortgrass prairie, sand-sage prairie, and woodlands along the Cimarron River.

The health of the grasslands ensures the health of the many animals that live there, so this is an important ecosystem. Pronghorn antelope, elk, and mule deer can be found on the Cimarron National Grassland. It's also home to a wide range of birds, making it a popular spot for birding. For example, it provides habitat for the lesser prairie chicken, which the US Fish and Wildlife Service listed as a threatened species under the Endangered Species Act in 2014. The Cimarron National Grassland also contains the state's only set of trails that are still open to covered wagons.

Contact: US Forest Service District Office, 242 E. Highway 56, PO Box 300, Elkhart, Kansas 67950; 620-697-4621; http://www.fs.usda.gov/psicc/cim.

Companion Trail, Cimarron National Grassland. (Photo by Kristin Conard)

Hours: Daylight hours.
Cost: Free.

FEATURED TRAIL: COMPANION TRAIL (TOP HISTORICAL TRAIL)

Trail access: Hike, bike, bridle, and covered wagon.
Distance: 6.2 miles, one-way.

In the 1800s the Santa Fe Trail stretched across 900 miles of plains from Missouri to Mexico (before the Mexican-American War, after which it stopped in New Mexico). It was used as a trade route and a thoroughfare for westward migrants, many of them traveling in covered wagons. In 1987 the trail was designated a National Historic Site, and the Cimarron National Grassland contains the largest section of the trail on public land: 23 miles of the Santa Fe Trail's Cimarron Route. The Companion Trail is a mowed grass path that runs alongside and sometimes on top of the historic Santa Fe Trail.

Running 19 miles between the Conestoga and Murphy trailheads, the clearest portion of the trail is the 6.2 miles between the Murphy trailhead and K-27. Both trailheads have restrooms, interpretive signs about the area's history, and water pumps (although there's no guarantee that the water will be running). From the Murphy trailhead, head northeast, parallel to the tracks of the Santa Fe Trail and north of Forest Service Road (FS) 600. Limestone posts mark the locations of archaeologically confirmed portions of the Santa Fe Trail, and where wagon ruts from that trail are evident, the Companion Trail runs next to it. Where the ruts aren't clear or have been eroded, the Companion Trail runs on top of the Santa Fe Trail. Sagebrush and cacti have been removed to help differentiate the trail from the surrounding grassland, and there are occasional brown flex trail markers along the way.

The Companion Trail is an exposed trail in a windy part of a windy state, and there's no water nearby, so a balmy day in spring or fall is the ideal time for this hike. You can follow the tradition of the Santa Fe Trail travelers and start near dawn — a good idea in the summer to try to beat the heat. Starting at the Murphy trailhead (37.08350, –101.99157), the relatively flat trail heads east through the shortgrass prairie. The trail is faint at times, and watching for the limestone markers of the original trail can help keep you oriented. The Companion Trail crosses a few farm roads on the way to Point of Rocks, which is one of the few landmarks along this vast stretch of prairie. You can take a side trail up to Point of Rocks (37.10367, –101.93853), where there's a small parking lot and an overlook, to take in the incredible view of the Cimarron River Valley from 3,540 feet. On clear days you can see for miles, and several interpretive signs provide more information about the area and its history.

Even though the trail runs through mostly flat, seemingly empty terrain, there's subtle beauty and a lot of life along the way. In the spring you're likely to see blooming yucca, and in the summer the buffalo gourds grow. A mile past Point of Rocks is the intersection with the road leading up to the Middle Spring picnic area (37.11288, –101.92708). Unlike the Cimarron River, which rarely flows aboveground, Middle Spring flows year-round, and it was an important watering spot along the Santa Fe Trail. The Middle Spring picnic area is less than 0.25 mile from the Companion Trail, and it offers tree cover and picnic tables, making it a great place to take a break. Continuing on the trail, it's another 0.75 mile to Point of Rocks ponds (37.11528, –101.91387). These man-made ponds are stocked by the KDWPT with channel catfish in the summer and trout in the winter. This could be your turnaround point, or you could continue another mile to the intersection of K-27 and FS 600. The trail continues past the intersection, but it can be challenging (though not impossible) to follow the trace trail, and there are no major landmarks along the rest of the trail.

Directions to the trailhead: For the Murphy trailhead: From the junction of US-56 and Morton Street in Elkhart, head east on US-56 for 1.8 miles, to the intersection of K-27. Turn left (north) on K-27 and drive for 8 miles. Turn left (west) on

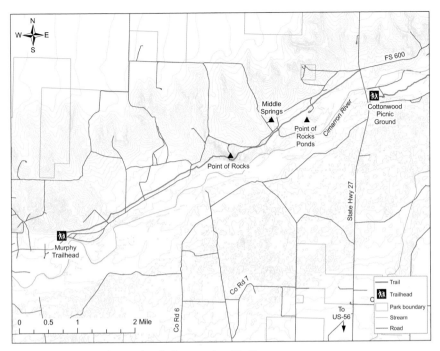

Cimarron National Grassland, Companion Trail

FS 600 after crossing the Cimarron River Bridge and continue on FS 600 for about 6 miles. The trailhead is on the right.

For the Conestoga trailhead: From the junction of US-56 and K-27 in Elkhart, drive east on US-56 for 6.6 miles to County Road 16. Turn left (north), and continue for approximately 10 miles. The trailhead is on your left.

Additional trails: The Companion Trail continues another 13 miles to the Conestoga trailhead, although the grass trace trail can be difficult to follow. If you'd like to link the western portion of the Companion Trail with the Turkey Trail, continue south on K-27 to the Cottonwood Picnic Grounds.

FEATURED TRAIL: TURKEY TRAIL

Trail access: Hike, bike, or bridle; ATV accessible between the Cimarron Recreation Area and the Cottonwood Picnic Grounds.

Distance: 5.1 miles, one-way.

The Turkey Trail officially runs between Wilburton Pond and the Cottonwood Picnic Grounds (37.11967, –101.89468). The most well-maintained and enjoyable portion of the trail is the 5.1-mile stretch between the Cimarron Recreation Area and the Cottonwood Picnic Grounds. It's also the most easily accessible, and it can

On the Turkey Trail at Cimarron National Grassland. (Photo by Joyce Conard)

be taken in either direction. The Turkey Trail got its name from the flocks of wild turkeys in the area, and it follows what was once a farm road.

If you're taking the trail from east to west, start at the north end of the Cimarron Recreation Area Campground (37.13865, −101.82325). Both the campground and the Cottonwood Picnic Grounds have pit toilets and wells that provide a potable water source, but because the wells may not be working, it's best to bring your own water. As a former primitive road, the trail is easy to follow and generally flat, although bikers may find the occasional sandy sections more challenging. Heading across the shortgrass prairie, the trail is exposed. The first landmark, about a mile from the campground, is a windmill. Take the track that heads south and around the windmill over a couple of cattle guards. After the windmill, the effects of the May 2011 Tunner fire become more obvious. The fire burned about 20,000 acres and closed the Cimarron Recreation Area through the spring of 2012. The white trunks of the dead cottonwoods can be seen along the trail; however, much of the ground cover and the sagebrush, prickly pear cactus, buffalo gourds, and grasses have returned. The ecosystem is actually well suited to fire. Fires burn out dead grass without damaging the roots, which keeps the grasslands primarily tree-free beyond the riverbanks. The US Forest Service conducts prescribed burns on the Cimarron National Grassland (the Tunner fire was not a prescribed burn).

Three miles from the Cimarron Recreation Area, a side road heads south to FS 700 at a gas well (37.13050, –101.86347). Natural gas has been pumped from the area since the early 1930s, and there are a few hundred oil and gas wells throughout the grassland. The trail continues past the gas well, roughly paralleling the Cimarron River. The river often seems dry aboveground, but the water running a few feet beneath the sand supports the cottonwood groves near the banks. The end of the area impacted by the 2011 fire is clear as the trail gets closer to the Cottonwood Picnic Grounds, where there are more thriving cottonwoods. You can check out the river 0.2 mile before the Cottonwood Picnic Grounds by taking a side trail to the north (37.12005, –101.89177). If you continue straight, the trail ends at the picnic grounds, where you'll find picnic tables, some playground equipment, and an old steam engine that was used in the 1950s to construct the nearby K-27 bridge.

Directions to the trailhead: For the Cottonwood Picnic Grounds trailhead: From the junction of US-56 and Morton Street in Elkhart, take US-56 east for 1.8 miles to the intersection of K-27. Turn left (north) on K-27 and follow it for 7.5 miles. Turn right (east) on FS 700. The Cottonwood Picnic Grounds is to the left (north) of FS 700. If you cross the K-27 bridge over the Cimarron River, you've gone too

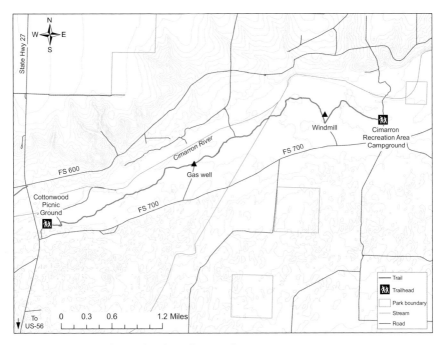

Cimarron National Grassland, Turkey Trail

far. For the Cimarron Recreation Area trailhead: From K-27, drive 4 miles east on FS 700.

Additional trails: The trail extends 4.5 miles to the east of the Cimarron Recreation Area, but the two-track trail becomes a single grass track that's harder to follow and not as well maintained. The Turkey Trail can also be linked to the Companion Trail: from the Cottonwood Picnic Grounds, head north on K-27 for 0.6 mile to FS 600; the trail picks up southwest of the FS 600 and K-27 intersection. There's also a short nature trail at the Middle Spring Picnic Grounds.

Camping: Cimarron Recreation Area has established campsites with pit toilets. There are no hookups, and open campfires aren't allowed. The wells should have water, but it's best to bring your own. Fee-free "primitive dispersed" camping is available throughout the grassland, except at the Cottonwood Picnic Grounds, Middle Spring Picnic Grounds, Point of Rocks, and Cimarron Recreation Area.

FRAZIER PARK

Frazier Park is a small oasis amidst the dry sand-sage prairie of southwestern Kansas. The park consists of a small, well-manicured area surrounding Frazier Lake. The dam for the lake was constructed in 1954, and the lake — originally known as Grant County State Lake — was filled with water that summer. A golf course and a picnic area were constructed near the lake, making it the first state park to have all three. Perhaps because of concern over siltation issues and a lack of water for the lake, the state deeded the lake to the City of Ulysses in 1959. The city took over the park and named it in honor of Bill Frazier, a member of the first park board.

Contact: City of Ulysses Parks Department, 1380 Frazier Park Road, Ulysses, KS 67880; 620-353-1720.

Hours: Daylight hours.

Cost: Free.

FEATURED TRAIL: FRAZIER PARK TRAILS

Trail access: Hike or bike.

Distance: 3 miles total.

The current trail network angles through scattered cottonwoods along a dry streambed and behind the lake itself. The trails are easily visible but are not marked or named. There is no marked trailhead either, but if you start from the parking lot by the driving range (37.56593, −101.33906), go south on a small dirt path that enters the woods along a dry streambed. From here, the trail can be followed clockwise to the east to form a loop. Going east, the trail is bounded by Frazier Lake to the north, but it stays tucked down amidst the scattered trees along the riparian zone of the intermittent stream. At several points along this section there are connecting trails to the asphalt path next to Frazier Lake. Continuing east, the trail network follows the edge of the lake as it bends to the north and will

Frazier Park. (Photo by Jonathan Conard)

eventually terminate at a small park road unless you choose one of the myriad options for looping back to the south and west. If you loop back, stay on the south part of the trail network for a few short but steep climbs through sandy dunes covered in sagebrush, which are scattered throughout this more open part of the trail. From the trailhead, it is also possible to take a shorter loop to the west. This western loop of the trail, which is more shaded and passes closer to the riverbed, follows a pleasant little stretch of trail with minimal elevation change.

257

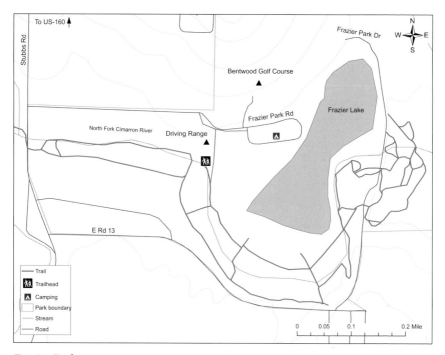

Frazier Park

Directions to the trailhead: From the intersection of K-25 and US-160 in Ulysses, go east on US-160 for 1 mile before turning right (south) onto Stubbs Road. Follow Stubbs Road for 0.7 mile and turn left (east) into Frazier Park. Follow the park road until you reach the first parking lot on the south side of the road by the driving range. Currently, there is no marked trailhead, but this parking lot is the best place to access the trails.

Additional trails: Along the trail network at the western edge of Frazier Park, you can take another trail that crosses Stubbs Road and continues west. West of Stubbs Road, this trail climbs steadily and turns northwest through an open pasture. This segment of the trail continues for approximately 0.65 mile (one-way) to an access point within the city of Ulysses.

Camping: Camping is allowed at Frazier Park. There are six full utility sites that can be reserved by calling the Bentwood Golf Course Clubhouse (620-356-3097).

LAKE SCOTT STATE PARK

Straddling the border between northwest and southwest Kansas in northern Scott County (14 miles north of Scott City) is Lake Scott State Park, which gets about 150,000 visitors annually. Located amidst the High Plains, the park features sedimentary cliffs and bluffs of the Ogallala Formation around the tree-lined banks of the 100-acre lake. Out on the shortgrass prairie, natural springs and wooded canyons are an unexpected and welcome sight, and the hills and canyons of western Kansas in and around what is now Lake Scott State Park have great historical significance, particularly for Native American tribes.

In 1664 Taos Indians migrated to the area to escape Spanish control, and they built pueblos and started raising crops. Thus, Lake Scott State Park is the site of the northernmost pueblo community in the country. The pueblo ruins were discovered by Herbert Steele, a homesteader who farmed in the area and even used the irrigation ditches originally dug by the Taos Indians hundreds of years before. Steele moved to the area in 1888, 10 years after the nearby Battle of Punished Woman's Fork between the Northern Cheyenne and the US Cavalry — the last Native American battle in Kansas.

The Northern Cheyenne had been sent to a Southern Cheyenne reservation in Oklahoma in 1877. They had little food, and when a measles outbreak hit the reservation, their chances of survival were slim. Two Cheyenne chiefs, Dull Knife

Battle Canyon near Lake Scott. (Photo by Mark Conard)

259

and Little Wolf, took matters into their own hands, and on the night of September 9, 1878, they left their fires burning and led more than 300 Cheyenne off the reservation. They were headed back to Yellowstone country, 1,500 miles away. By September 13, US troops had found them, and they were offered the option of surrender. Dull Knife refused to go back to the reservation, so the fighting began.

A cat-and-mouse game continued through the next week, as the Cheyenne tried to get away. They finally reached Punished Woman's Fork on September 25 — a place specifically chosen for their last stand. The remote canyon had a natural cave at one end where women, children, and the elderly could take shelter; along the hills and bluffs, rifle pits could be dug to provide cover for the Cheyenne fighters. The plan was to lure US soldiers into the canyon (now known as Battle Canyon) and ambush them, using the landscape as a weapon.

One of the Cheyenne fighters described the incoming soldiers: "A great angry snake of whites come against us in the morning." On September 27, those who were not fighting took shelter in the cave, and the battle began. The Cheyenne were forced into Battle Canyon, but they drove the army back and killed Lieutenant Colonel Lewis, commander of Ford Dodge, Kansas, who had once said, "I will run the Cheyenne to ground or leave my body on the prairie." He did the latter. On the night of September 27, the army pulled back to its camp, and the Cheyenne once again made their escape in the dark, leaving their fires burning, and headed north.

Although Battle Canyon is not within park boundaries, the reconstruction of the foundation of El Cuartelejo Pueblo is. In 1964 it was designated a National Historic Landmark, and a few years later it was excavated and restored. As you walk around the historic site, know that your view of the nearby hills and bluffs is similar to that of the pueblo dwellers hundreds of years earlier. The Steele home is another historic site that has been preserved for viewing. The park is a popular fishing destination, and the lake, created with the damming of Ladder Creek in 1930, has swimming beaches and playground areas amidst the surprisingly rugged landscape.

Contact: Lake Scott State Park, 101 W. Scott Lake Drive, Scott City, KS 67871; 620-872-2061.

Hours: 24/7.

Cost: State park fee.

FEATURED TRAIL: MULTIUSE TRAIL (TOP HISTORICAL TRAIL, TOP BRIDLE TRAIL, AND TOP 10 TRAIL)

Trail access: Hike, bike, or bridle.

Distance: 6.2-mile loop.

The narrow, unnamed multiuse trail that circles the entire lake is primarily packed dirt with occasional mowed grass sections. If you're hiking or biking, you can pick up the trail just north of the park office at the southern end of the lake (which means access to flush toilets and water when the office is open). If you're on horseback, the horse unloading and camping area is on the northeast side at the Timber Canyon Campground.

The trail can be taken either clockwise or counterclockwise, but the western side of the lake has more diverse terrain and more hills. To start with the more challenging sections and take the loop clockwise, head left away from the road north of the park office (38.66617, −100.91978). The trail starts beneath shade trees, and the lake is surrounded by stands of willows, elms, cottonwoods, and more. At 0.25 mile from the park office, there's a turn-off to the east for the Big Springs Nature Trail and Picnic Area. Shortly after that, the trail emerges from the trees and is more exposed as it parallels W. Scott Lake Drive. To the left (west) of the trail is a sign for the Boy Scout ranch adjacent to the park. After 0.7 mile of rolling hills, you'll be east of and below the Steele Monument (38.67446, −100.91913). The small stone house atop a hill is a monument to the Steele family, who sold 620 acres of their land to the Kansas State Forestry, Fish, and Game Commission in 1928. This land now makes up half the park's total acreage (1,280 acres). A primitive, faint side trail heads up toward the monument while the main trail continues north.

Lake Scott State Park bluffs. (Photo by Kristin Conard)

El Cuartelejo Pueblo is east of the trail across the park road, 0.25 mile past the Steele Monument. The pueblo is worth a visit, even though these aren't the original ruins. The reproduction of the foundation and the rendition of what the original pueblo looked like can help you envision life in the valley.

The trail continues north and starts to bear west, heading into and out of a few small gullies. Bluffs rise to the west, and yucca plants dot the hillsides; during May and June the yucca flowers are in bloom. Fairly steep side trails to the west lead up to the cliff tops, where you can take in the views. Side trails to the east take you to the road and the nearby campgrounds, while the main trail continues northwest. After crossing a dirt park road that leads down to the Circle Drive Campground (38.68475, –100.92413), you'll head back into the trees and start climbing uphill as you make your way along Horse Thief Canyon and Suicide Bluff. Past Suicide Bluff there's a trail junction (38.6872, –100.93105), where you can bear right (north) for 0.3 mile to link up with the main trail on the north side of N. Juniper Road; this cutoff takes 0.2 mile off the trail. Following the trail to the left (southwest) takes you west around the Timber Canyon Campground (38.68646, –100.93484). If you're on horseback, this is the end of the trail, as there is horse unloading and camping at this campground. The 0.5 mile of trail around the campground and across N. Juniper Road is mostly shaded, with the same flowing and occasionally steep but short hills common on the western side of the lake. Wildlife abounds at the park, and as you head through the trees you might see wild turkeys and white-tailed or mule deer.

Shortly after the intersection of the cutoff trail and the main trail north of the park road (38.68803, –100.93358), the trail emerges from the trees. More stone bluffs rise to the north, and as you head toward the dam and spillway, there are pleasant views out over the lake. Past the concrete spillway and at its northern-most portion (38.69369, –100.92436), the trail follows the park road for about 100 feet before heading back south. The trail continues south on the west side of E. Scott Lake Drive for approximately 0.15 mile before it turns east and crosses that road. The trail winds east around and past Bull Canyon South Campground, and it crosses the park road again as it turns south.

From there, the trail stays between the paved park road and the lake. The path occasionally becomes faint, but if you keep the road to the east, you'll be on the right track. Primarily exposed, but with more gradual elevation changes, the trail on the northeast side of the lake provides good views of the water, and it takes you across a side park road and past United Methodist Church Camp Lakeside (38.68248, –100.91571). The trail curves around the lake, in and out of groves of trees, and across shortgrass meadows. About 0.6 mile past Camp Lakeside, the trail heads away from the lake (say good-bye to the lake views) and around a dry pond, closely paralleling K-95. You'll head through more timber before crossing W. Road 280 (38.67037, –100.91528). From there, the trail opens up again and remains primarily exposed for the last 0.5 mile back to the end of the loop.

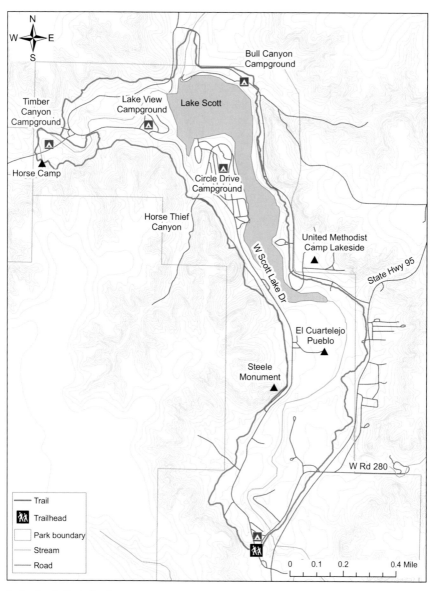

Lake Scott State Park

Directions to the trailhead: From Scott City, take US-83N for 9.7 miles. Turn left onto K-95N and continue for 3.1 miles to W. Scott Lake Drive. Turn left (west) off W. Scott Lake Drive approximately 150 feet from K-95, where there's parking for the park office and the trailhead.

Additional trails: A couple of shorter nature trails and variations on the main trail are available. On the west side of the lake, a handful of side trails lead you up to the top of the bluffs near Horse Thief Canyon and Suicide Bluff. These trails are accessible only on foot and they aren't officially maintained, so hike them at your own risk.

At the southern end of the lake near the park office is the Big Springs Nature Trail — a short, easy loop hike. On the east side, north of the Elm Grove Camping Area, is the Dry Pond Loop, another short, easy trail. You can make a 0.8-mile loop near the Timber Canyon Campground by combining the cutoff section with the 0.5-mile loop around the campground.

Camping: The park has two modern cabins and a horse camp. It also has utility and primitive campsites. All the campgrounds have toilets, and the Circle Drive Campground and Elm Grove Camping Area have shower houses.

CHAPTER 9

LONG-DISTANCE
RAIL TRAILS

Railway termini are our gates to the glorious and the unknown.

E. M. FORSTER

Mural near the Prairie Spirit trailhead in Ottawa. Photo by Mark Conard

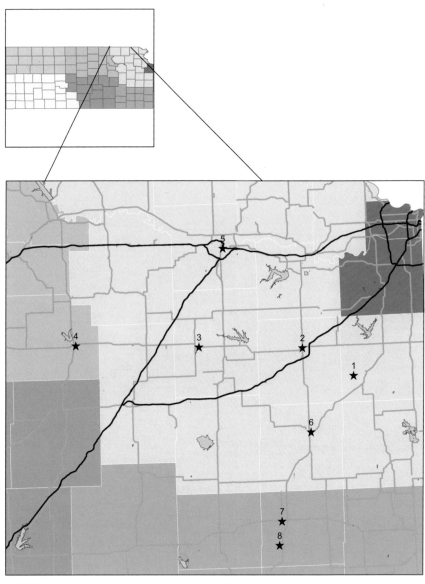

Rail Trails

1. Flint Hills Nature Trail – Osawatomie
2. Flint Hills Nature Trail / Prairie Spirit
   Trail – Ottawa
3. Flint Hills Nature Trail – Osage City
4. Flint Hills Nature Trail – Council Grove
5. Landon Nature Trail – Topeka
6. Prairie Spirit Trail – Garnett
7. Prairie Spirit Trail – Iola
8. Southwind Rail Trail – Humboldt

Native American tribes that used the land for hunting made the first trails in Kansas. Some of these Native American trails were then used to create routes such as the Santa Fe Trail and the Oregon Trail, which in turn had rail lines built along them. After the Civil War, the West was being developed and the rail system expanded rapidly. The railroads connected the various parts of the United States and made it easier to move goods and people around the nation. The Kansas-Nebraska Act of 1854 was designed to help open the Midwest to settlement, and the first railroad in what is now Kansas was a 5-mile stretch between Elwood and Wathena. The Santa Fe Railroad; the Union Pacific Railroad; the Atchison, Topeka, and Santa Fe Railroad; the Missouri, Kansas, and Texas Railway (aka the Katy); and others became major players in the development of the state. The railroads helped build Kansas and gave life to many of the smaller towns along the rail lines. Millions of Texas cattle were shipped via Kansas rail, and coal was shipped out of southeastern Kansas. Even today, the railroad is used to transport Kansas wheat to the rest of the world.

But with the development of the automobile and the airplane, many rail lines were decommissioned as the railroads went out of business or consolidated. These unused rail lines could have been forgotten, allowed to become overgrown and worthless, but many have now been remade as trails. The National Trails System Act of 1968 was designed "to promote the preservation of public access to, travel within, and enjoyment and appreciation of the open-air, outdoor areas and historic resources of the Nation." Nothing typifies these ideals more than the rail trails. As explained by Clark Coan, former director of development at the Kanza Rail-Trails Conservancy, a nonprofit devoted to converting abandoned railways to trails: "Tourism from rail-trails can help small towns survive. Trail users need food, gas, lodging and souvenirs. The boost to a small town's economy may help it stay alive. They allow Kansans to have adventures close to home."

Under the National Trails System Act, "rail banking" is an agreement between the railroad and the trail agency that, if the need ever arises, the route can be used again by the railroad; in the meantime, it can be developed as a multiuse trail. Kansas has more than 100 miles of converted rail trails throughout the state, with many others in the planning stages. It is a huge undertaking to build these routes. It takes thousands of volunteer hours to obtain funding, clear brush, install crushed limestone, and put up signage. And once a trail is set, it requires continuous maintenance to keep it in good shape. The first rail trail in Kansas, the 38-mile Landon Nature Trail between Topeka and Pomona, was started in 1987. What will eventually be the state's longest trail — the 117-mile Flint Hills Nature Trail — may someday (ideally) be linked with the Katy Trail in Missouri. These are some of Kansas's newer trails, and most are open for hiking, biking, and horseback riding. Because they are topped primarily with crushed limestone, the hard-packed surface provides an easy ride suitable for wheelchairs, strollers, and road bikes.

The long-term goal is to create a long-distance trail system, and plans are in the works to create and link more of these trails. Some currently undeveloped portions will be developed within the next few years. For updates, visit our website (kansastrailguide.com). Another long-distance trail through Kansas, though not a rail trail, is the American Discovery Trail. Following mostly back roads, it is part of a coast-to-coast trail (for more information, go to discoverytrail.org/states /kansas/).

FLINT HILLS NATURE TRAIL

As the longest rail trail in Kansas and the seventh longest rail trail in the country, the Flint Hills Nature Trail has gained national recognition. It crosses the Flint Hills — home to one of the world's last remaining stretches of tallgrass prairie — on what was once a Missouri-Pacific rail line. The nonprofit Kanza Rail-Trails Conservancy was founded in 2001 as a grassroots, all-volunteer organization dedicated to converting former rail lines into public trails, and the Flint Hills Nature Trail is one of its most impressive projects. It is still a work in progress, and about $2.4 million in grants were awarded in 2013 to finish the trail, which will eventually cover 117 miles. Some portions of the trail that are not completed, as of this writing, are mentioned as additional trails in the descriptions.

Contact: Kanza Rail-Trails Conservancy, info@kanzatrails.org; kanzatrails.org.
Hours: Daylight hours.
Cost: Free.

FEATURED TRAIL: FLINT HILLS NATURE TRAIL — OSAWATOMIE TO OTTAWA

Trail access: Hike, bike, or bridle.
Distance: 18.4 miles, one-way.

As of this writing, the best place to pick up the Flint Hills Nature Trail in Osawatomie is 0.5 mile east of the intersection of W. 347th Street and Indianapolis Road (38.49895, –95.00216). (Eventually, the plan is to start the trail at the Karl E. Cole Sports Complex at 12th and Walnut in Osawatomie.) You can park along the side of the trail, although there isn't much in the way of signage or notification. The trail heads toward Rantoul, 7.1 miles to the northwest, along a lightly tree-lined corridor. The path is wide and relatively smooth, with a fine gravel surface, and for the first 2 miles, you can see the croplands bordering the trail through breaks in the trees. The elevation stays fairly consistent, with a few gradual ups and downs. After crossing Pressonville Road, the trail turns more toward the west, and the trees become denser as the trail runs along the bluffs above the Marais des Cygnes River and curves northwest. Once you cross Virginia Road and Jackson Road, you'll be in an open field, where you'll have a view across the croplands as you travel the last mile into Rantoul.

The Rantoul trailhead is 0.12 mile north of the intersection of W. Main Street and N. McGinnis Avenue (38.55183, –95.10262). From Rantoul to Ottawa, it's 11.3 miles. The stretch of trail out of Rantoul is shady, flat, and easy, and it crosses

Flint Hills Nature Trail. (Photo by Mark Conard)

two bridges before turning west along Kingman Road. You're still close to the river, so you'll cross a total of nine bridges between Rantoul and Ottawa. Many of them span small streams or tributaries to the river, making them good places to stop and look for wildlife. Many of the east-west roads have gates across them to prevent motor vehicles from accessing the trail, but it's easy to ride or walk around them as you continue northwest. Overall, the elevation increases a bit from Rantoul to Ottawa, with some long, slow ups and downs along the trail. At 8.6 miles from Rantoul, the trail passes beneath I-35, and in another 1.25 miles you'll be on the eastern edge of Ottawa. Along the levee, 0.5 mile of the rail trail is grassy and unfinished and can be difficult to navigate on a bike. The trail briefly joins with the levee system trails before you turn onto E. 1st Street. The trail passes through Ottawa along 1st Street, and if you want a convenient spot to meet or end the trail in Ottawa, you can turn right (north) at S. Walnut Street for the Old Depot Museum and the Prairie Spirit trailhead (38.62032, –95.27014).

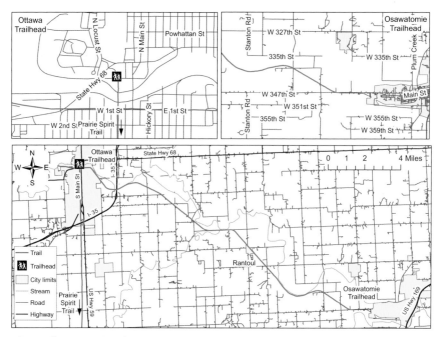

Flint Hills Nature Trail, Osawatomie to Ottawa

Directions to the trailhead: For the current Osawatomie trailhead: From US-169S/K-7, take the Main Street exit into Osawatomie. Continue on Main Street for 1.5 miles and turn right (north) onto 12th Street; follow it to the left (west) as it turns into Parker Avenue and then W. 347th Street. The trail starts off of 347th Street, between Bethel Church Road and Indianapolis Road.

For the Ottawa trailhead: From I-35, turn north onto US-59, which turns into S. Princeton Street and then S. Main Street. Drive for 3 miles and cross the Marais des Cygnes River; turn left onto Tecumseh Street. The Old Depot Museum and the trailhead are on the right.

FEATURED TRAIL: FLINT HILLS NATURE TRAIL — OTTAWA TO OSAGE CITY

Trail access: Hike, bike, or bridle.
Distance: 20.8 miles, one-way; eventually, 32.1 miles total.

From Ottawa to Osage City, the trail runs past and through Pomona, the Landon Nature Trail junction (Lomax Junction), and Vassar. Currently, the trail follows 1st Street, and it's in good condition for 1.2 miles as it heads west past the ball fields of the Orlis Cox Sports Complex and to a bridge over the river. For the next 7 miles, to outside of Pomona, the trail is unfinished. A short, 2-mile section of trail is open east of Pomona from Colorado Road, a block south of 1st Street (38.60229, –95.45283), to Florida Road (38.60315, –95.41573). For the next 4 miles—

from Pomona to S. Stubbs Road, 0.5 mile south of E. 253rd Street/Highway 268 — the trail is unfinished. As work continues on this section, check the Kanza website for construction updates and the current status of the trail (www.kanzatrails .org). At Stubbs Road, just west of the intersection with the Landon Nature Trail (38.60038, –95.52714), you can pick up the Flint Hills Nature Trail as it heads uphill and northwest past E. 237th Street and then southwest for 6.5 miles into Vassar.

In Vassar, you can take a break and get some food before continuing west. The trail crosses a large bridge over US-75, and the route from Vassar to Osage City is 11.1 miles long. Heading west, the trail is downhill overall, but it has the same long, low hills that are typical of this trail. The path here may be more uneven than in the portion east of Ottawa, and riding a road bike may be difficult. Some of the railroad bridge crossings are not finished and may consist of open ties; however, the ties are spaced close together, so walking across them is relatively easy. The trail runs through the countryside, with croplands visible beyond the tree line, and it tracks nearly due west as it heads into Osage City. When the trail starts to bear south, you're 0.5 mile from town. At S. Indian Hills Road, at the eastern edge of Osage City, the trail is grassy and more difficult to ride as it heads through the neighborhoods there. At S. Auburn Road (38.63895, –95.82004), turn left (south) for a block on the city streets, as the trail currently dead-ends at the active train line. Turn right (west) onto Lakin Street, follow it past the train tracks, and take

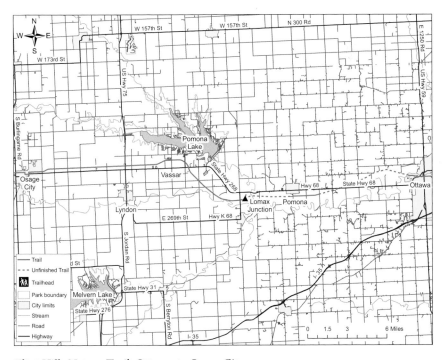

Flint Hills Nature Trail, Ottawa to Osage City

271

a right onto N. 6th Street, where you can pick up the trail as it heads west out of town (38.63887, –95.82563). After traveling 0.7 mile through the northwestern blocks of Osage City, you'll cross N. Martin Street and leave the city behind as you return to the tree-lined trail.

Directions to the trailhead: For the Ottawa trailhead: From I-35, turn north onto US-59, which turns into S. Princeton Street and then S. Main Street. Drive for 3 miles and cross the Marais des Cygnes River; turn left onto Tecumseh Street. The Old Depot Museum and trailhead are on the right.

For the Osage City trail on the east side of town: From US-75, turn west onto K-31/W. 237th Street. Follow it for 7.3 miles into Osage City and turn right (north) onto N. 9th Street/S. Auburn Road. The trail starts 0.1 mile after the turn.

FEATURED TRAIL: FLINT HILLS NATURE TRAIL — OSAGE CITY TO COUNCIL GROVE

Trail access: Hike, bike, or bridle.

Distance: 39.7 miles, one-way.

Heading out of Osage City (38.63887, –95.82563) on the way to Council Grove, you'll pass west of Miller and through the towns of Admire, Allen, and Bushong. It's 15.5 miles from Osage City to Admire. From Osage City, the trail heads west and crosses several bridges. At 5.25 miles from the western edge of Osage City, the trail curves southwest, and the tree cover ends. You can see out across the croplands and prairie grasses, and the increasingly open terrain stands in sharp contrast to the shady Osawatomie-to-Ottawa section. There's a brief break in the openness as you cross a bridge over the Marais des Cygnes River. You'll traverse the countryside as you head beneath the turnpike and start bearing northwest. Intermittent tree cover returns as you approach Admire (38.64081, –96.10386).

From Admire, the trail continues west and crosses Hill Creek (38.65618, –96.13869) before reaching Allen. From the trailhead in Allen, the trail skirts the southern edge of the small town and continues west. West of Allen, the trail currently passes through a gate and crosses Allen Creek (38.64525, –96.22598); it passes through a second gate in about 1.1 miles. The section of trail between the gates is accessible to the public, but make sure you close the gates after you pass through, since the surrounding area may be used as pasture. The trail passes along the southern edge of Bushong (no services available) and continues west. Around Bushong, the trail truly enters the heart of the Flint Hills, proceeding through expanses of tallgrass prairie in one of the trail's most scenic sections. Here, it also passes through areas where the railroad made deep cuts in the limestone hills to level the grade; along one of these cuts, the limestone has begun to erode, and the huge fallen boulders are an impressive sight (38.63157, –96.33513). This section is one of the most remote portions of the route, with few major road intersections until the trail crosses Dunlap Road just west of Rock Creek.

As the trail continues through the Flint Hills, watch for a gravel road leading to Allegawaho Memorial Heritage Park on the north side of the trail, about 3.25

Flint Hills Nature Trail. (Photo by Jonathan Conard)

miles west of Dunlap Road. Ruins of a large limestone building on the site of the former Kaw Indian reservation (38.62487, –96.43199) are visible from the trail itself. If you're interested in a short side trip or want to learn more about the history of the area, see the description for Allegawaho Memorial Heritage Park in chapter 5. After this point, the trail enters the historic town of Council Grove. As one of the last stopping points for traders heading west along the Santa Fe Trail, this town is rich in history and worth a visit. The trail eventually continues west through Council Grove to the town of Herington.

Directions to the trailhead: For the Osage City trailhead on the west side of town: From US-75, turn west onto K-31/W. 237th Street. Follow it for 7.3 miles into Osage City, and continue straight onto Lakin Street. After 0.3 mile, turn right (north) onto N. 6th Street. The trail picks up after half a block.

For the Council Grove trailhead: From US-56 in Council Grove, turn south onto 8th Street and drive for 2 blocks until you reach Donnon Street. Turn west onto Donnon Street and continue for 2 blocks. The trailhead is just before the Walnut Street intersection.

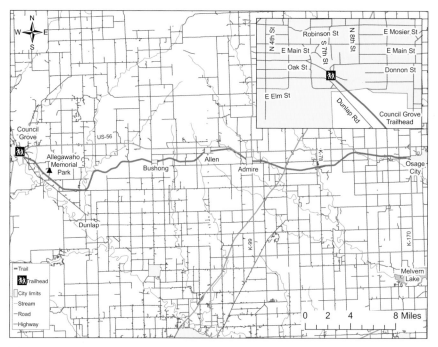

Flint Hills Nature Trail, Osage City to Council Grove

Additional trails: In Ottawa, the trail intersects with the north-south Prairie Spirit Trail at the Old Depot Museum on the north side of town. It also intersects with the Landon Nature Trail near Pomona.

Camping: No camping is allowed on the Flint Hills Nature Trail. A short side trip to Pomona Lake (5260 Pomona Dam Road, Vassar, KS 66543; 785-453-2201) or to Council Grove Lake (945 Lake Road, Council Grove, KS 66846; 620-767-5195) would provide options for campers.

LANDON NATURE TRAIL

As part of an ambitious project spearheaded by the Kanza Rail-Trails Conservancy, the Landon Nature Trail will eventually stretch 38 miles south from Topeka and connect with the Flint Hills Nature Trail. Upon completion, this will be the longest network of trails in the state. Currently, the wide, crushed limestone Landon Nature Trail travels along the old Missouri-Pacific rail bed through the southern part of Topeka before opening up into pastoral farmland and wooded streambeds as it winds south. The Landon Nature Trail was the first long-distance trail to be rail-banked in the state of Kansas, and it was named in honor of former governor Alf Landon. When complete, the trail will intersect both the historic Oregon Trail and the Santa Fe Trail.

Contact: Kanza Rail-Trails Conservancy, info@kanzatrails.org.

Hours: Daylight hours.
Cost: Free.

Trail access: Hike, bike, or bridle.
Distance: 12.5 miles, one-way.

The trail starts at a parking lot southeast of the *Brown v. Board of Education* Historic Site (1515 SE Monroe Street), which recounts the history of and circumstances surrounding the pivotal US Supreme Court case that ended school segregation in 1954. From the historic site, the trail starts south along a paved route before intersecting with the paved Shunga Trail at a unique bicycle roundabout (39.03337, –95.67602). Bikers and hikers can explore the Shunga Trail, which runs east-west through the city of Topeka along Shunganunga Creek. Continuing south, the Landon Nature Trail crosses Shunganunga Creek and heads through the city of Topeka. Within the city, the trail is paved and passes through a mix of urban and woodland areas. Be careful when crossing the city streets, including a particularly busy intersection where the trail crosses SE 29th Street (39.01505, –95.67955). The trail is believed to intersect the former Union Ferry Branch of the Oregon Trail in the vicinity of SE 42nd Street in Topeka. There are few traces of the Oregon Trail left in the city, and it is clear that the landscape has changed greatly since the route was used by wagon trains heading west.

At around 4 miles, the concrete surface is replaced by a smooth dirt surface that transitions to crushed limestone shortly thereafter (38.97636, –95.6801), before passing Herrman's Trailhead and crossing SE 53rd Street. If you want to avoid the more urban section of the trail in Topeka, Herrman's Trailhead is an excellent choice for an access point; the gravel parking lot is located on the north side of SE 53rd Street, just west of SE Adams Street.

From here, the trail continues south and crosses Berryton Road, just south of the tiny hamlet of Berryton. It passes through farmsteads, fields, and mixed woodlands. Elms, black walnuts, and occasional red cedars shade the route as it parallels wooded Lynn Creek to the east. Between Berryton and 77th Street, the trail is narrower and appears to be less frequently used, but it is certainly passable. The last completed section of the trail opens up and offers a wider view of the rolling pastures of the Flint Hills to the east. The trail currently ends at the 12.5-mile point, just before intersecting SE 89th Street.

Directions to the trailhead: For the *Brown v. Board of Education* Historic Site trailhead: From I-70, take exit 363 for Adams Street toward Branner Trafficway. Turn left (southwest) onto SE Adams Street, and take the first right (northwest) onto SE 15th Street. After 0.4 mile, turn left (southwest) onto SE Monroe Street.

Additional trails: When completed, the Landon Nature Trail will continue south and intersect with the Flint Hills Nature Trail. Currently, a short section of trail

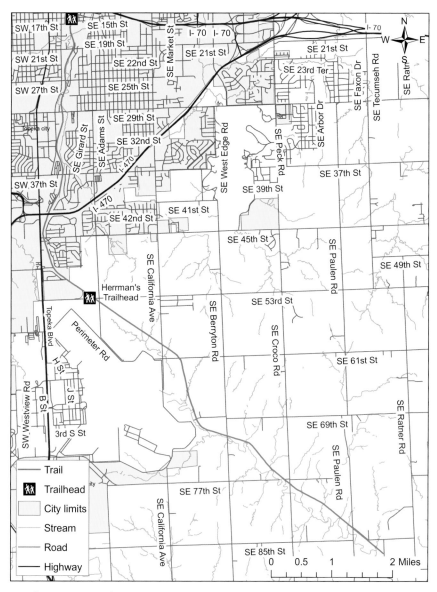

Landon Nature Trail

running south from a trailhead in Overbrook has been completed. The City of
Topeka has a wide array of trails, including the featured hiking and biking trails
at MacLennan Park and Kaw River State Park (see chapter 3). For a fascinating
history of the Sunflower State, including more information about the Oregon and
Santa Fe Trails, visit the Kansas Museum of History in Topeka, where you can also
enjoy 2.5 miles of nature trails around the museum (6425 SW 6th Avenue).

Camping: No camping is allowed along the Landon Nature Trail, but there are campgrounds east of the trail at Lake Shawnee. Lake Shawnee has tent and RV campsites, along with a swimming beach, shower house, and marina (3137 SE 29th Street, Topeka, KS 66505; 785-267-1156).

PRAIRIE SPIRIT TRAIL (TOP 10 TRAIL, COMBINED WITH SOUTHWIND RAIL TRAIL)

Part of Kansas's first north-south rail line, built in the 1860s, has been converted to a state park and a 51.4-mile rail trail that runs from Ottawa to Iola. This is the state park system's only rail trail, and along the way you'll pass through six small towns. Since it's a north-south route, the trail is mostly shaded during the mornings and evenings. The trailhead in each town is well marked, and parking is available; there is also a self-pay station for the required trail-use permit, along with picnic tables, water, and bathrooms. In Ottawa and Garnett, these facilities are open year-round; elsewhere, they are available from April through October.

Common scene on the Prairie Spirit Trail. (Photo by Mark Conard)

Contact: Garnett Area Chamber of Commerce, 419 S. Oak, Garnett, KS 66032; 785-448-6767.

Hours: Daylight hours.

Cost: $3.50 per day; annual pass, $12.50. No permit is required within the city limits of Iola, Garnett, and Ottawa.

FEATURED TRAIL: PRAIRIE SPIRIT TRAIL — OTTAWA TO GARNETT

Trail access: Hike, bike, or bridle.

Distance: 25.1 miles, one-way.

Although the trail can be taken from either north to south or south to north, or even broken up into smaller portions, a north-to-south route means that you can easily hook up with the Southwind Rail Trail. The northern trailhead is at the Old Depot Museum in Ottawa (38.62032, –95.27014), at 135 W. Tecumseh. The Atchison, Topeka, and Santa Fe Railroad gifted the 1888 depot building to the Franklin County Historical Society in 1962, and it has exhibits on the history of both the county and the state, including a model schoolroom, a Victorian parlor, and a dentist's office. The first part of the trail through the city of Ottawa is along pavement, and a sidewalk takes you across the bridge over the Marais des Cygnes River. From the bridge, stay on S. Walnut Street until 7th Street, where the trail moves over onto a sidewalk that parallels S. Walnut. At about 1.5 miles in, you'll pass the first rest stop at Kanza Park; from there, it's 4.5 miles to the southern edge of town. The trail deviates from its straight path to jog east and take the underpass at the intersection of US-59 and I-35. Shortly thereafter, the trail becomes a fine, crushed limestone path through a tree-lined corridor.

The trail roughly parallels US-59, and it's a slow and steady climb up to about mile 8, outside of Princeton. The trail is generally smooth, although the country roads can be a bit bumpy at times. Between Ottawa and Princeton, there are a couple of benches along the way. The Princeton trailhead is near the center of town, half a block off of High Street (38.48977, –95.27432). The town has a gas station and a small restaurant if you need to refuel before continuing.

After going south for 3 blocks, you'll be out of Princeton. The next town, Richmond, is 6.5 miles away. Outside of Princeton, the thick tree line on both sides of the trail begins to thin out after a few miles, which means that the slight uphill grade can be more challenging on windy days. You can take a break just after mile 12; there's a bench where you can enjoy the view of the fields and farmlands. As the tree line becomes thicker again, you'll know you're getting closer to Richmond. You can use the grain elevator as a guide; the Richmond trailhead (38.39800, –95.25505) is close to the elevator, on the southwestern side of town. The small town has some diners and restaurants, as well as free camping at Richmond Lake (Allen Road–NW 2500 Road), about 1.25 miles east of the trail's intersection with Allen Road (38.39127, –95.22536).

From the Richmond trailhead, the trail bears east toward Garnett, and you'll cross beneath US-59 at Allen Road. At this point, the trail goes downhill for a couple of miles, but at around mile 20, it's a steady 125-foot climb for the handful of miles remaining before you arrive in Garnett. There are plenty of benches along this mostly tree-lined section as the trail crosses Scipio Road, winds through the countryside, crosses Pottawatomie Creek (the bridge here was washed out in 2007 but has since been replaced), and passes Garnett Lake.

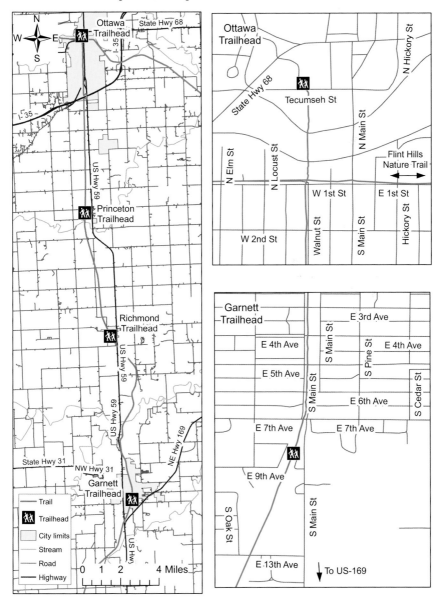

Prairie Spirit Trail, Ottawa to Garnett

In Garnett, one of the larger towns along this stretch, the trail turns to pavement, and you have some options for dining and taking a break. The trailhead is at the southern edge of town at the old Santa Fe Depot, which is also a Tourist Information Center (38.27648, –95.24067).

Directions to the trailhead: For the Ottawa trailhead: From I-35, turn north onto US-59, which turns into S. Princeton Street and then S. Main Street. Drive for 3 miles, cross the Marais des Cygnes River, and turn left onto Tecumseh Street. The Old Depot Museum and the trailhead are on the right.

For the Garnett trailhead: From US-59, turn east onto W. 7th Avenue; after 0.5 mile, turn right (south) onto S. Main Street. The trailhead is on the right.

FEATURED TRAIL: PRAIRIE SPIRIT TRAIL — GARNETT TO IOLA

Trail access: Hike, bike, or bridle.

Distance: 26.3 miles, one-way.

From the Garnett trailhead (38.27648, –95.24067), it's 8.4 miles to the Welda trailhead. Outside of Garnett, after passing Crystal Lake, the trail crosses to the west side of US-59/169 and starts heading southwest. Once it crosses the highway, the trail slowly gains elevation toward Welda. There are a few benches along the way, and you can observe the gradual change from wooded area to prairie. The trail alternates from tree lined to open in its more remote portion. The trail flattens out as you get to Welda, and the Welda trailhead is near the center of town (38.16929, –95.29506). About 0.5 mile south of the trailhead, you'll cross beneath Highway 169 and continue toward the southwest, paralleling the highway. The 7.8 miles between Welda and Colony are mostly flat, with a couple of benches along the way. There are fewer trees along this stretch, and you can see out over the low hills. The Colony trailhead (38.07460, –95.36717) is on the northern side of the small town. There's a small diner on Broad Street, where you can fuel up before you leave.

From Colony to Carlyle it's 5.6 miles — mostly downhill. The trail starts out fairly open and exposed, highlighting the Kansas vistas. Once you pass beneath the highway, the trail becomes shaded and tree lined again, which can be nice if it's sunny or windy. The trailhead in Carlyle (37.99437, –95.38778) is 4.5 miles northeast of the Iola trailhead, and the terrain is flat. A bridge crosses the Neosho River, and the trail is mostly shaded. The trail turns to pavement as you enter Iola, and the trailhead is on the southern edge of town (37.93241, –95.40957).

Additional trails: The Southwind Rail Trail is essentially a continuation of the southern end of the Prairie Spirit Trail. It's 6.5 miles from Iola to Humboldt; see the following featured trail.

Camping: Camping is not allowed on the trail, but you can camp at Richmond Lake. In Garnett, there's tent and RV camping available at Lake Garnett (500 N. Lake Road, Garnett, KS 66032; 785-448-5496) and RV camping on the south side of Crystal Lake.

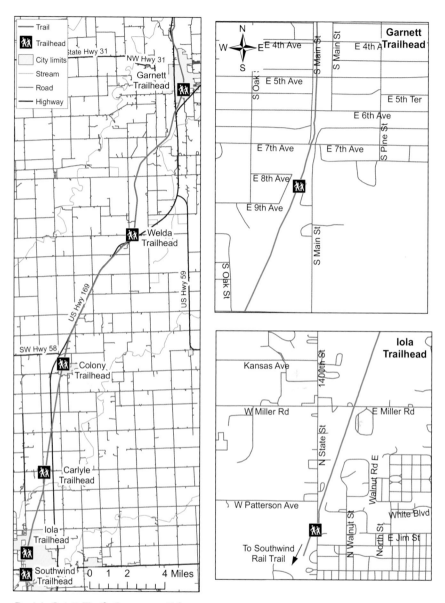

Prairie Spirit Trail, Garnett to Iola

SOUTHWIND RAIL TRAIL (TOP 10 TRAIL, COMBINED WITH PRAIRIE SPIRIT TRAIL)

The Southwind Rail Trail starts at the southern end of the Prairie Spirit Trail; if you're combining the trails, continue south on the paved trail to Riverside Park on the southern edge of Iola.

Running between Iola and Humboldt, the Southwind Rail Trail was opened in 2013. It was once a line of the Atchison, Topeka, and Santa Fe Railway. The trail was created thanks to a partnership between Allen County and volunteer organizations, which is particularly interesting in terms of politics; in other places in Kansas, counties have blocked the development of such trails. The Sunflower Rail-Trails Conservancy maintains the trail, keeping it free of weeds and obstructions and open for hikers and bikers (no horses).

The authors on the Southwind Rail Trail. (Photo by Mark Conard)

Contact: Thrive Allen County, 12 W. Jackson Avenue, Iola, KS 66749; 620-365-8128; info@thriveallencounty.org.
Hours: Daylight hours.
Cost: Free.

FEATURED TRAIL: SOUTHWIND RAIL TRAIL

Trail access: Hike or bike.
Distance: 7.2 miles, one-way.

This wide trail of smooth gravel is an easy and fun hike or ride. You can take the Southwind Rail Trail either from Iola to Humboldt (north to south) or from Humboldt to Iola. To tack this trail onto the end of the Prairie Spirit Trail, travel north to south.

Officially, the Southwind Rail Trail begins in Iola's Riverside Park, in the southern part of town (37.91849, −95.41078). The park has restrooms and a pool (who wouldn't enjoy a quick dip after a long trek on a hot day?). The trail heads south and crosses Elm Creek on a truss bridge shortly after it leaves town. The railings on this restored rail bridge across the creek (37.90856, −95.41041) were specially designed by a local craftsman for this project. The trail roughly parallels State Street to the east as it passes Lake Bassola and then heads into a tree-lined corridor through the fields. Crossing a handful of roads, it continues south-southwest with a few long, gradual ups and downs. Despite the trees lining the trail, some parts of it get direct sun at midday, which can be pleasant on a cool day but uncomfortable in the midst of summer. Take the trail early in the morning or in the evening to keep yourself in shade for most of the journey. Along the way, keep an eye out for rabbits and the occasional turkey, as well as the breaks in the tree line that allow you a glimpse of the fields beyond the trail corridor. During spring and summer, you'll see wildflowers blooming. The trail ends (or begins) near the intersection of Franklin Street and Hawaii Road in northeastern Humboldt (37.82037, −95.42859). A big wooden sign marks the trailhead at Humboldt, and there's a large parking area nearby.

Directions to the trailhead: For the Iola trailhead: From US-169, take US-54W/East Street to Iola. Follow US-54W for about 1.7 miles, as it changes from East Street to E. Madison Avenue. Turn left (south) onto S. State Street, and then turn right (west) onto W. Bruner Street.

For the Humboldt trailhead: From US-169, take the K-224 exit toward Humboldt. Drive for 1.1 miles to Hawaii Road. The trailhead is on the right (north), near the intersection of Hawaii Road and Franklin Street.

Additional trails: Several trails are in the works. One will wind along the Coon Creek Canal in downtown Iola. The Missouri-Pacific (MoPac) Trail will be a short trail that connects the Prairie Spirit Trail and the Southwind Rail Trail with central Iola and the courthouse. It will be an off-road option along Benton Street. Another trail being developed in Iola is the Lehigh Portland Rail Trail. It will begin south of

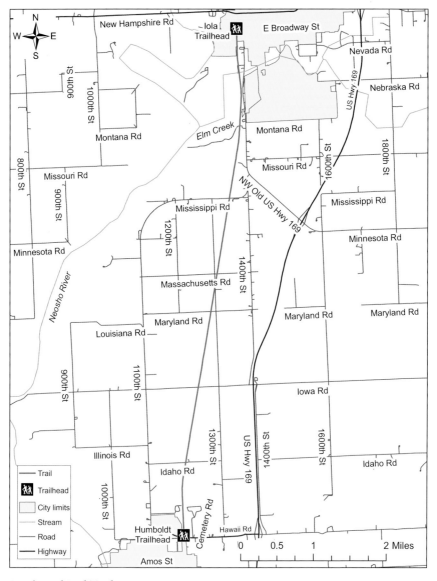

Southwind Rail Trail

Iola at Elm Creek South Park and will include a main path of crushed limestone, along with single-track side trails for mountain bikers.

Camping: No camping is allowed along the Southwind Rail Trail. The closest camping is RV and tent camping at Iola RV Park and Storage (1327 US-54, Iola, KS 66749; 620-365-2200).

Bibliography

Archaeology Laboratory, University of South Dakota. "A 1993 Cultural Resources Inventory at Pomona Lake in Osage County, Kansas." US Army Corps of Engineers–Kansas City District, 1995.

Bike Prairie Spirit. 2012. http://www.bikeprairiespirit.com/ (accessed July 5, 2013).

Buchanan, R. C., ed. *Kansas Geology: An Introduction to Landscape, Rocks, Minerals, and Fossils.* Lawrence: University Press of Kansas, 1984.

Buchanan, R. C., and J. R. McCauley. *Roadside Kansas: A Traveler's Guide to Its Geology and Landmarks.* Lawrence: University Press of Kansas, 1987.

Centers for Disease Control and Prevention. "Ticks." July 26 2012. http://www.cdc.gov/ticks/ (accessed October 12, 2012).

Cirlincuina, Julie. *Kansas Outdoor Treasures: A Guide to Over 60 Natural Destinations.* Weiser, ID: Trail Guide Books, 2008.

Collins, J. T., ed. *Natural Kansas.* Lawrence: University Press of Kansas, 1985.

Cutler, W. G. *History of the State of Kansas.* Chicago: A. T. Andreas, 1883.

Dary, D. *The Santa Fe Trail: Its History, Legends, and Lore.* New York: Knopf, 2000.

Duncan, Dayton, and Ken Burns. *The Dust Bowl: An Illustrated History.* 1st ed. San Francisco: Chronicle Books, 2012.

EarthRiders Mountain Bike Club. 2010. http://earthriders.com (accessed December 2013).

Evans, Catherine S. *From Sea to Prairie: A Primer of Kansas Geology.* Lawrence: Kansas Geological Survey, 1988.

Fry, T. S. "The Unknown Indian Monument." *Heritage of the Great Plains* 23, 4 (1990): 19–24.

Goodin, D. G., J. E. Mitchell, M. C. Knapp, and R. E. Bivens. *Climate and Weather Atlas of Kansas.* Lawrence: Kansas Geological Survey, 1995.

Gower, C. W. "The Pike's Peak Gold Rush and the Smoky Hill Route, 1859–1860." *Kansas Historical Quarterly* 25, 12 (1959): 158–171.

Gress, B., and G. Potts. *Watching Kansas Wildlife: A Guide to 101 Sites.* Lawrence: University Press of Kansas, 1993.

Hartman, Joe, and Mechele MacDonald. "The Cornerstone of Kansas." *Kansas Wildlife & Parks* 45 (1988): 9–13.

Hauber, Catherine M., and John W. Young. *Hiking Guide to Kansas.* Lawrence: University Press of Kansas, 1999.

Hill, Matthew W., Jr. "Before Folsom: The 12 Mile Creek Site and the Debate over the Peopling of the Americas." *Plains Anthropologist* 51, 198 (May 2006): 141–156.

Hygnstrom, S. E., and Dallas R. Virchow. "Prairie Dogs and the Prairie Ecosystem." Paper 36 in *Papers in Natural Resources University of Nebraska–Lincoln* (September 7, 2002). Digitcalcommons.unl.edu/natrespapers/36 (accessed December 2013).

Ingalls, John James. *A Collection of the Writings of John James Ingalls.* Kansas City, MO: Hudson-Kimberly Publishing, 1903.

Johnson County Park & Recreation District. "Trail Guide." 2013. http://www.jcprd.com/parks_facilities/trailguide.cfm (accessed January 2014).

Kansas Cyclist. January 2014. http://www.kansascyclist.com/ (accessed January 2014).

Kansas Department of Transportation. "History of Kansas Railroads." N.d. http://www.ksdot.org/burrail/rail/railroads/history.asp (accessed November 10, 2013).

Kansas Department of Wildlife, Parks and Tourism. 2013. http://www.kdwpt.state.ks.us/ (accessed 2013).

Kansas Horse Council. 2012. http://www.kansashorsecouncil.com/ (accessed June 2013).

Kansas Singletrack Society. May 2013. http://www.kssingletrack.com/ (accessed June 2013).

Kanza Rail-Trails Conservancy. N.d. http://kanzatrails.org/ (accessed December 12, 2013).

Kindscher, Kelly. *Edible Wild Plants of the Prairie*. Lawrence: University Press of Kansas, 1987.

Knapp, A. K., J. M. Briggs, D. C. Hartnett, and S. L. Collins, eds. *Grassland Dynamics: Long-Term Ecological Research in Tallgrass Prairie*. New York: Oxford University Press, 1998.

Least Heat-Moon, William. *PrairyErth (A Deep Map)*. New York: Mariner Books, 1999.

Lee, W. C., and H. C. Raynesford. *Trails of the Smoky Hill*. Caldwell, ID: Caxton Printers, 1980.

Lewis, Meriwether, William Clark, et al. *The Journals of the Lewis and Clark Expedition*, ed. Gary Moulton. Lincoln: University of Nebraska Press/University of Nebraska–Lincoln Libraries Electronic Text Center, 2005. http://lewisandclarkjournals.unl.edu /read/?_xmlsrc=1804-07-04.xml&_xslsrc=LCstyles.xsl#n04070419 (accessed September 1, 2012).

Linsemayer, P. T. "Kansas Settlers on the Osage Diminished Reserve: A Study of Laura Ingalls Wilder's *Little House on the Prairie*." *Kansas History* 24, 3 (2001): 186–199.

McCoy, S., and J. Gruber. *1001 Kansas Place Names*. Lawrence: University Press of Kansas, 1989.

Muilenberg, G., and A. Swinford. *Land of the Post Rock*. Lawrence: University Press of Kansas, 1975.

National Park Service. "Santa Fe Trail: Official Map and Guide." US Department of the Interior, 1995.

Otte, C. "Poison Ivy: Identification and Control Guide." Kansas State University–Geary County Extension, n.d. http://gearycountyextension.com/poisonivy.htm (accessed September 14, 2012).

Penner, M. *The Kansas Guidebook for Explorers*. Newton, KS: Mennonite Press, 2006.

Reichman, O. J. *Konza Prairie*. Lawrence: University Press of Kansas, 1987.

———. *Living Landscapes of Kansas*. Lawrence: University Press of Kansas, 1995.

Richmond, R. W. *Kansas: A Land of Contrasts*. St. Charles, MO: Forum Press, 1974.

Ruetti, O. *It Happened Here: Stories from Marshall County, Kansas*. Hillsboro, KS: Print Source Direct, 2002.

US Army Corps of Engineers. N.d. http://www.usace.army.mil/ (accessed 2013).

USDA Forest Service National Grasslands. "About Us." March 24, 2013. http://www.fs.fed .us/grasslands/aboutus/ (accessed October 12, 2013).

———. "Pike and San Isabel National Forests, Cimarron and Comanche National Grasslands." N.d. http://www.fs.usda.gov/detail/psicc/news-events/?cid=STELPRDB5368151 (accessed November 10, 2013).

Vail, Jake, Doug Hitt, and Lisa Grossman. *A Kansas Bestiary*. Lawrence, KS: Mammoth Publications, 2012.

Wellman, Paul. *The Walls of Jericho*. Philadelphia: Lippincott, 1947.

White, Wayne. "Federal Grant Sparks $2.4 Million Investment into Flint Hills Nature Trail." *Osage County News*, June 25, 2013. http://www.osagecountyonline.com/archives/2981 (accessed January 1, 2013).

Index